D1129772

THE INVINCIBLE
IRON MAN
LONG WAY DOWN

INVINCIBLE IRON MAN VOL. 10: LONG WAY DOWN. Contains material originally published in magazine form as INVINCIBLE IRON MAN #516-520. First printing 2012. Hardcover ISBN# 978-0-7851-6048-9. Softcover ISBN# 978-0-7851-6049-6. Published by MARVEL WORLDWIDE, INC., a subsidiary of MARVEL ENTERTAINMENT, LLC. OFFICE OF PUBLICATION: 135 West 50th Street, New York, NY 10020. Copyright © 2012 Marvel Characters, Inc. All rights reserved. Hardcover: $19.99 per copy in the U.S. and $21.99 in Canada (GST #R127032852). Softcover: $16.99 per copy in the U.S. and $18.99 in Canada (GST #R127032852). Canadian Agreement #40668537. All characters featured in this issue and the distinctive names and likenesses thereof, and all related indicia are trademarks of Marvel Characters, Inc. No similarity between any of the names, characters, persons, and/or institutions in this magazine with those of any living or dead person or institution is intended, and any such similarity which may exist is purely coincidental. **Printed in the U.S.A.** ALAN FINE, EVP - Office of the President, Marvel Worldwide, Inc. and EVP & CMO Marvel Characters B.V.; DAN BUCKLEY, Publisher & President - Print, Animation & Digital Divisions; JOE QUESADA, Chief Creative Officer; TOM BREVOORT, SVP of Publishing; DAVID BOGART, SVP of Operations & Procurement, Publishing; RUWAN JAYATILLEKE, SVP & Associate Publisher, Publishing; C.B. CEBULSKI, SVP of Creator & Content Development; DAVID GABRIEL, SVP of Publishing Sales & Circulation; MICHAEL PASCIULLO, SVP of Brand Planning & Communications; JIM O'KEEFE, VP of Operations & Logistics; DAN CARR, Executive Director of Publishing Technology; SUSAN CRESPI, Editorial Operations Manager; ALEX MORALES, Publishing Operations Manager; STAN LEE, Chairman Emeritus. For information regarding advertising in Marvel Comics or on Marvel.com, please contact Niza Disla, Director of Marvel Partnerships, at ndisla@marvel.com. For Marvel subscription inquiries, please call 800-217-9158. **Manufactured between 7/23/2012 and 9/3/2012 (hardcover), and 7/23/2012 and 3/4/2013 (softcover), by R.R. DONNELLEY, INC., SALEM, VA, USA.**

10 9 8 7 6 5 4 3 2 1

THE INVINCIBLE IRON MAN
LONG WAY DOWN

WRITER: **MATT FRACTION**
ARTIST: **SALVADOR LARROCA**
COLORS: **FRANK D'ARMATA**
LETTERS: **VC'S JOE CARAMAGNA**
COVER ART: **SALVADOR LARROCA** & **FRANK D'ARMATA**
ASSISTANT EDITORS: **JAKE THOMAS** & **JON MOISAN**
EDITOR: **MARK PANICCIA**
EXECUTIVE EDITOR: **TOM BREVOORT**

COLLECTION EDITOR: **JENNIFER GRÜNWALD**
ASSISTANT EDITORS: **ALEX STARBUCK** & **NELSON RIBEIRO**
EDITOR, SPECIAL PROJECTS: **MARK D. BEAZLEY**
SENIOR EDITOR, SPECIAL PROJECTS: **JEFF YOUNGQUIST**
SENIOR VICE PRESIDENT OF SALES: **DAVID GABRIEL**
SVP OF BRAND PLANNING & COMMUNICATIONS: **MICHAEL PASCIULLO**

EDITOR IN CHIEF: **AXEL ALONSO**
CHIEF CREATIVE OFFICER: **JOE QUESADA**
PUBLISHER: **DAN BUCKLEY**
EXECUTIVE PRODUCER: **ALAN FINE**

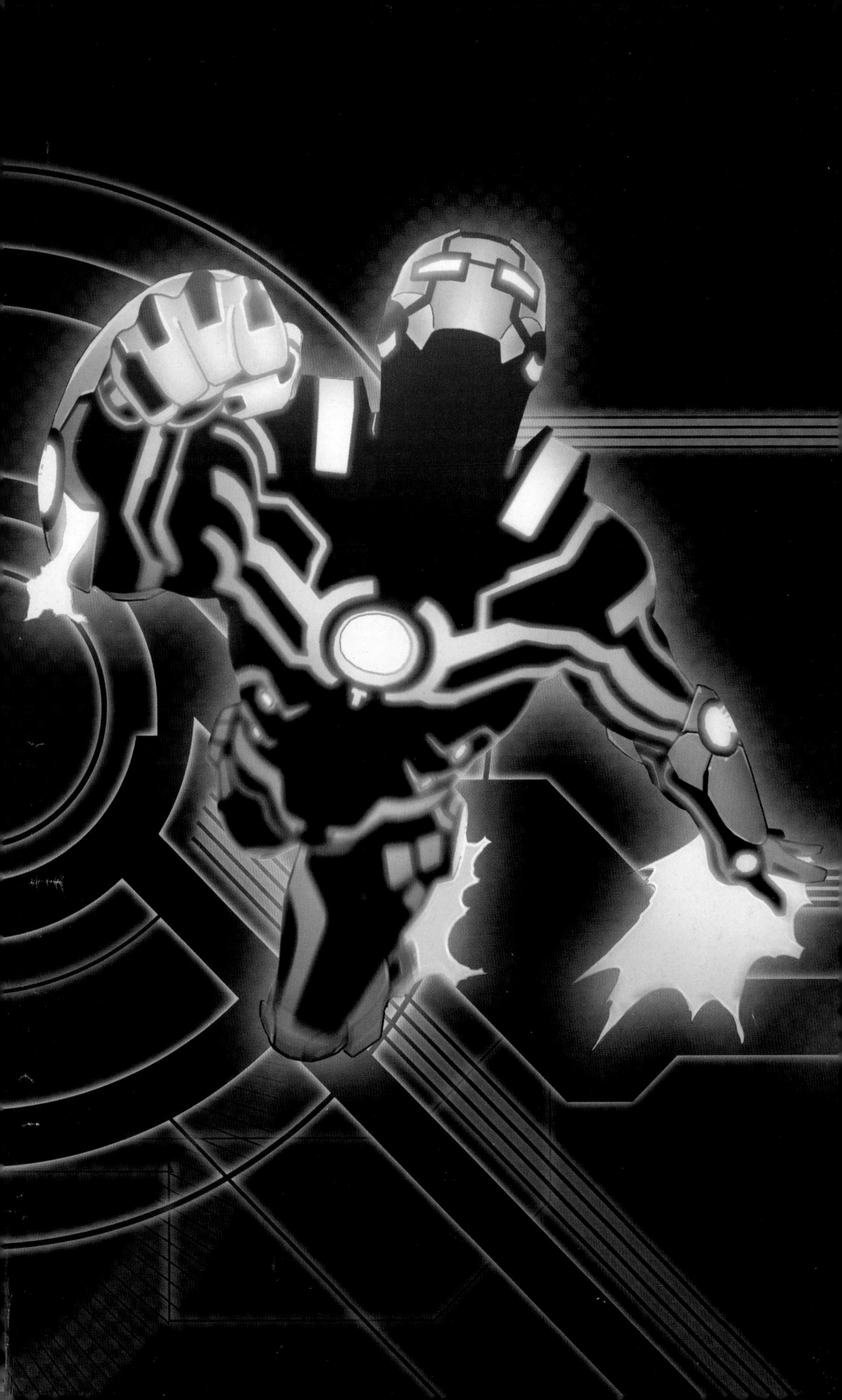

PREVIOUSLY:

FACED WITH WHAT HE THOUGHT WAS HIS LAST NIGHT ON EARTH, TONY STARK GOT DRUNK...AND NOW PEOPLE KNOW.

THE MANDARIN, EZEKIEL STANE, AND JUSTINE HAMMER JOINED FORCES TO MANIPULATE NOT JUST OUR GOVERNMENT, BUT THE WHOLE WORLD INTO BELIEVING THAT TONY WAS DANGEROUS, INEFFECTIVE AND UNFIT TO BE IRON MAN. ADDITIONALLY, TONY'S GREATEST FOES — UPDATED AND DEADLIER THAN EVER — UNLEASHED GLOBAL CALAMITY THROUGH A SERIES OF PRECISELY ORCHESTRATED ATTACKS.

WITH NO CHOICE, THE GOVERNMENT ISSUED TONY A MONITOR FOR HIS SUIT WHICH ALLOWS THEM TO SHUT HIM DOWN AT A MOMENT'S NOTICE. HIS OPTIONS: WEAR THE MONITOR AND BE AT THE MERCY OF SOMEONE ELSE, OR FORFEIT ALL OF HIS ASSETS TO THE U.S. GOVERNMENT. WITH NO OTHER CHOICE, TONY RELENTED.

AFTER BEING SHUT DOWN BY H.A.M.M.E.R., TONY WATCHED AS WAR MACHINE, JIM "RHODEY" RHODES, WAS FORCED TO FACE THE WHIRLWIND, THE MELTER, AND THE LIVING LASER. DESPITE PUTTING UP A VALIANT FIGHT, RHODEY WAS SEEMINGLY KILLED BEFORE PEPPER POTTS, SUITED UP IN HER OWN SET OF ARMOR, COULD ARRIVE ON THE SCENE.

HOWEVER, IT WAS REVEALED THAT RHODEY HAD FAKED HIS DEATH AS A PART OF TONY'S PLAN TO STRIKE BACK AT HIS ENEMIES. NOW, AS EZEKIEL STANE CONSTRUCTS THE MANDARIN'S DEATH MACHINE, TONY STARK HAS DONE SOMETHING HE HASN'T IN A VERY LONG TIME...ASK FOR HELP.

TONY STARK HAS BEEN SOBER FOR TWENTY-ONE DAYS.

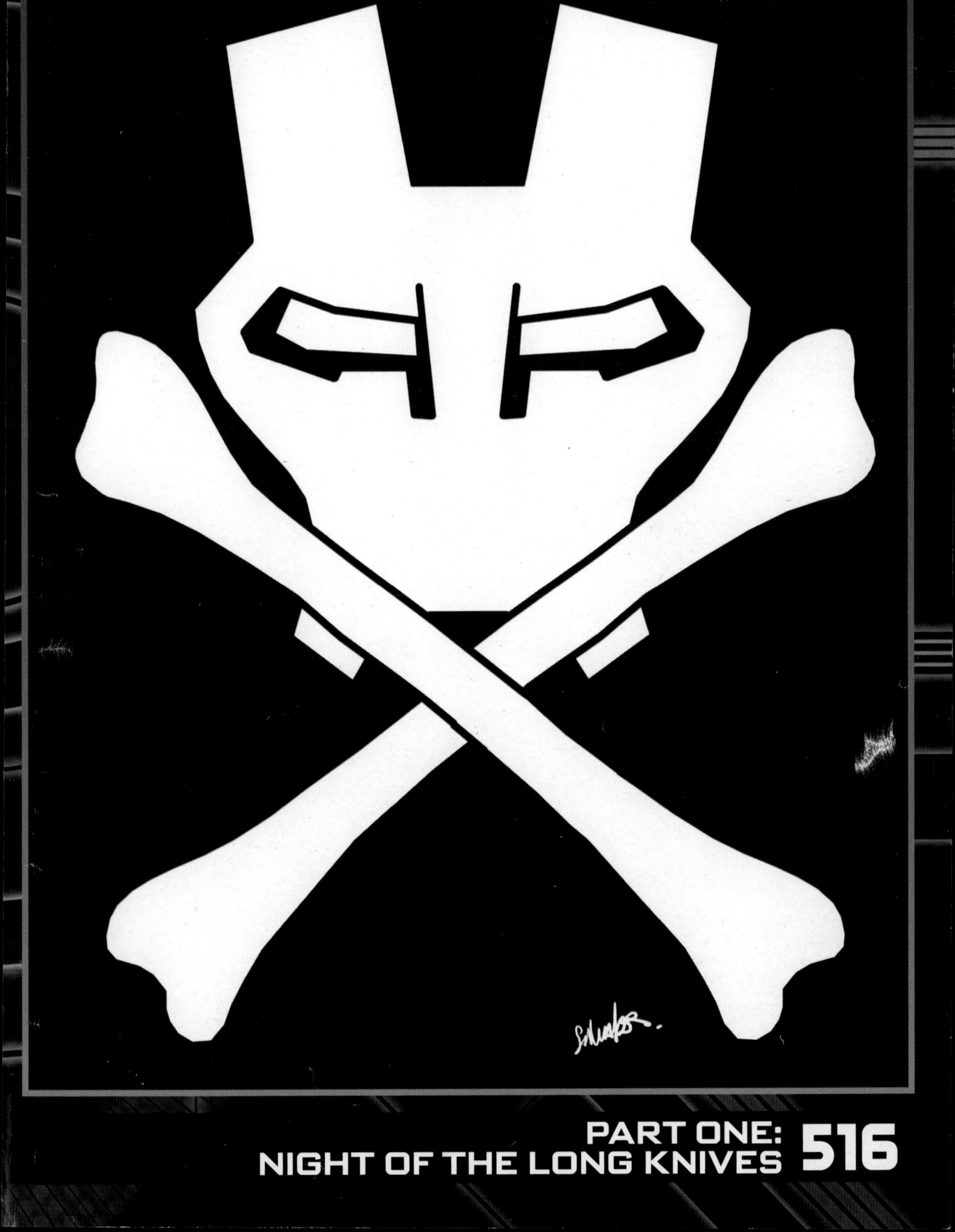

PART ONE: NIGHT OF THE LONG KNIVES 516

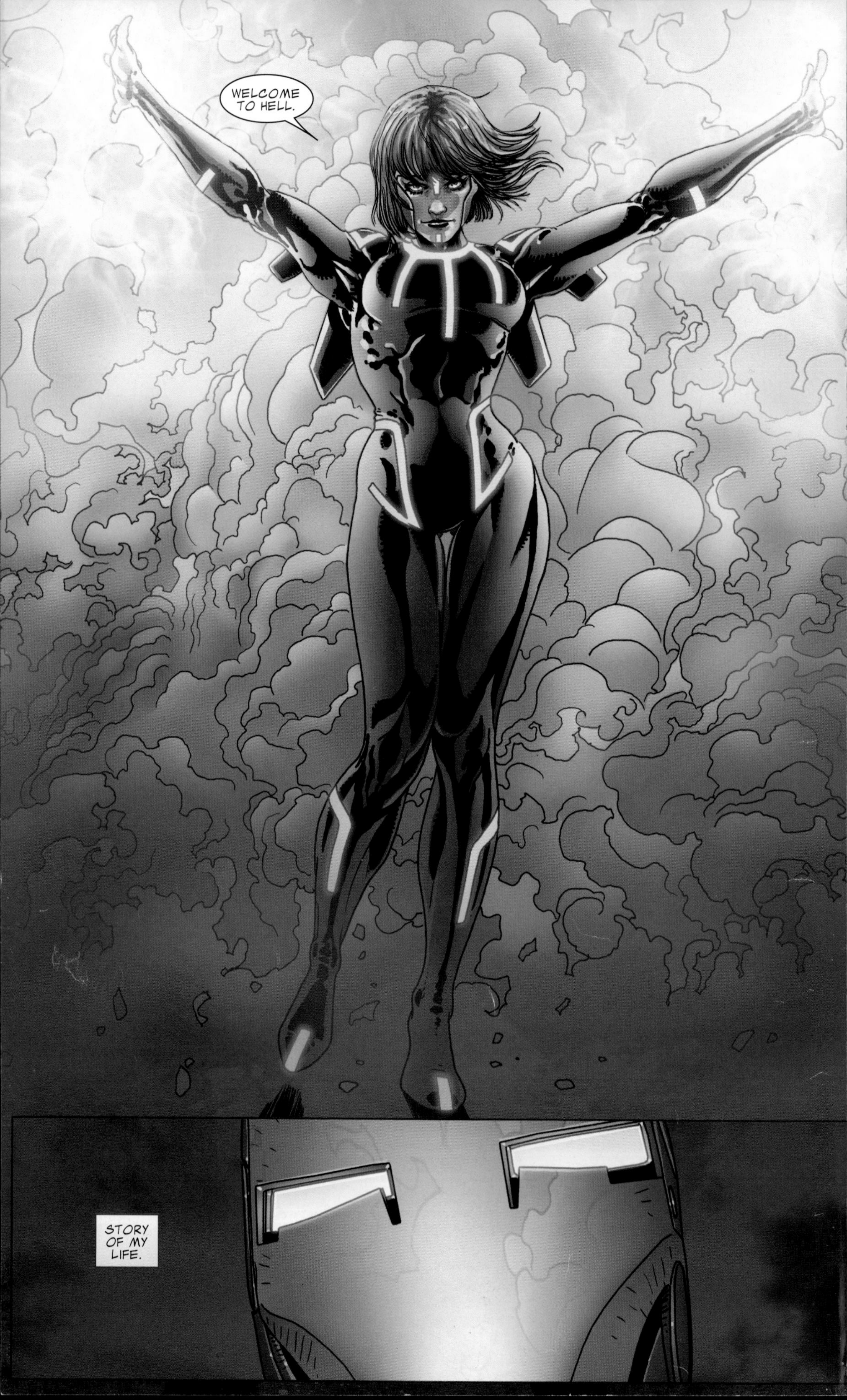
WELCOME TO HELL.
STORY OF MY LIFE.

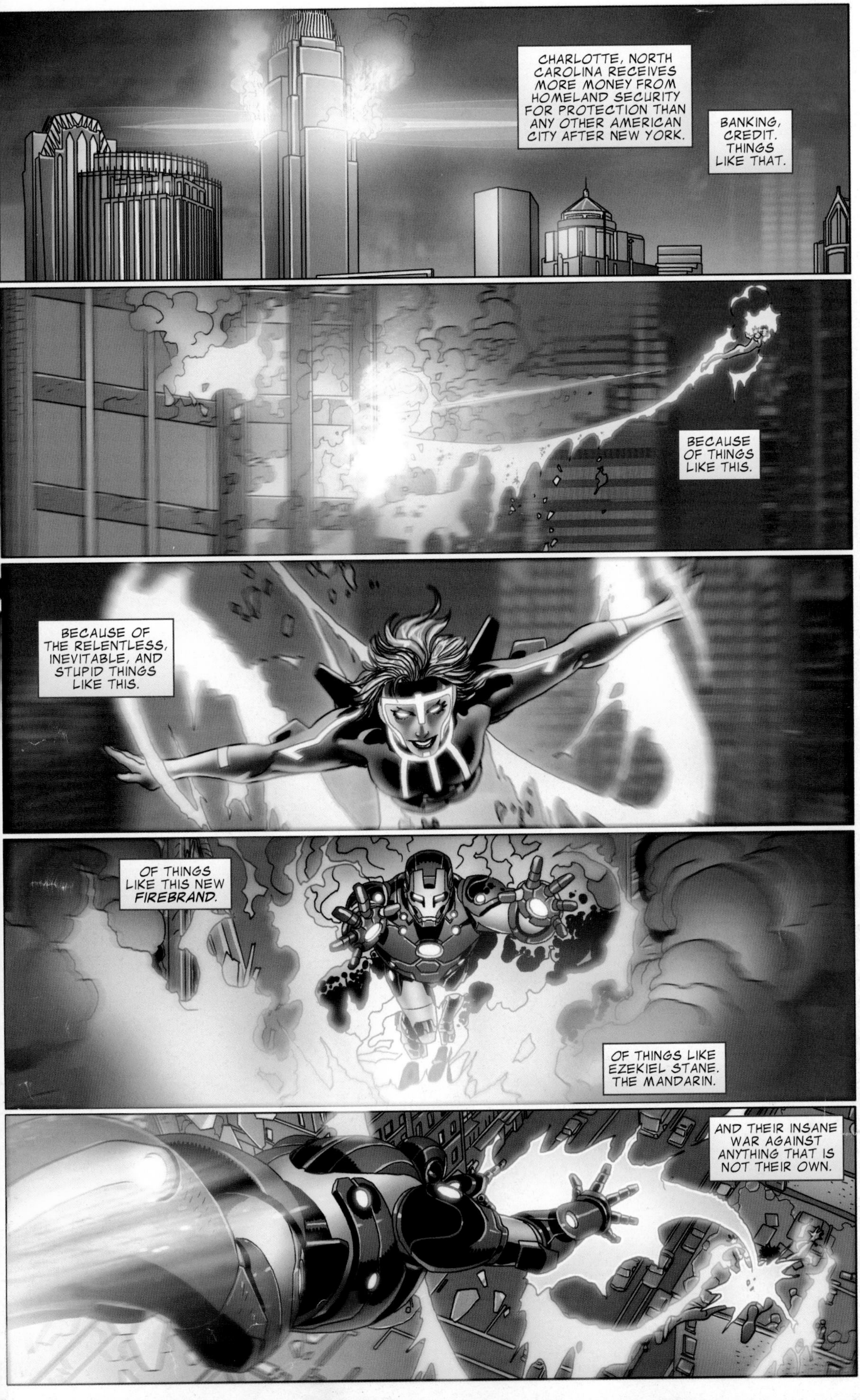
CHARLOTTE, NORTH CAROLINA RECEIVES MORE MONEY FROM HOMELAND SECURITY FOR PROTECTION THAN ANY OTHER AMERICAN CITY AFTER NEW YORK.
BANKING, CREDIT. THINGS LIKE THAT.
BECAUSE OF THINGS LIKE THIS.
BECAUSE OF THE RELENTLESS, INEVITABLE, AND STUPID THINGS LIKE THIS.
OF THINGS LIKE THIS NEW FIREBRAND.
OF THINGS LIKE EZEKIEL STANE. THE MANDARIN.
AND THEIR INSANE WAR AGAINST ANYTHING THAT IS NOT THEIR OWN.

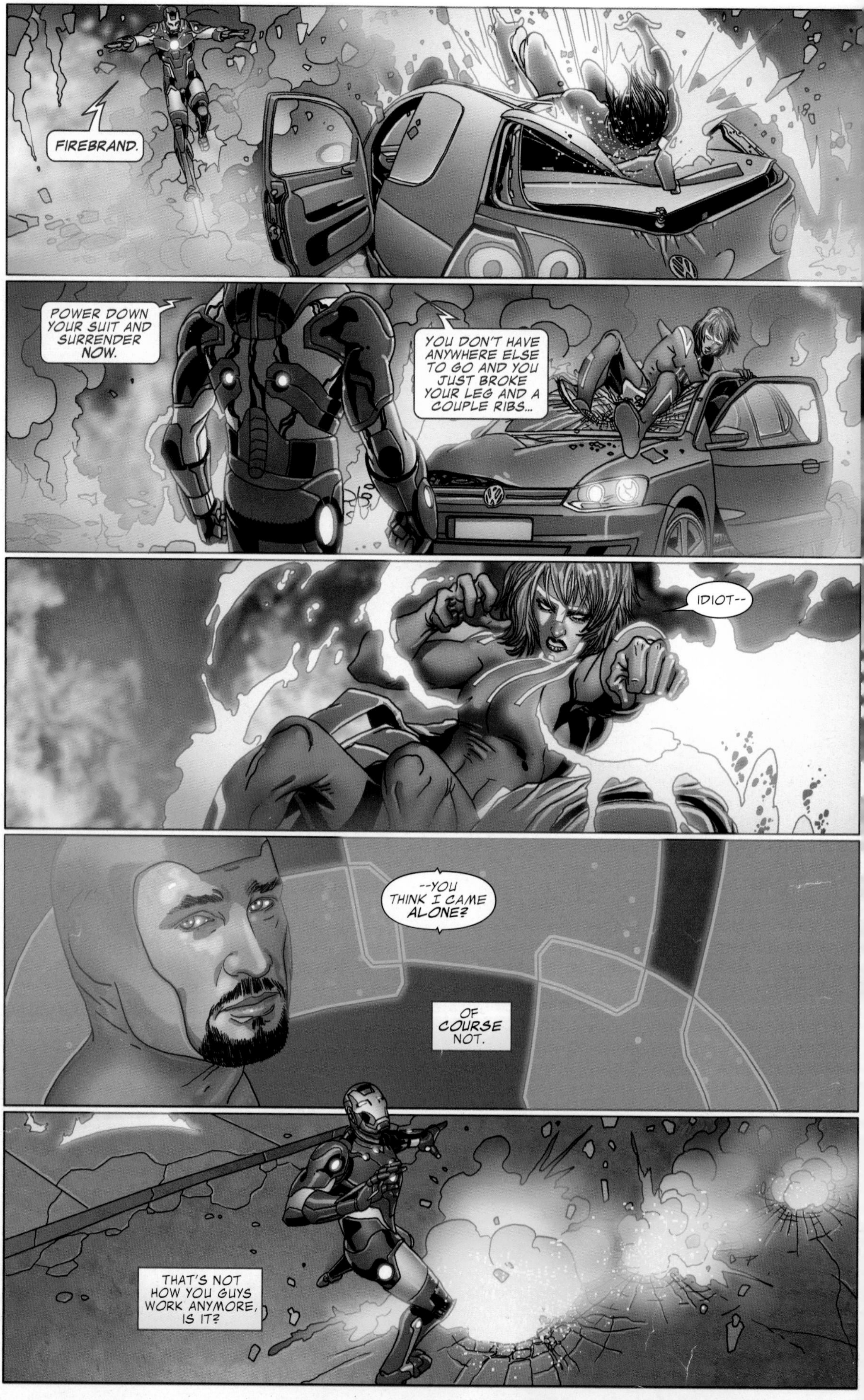

FIREBRAND.
POWER DOWN YOUR SUIT AND SURRENDER NOW.
YOU DON'T HAVE ANYWHERE ELSE TO GO AND YOU JUST BROKE YOUR LEG AND A COUPLE RIBS...
IDIOT--
--YOU THINK I CAME ALONE?
OF COURSE NOT.
THAT'S NOT HOW YOU GUYS WORK ANYMORE, IS IT?

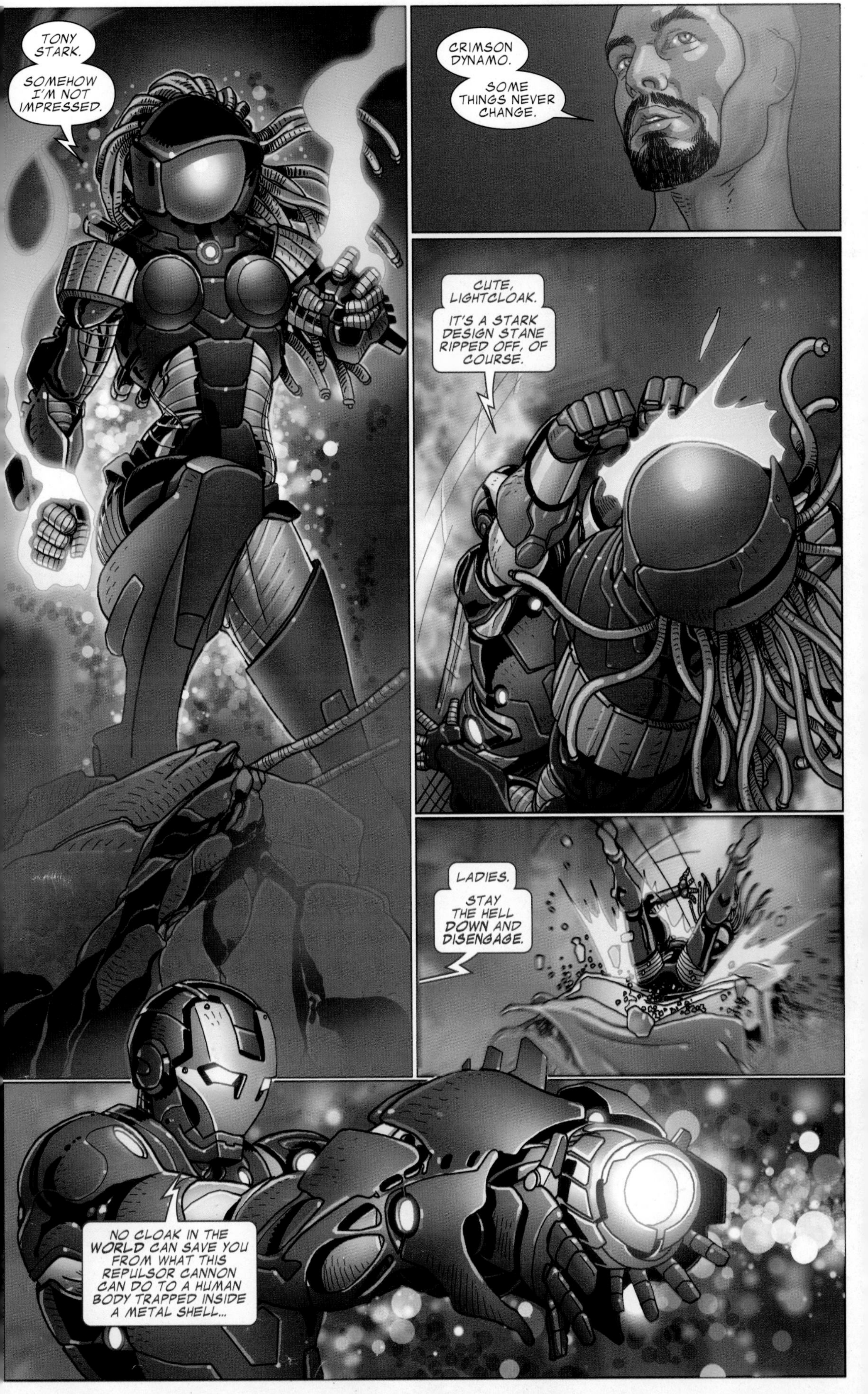
TONY STARK.
SOMEHOW I'M NOT IMPRESSED.
CRIMSON DYNAMO.
SOME THINGS NEVER CHANGE.
CUTE, LIGHTCLOAK.
IT'S A STARK DESIGN STANE RIPPED OFF, OF COURSE.
LADIES.
STAY THE HELL DOWN AND DISENGAGE.
NO CLOAK IN THE WORLD CAN SAVE YOU FROM WHAT THIS REPULSOR CANNON CAN DO TO A HUMAN BODY TRAPPED INSIDE A METAL SHELL...

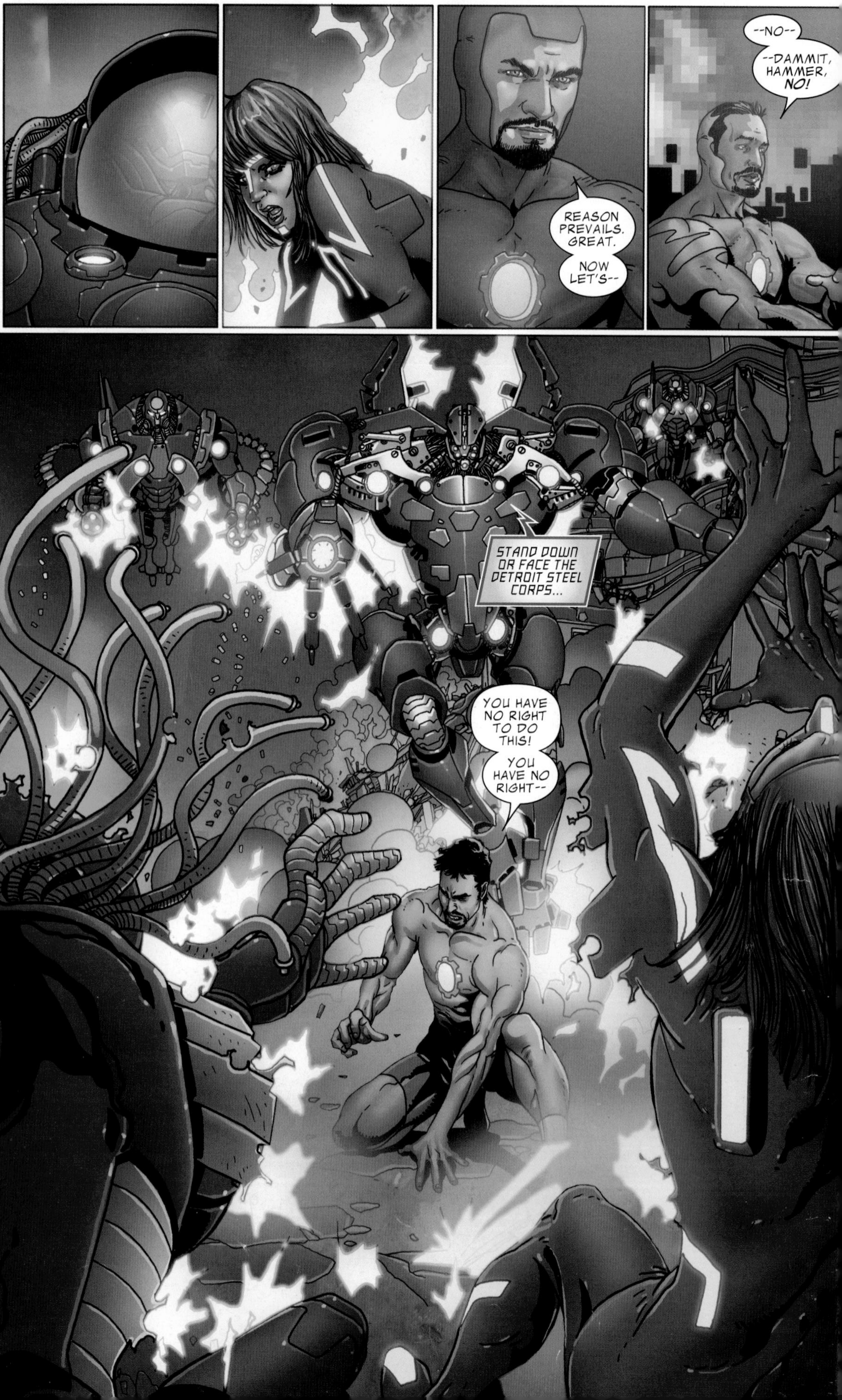

REASON PREVAILS. GREAT.
NOW LET'S--
--NO--
--DAMMIT, HAMMER, NO!
STAND DOWN OR FACE THE DETROIT STEEL CORPS...
YOU HAVE NO RIGHT TO DO THIS!
YOU HAVE NO RIGHT--

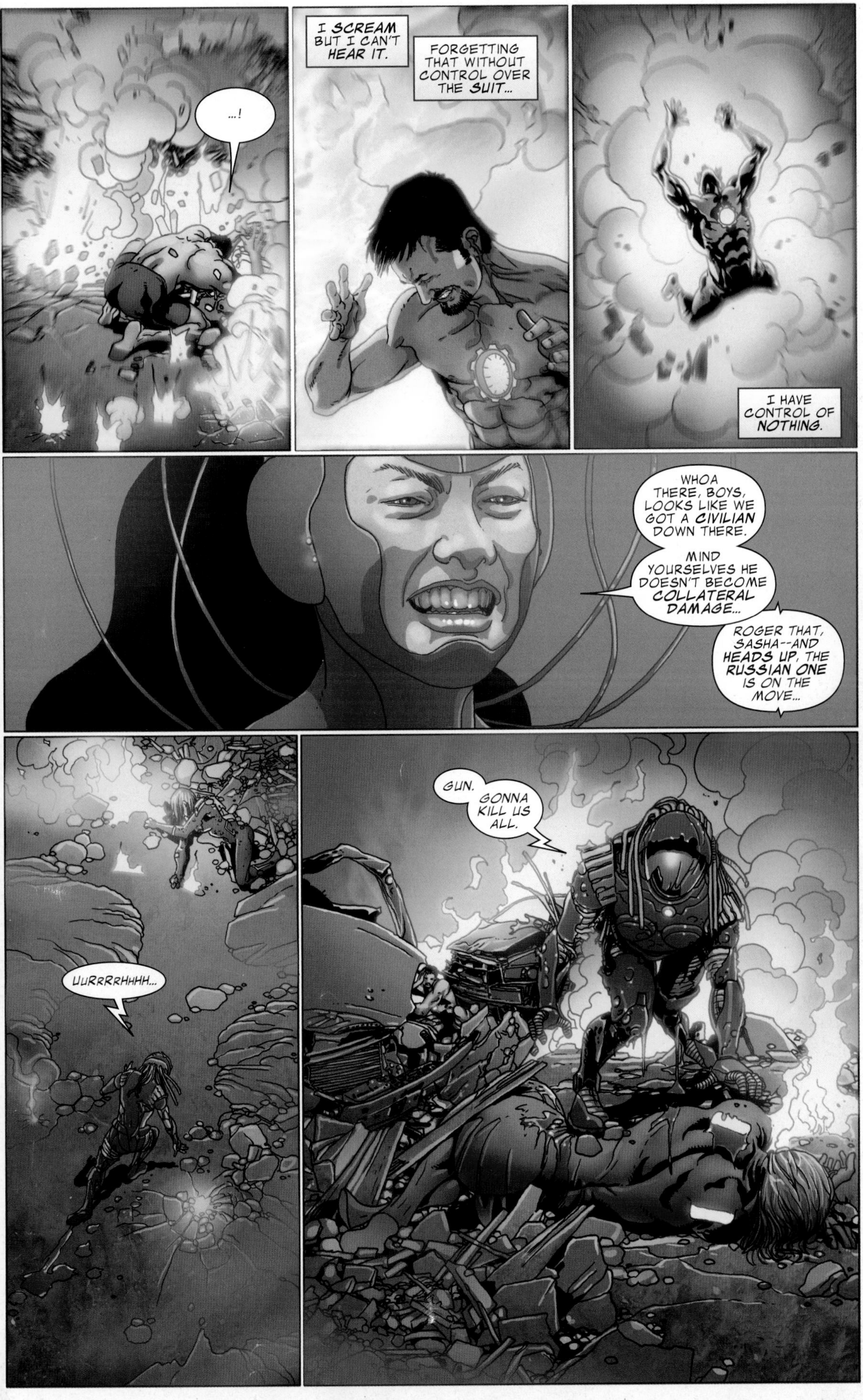
...!
I SCREAM BUT I CAN'T HEAR IT.
FORGETTING THAT WITHOUT CONTROL OVER THE SUIT...
I HAVE CONTROL OF NOTHING.
WHOA THERE, BOYS, LOOKS LIKE WE GOT A CIVILIAN DOWN THERE.
MIND YOURSELVES HE DOESN'T BECOME COLLATERAL DAMAGE...
ROGER THAT, SASHA--AND HEADS UP, THE RUSSIAN ONE IS ON THE MOVE...
UURRRRHHHH...
GUN.
GONNA KILL US ALL.

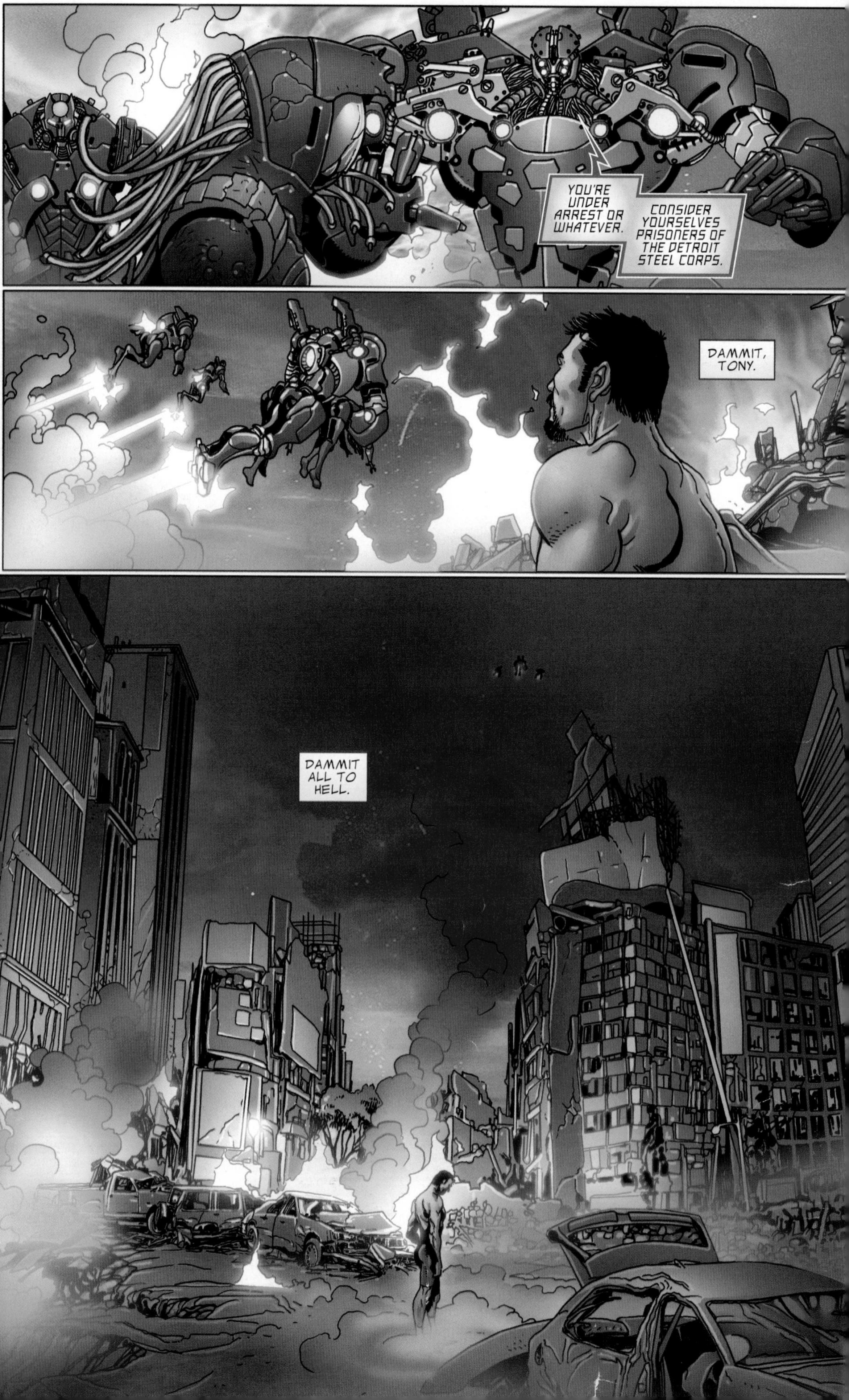
YOU'RE UNDER ARREST OR WHATEVER.
CONSIDER YOURSELVES PRISONERS OF THE DETROIT STEEL CORPS.
DAMMIT, TONY.
DAMMIT ALL TO HELL.

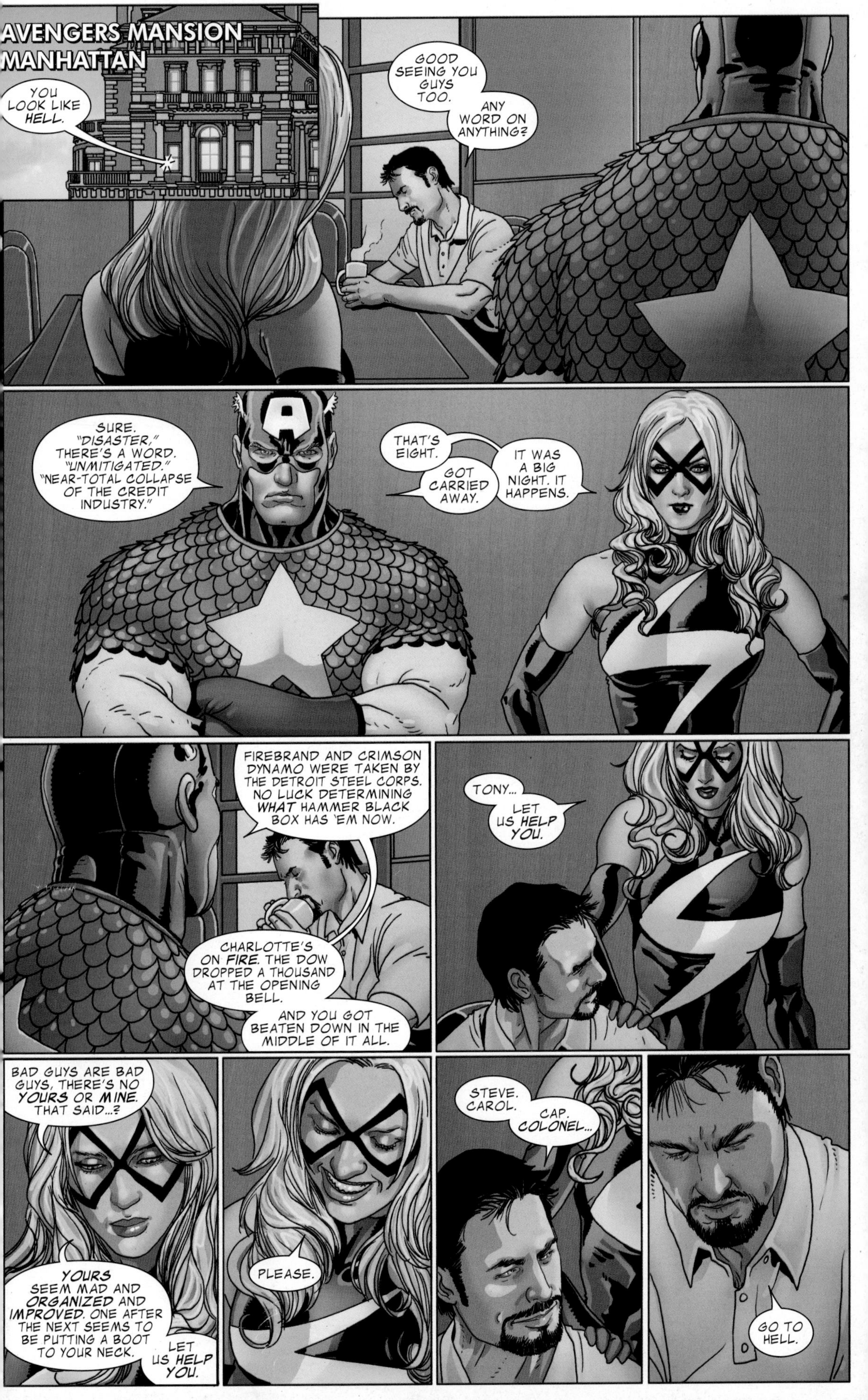
AVENGERS MANSION
MANHATTAN
YOU LOOK LIKE HELL.
GOOD SEEING YOU GUYS TOO.
ANY WORD ON ANYTHING?
SURE. "DISASTER," THERE'S A WORD. "UNMITIGATED." "NEAR-TOTAL COLLAPSE OF THE CREDIT INDUSTRY."
THAT'S EIGHT.
GOT CARRIED AWAY.
IT WAS A BIG NIGHT. IT HAPPENS.
FIREBRAND AND CRIMSON DYNAMO WERE TAKEN BY THE DETROIT STEEL CORPS. NO LUCK DETERMINING WHAT HAMMER BLACK BOX HAS 'EM NOW.
CHARLOTTE'S ON FIRE. THE DOW DROPPED A THOUSAND AT THE OPENING BELL.
AND YOU GOT BEATEN DOWN IN THE MIDDLE OF IT ALL.
TONY...
LET US HELP YOU.
BAD GUYS ARE BAD GUYS, THERE'S NO YOURS OR MINE. THAT SAID...?
YOURS SEEM MAD AND ORGANIZED AND IMPROVED. ONE AFTER THE NEXT SEEMS TO BE PUTTING A BOOT TO YOUR NECK.
LET US HELP YOU.
PLEASE.
STEVE. CAROL.
CAP. COLONEL...
GO TO HELL.

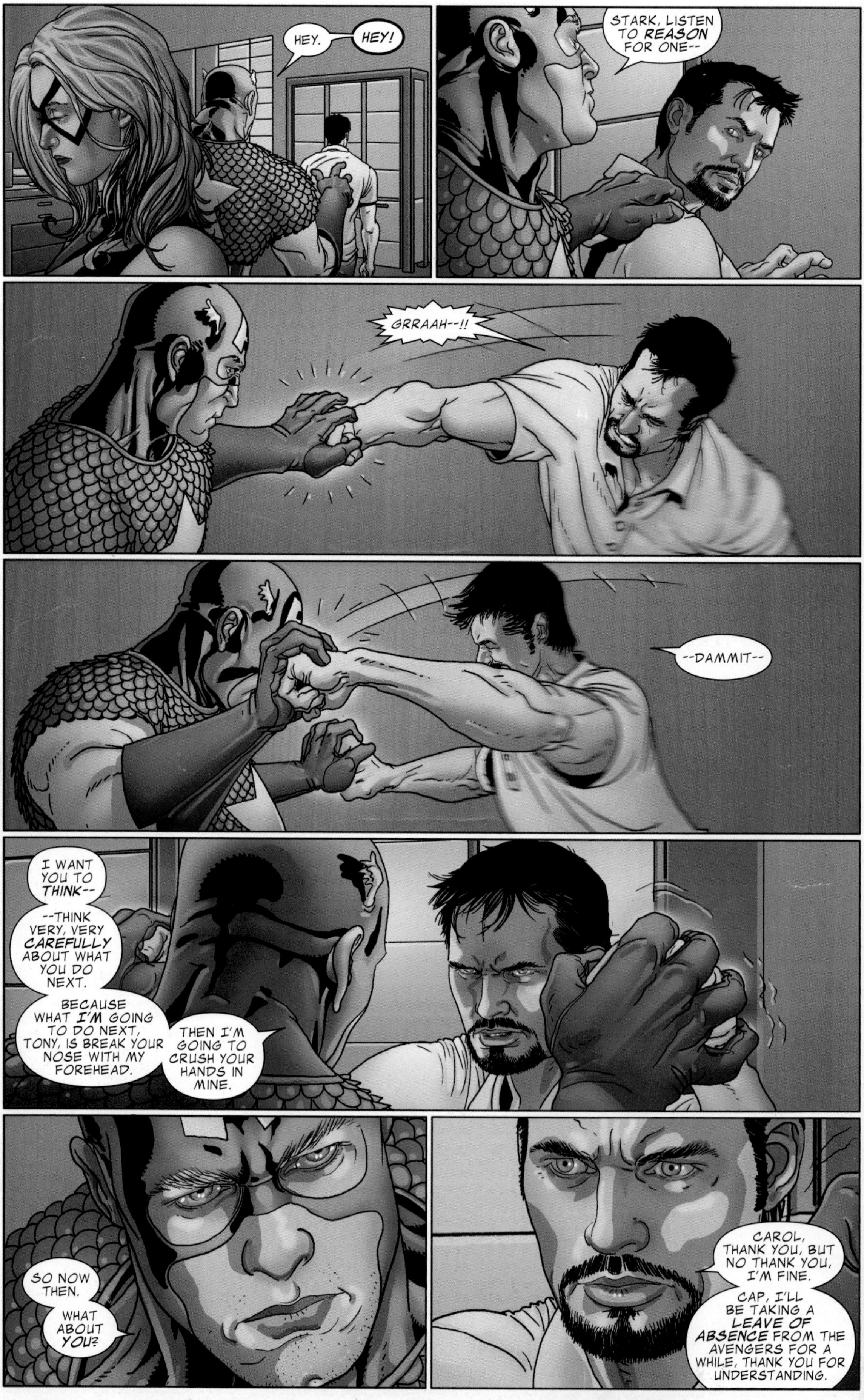
HEY.
HEY!
STARK, LISTEN TO REASON FOR ONE--
GRRAAH--!!
--DAMMIT--
I WANT YOU TO THINK--
--THINK VERY, VERY CAREFULLY ABOUT WHAT YOU DO NEXT.
BECAUSE WHAT I'M GOING TO DO NEXT, TONY, IS BREAK YOUR NOSE WITH MY FOREHEAD.
THEN I'M GOING TO CRUSH YOUR HANDS IN MINE.
SO NOW THEN.
WHAT ABOUT YOU?
CAROL, THANK YOU, BUT NO THANK YOU, I'M FINE.
CAP, I'LL BE TAKING A LEAVE OF ABSENCE FROM THE AVENGERS FOR A WHILE, THANK YOU FOR UNDERSTANDING.

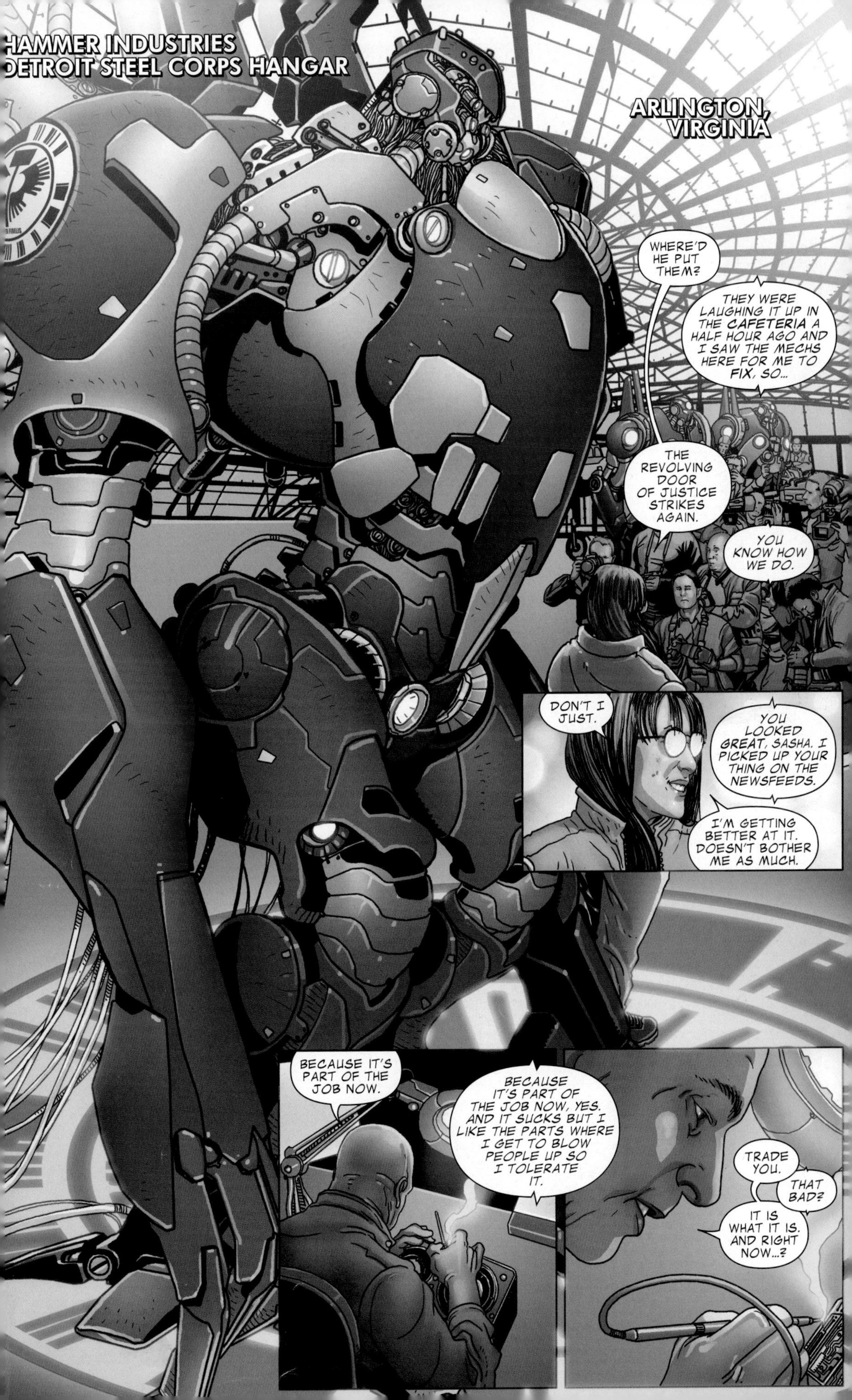
HAMMER INDUSTRIES
DETROIT STEEL CORPS HANGAR
ARLINGTON, VIRGINIA
WHERE'D HE PUT THEM?
THEY WERE LAUGHING IT UP IN THE CAFETERIA A HALF HOUR AGO AND I SAW THE MECHS HERE FOR ME TO FIX, SO...
THE REVOLVING DOOR OF JUSTICE STRIKES AGAIN.
YOU KNOW HOW WE DO.
DON'T I JUST.
YOU LOOKED GREAT, SASHA. I PICKED UP YOUR THING ON THE NEWSFEEDS.
I'M GETTING BETTER AT IT. DOESN'T BOTHER ME AS MUCH.
BECAUSE IT'S PART OF THE JOB NOW.
BECAUSE IT'S PART OF THE JOB NOW, YES. AND IT SUCKS BUT I LIKE THE PARTS WHERE I GET TO BLOW PEOPLE UP SO I TOLERATE IT.
TRADE YOU.
THAT BAD?
IT IS WHAT IT IS. AND RIGHT NOW...?

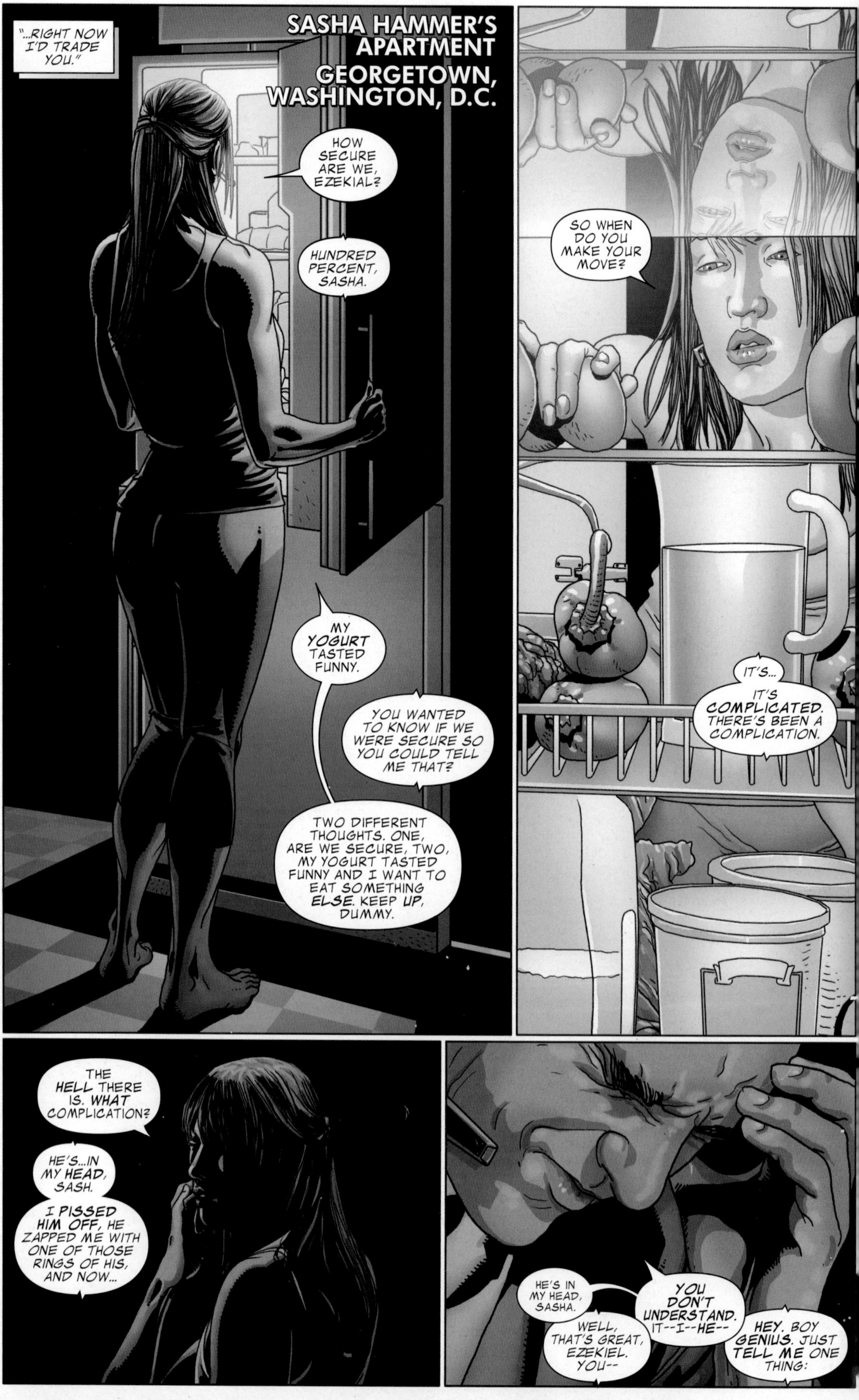
"...RIGHT NOW I'D TRADE YOU."
SASHA HAMMER'S APARTMENT
GEORGETOWN, WASHINGTON, D.C.
HOW SECURE ARE WE, EZEKIAL?
HUNDRED PERCENT, SASHA.
MY YOGURT TASTED FUNNY.
YOU WANTED TO KNOW IF WE WERE SECURE SO YOU COULD TELL ME THAT?
TWO DIFFERENT THOUGHTS. ONE, ARE WE SECURE, TWO, MY YOGURT TASTED FUNNY AND I WANT TO EAT SOMETHING ELSE. KEEP UP, DUMMY.
SO WHEN DO YOU MAKE YOUR MOVE?
IT'S...
IT'S COMPLICATED. THERE'S BEEN A COMPLICATION.
THE HELL THERE IS. WHAT COMPLICATION?
HE'S...IN MY HEAD, SASH.
I PISSED HIM OFF, HE ZAPPED ME WITH ONE OF THOSE RINGS OF HIS, AND NOW...
HE'S IN MY HEAD, SASHA.
WELL, THAT'S GREAT, EZEKIEL. YOU--
YOU DON'T UNDERSTAND. IT--I--HE--
HEY. BOY GENIUS. JUST TELL ME ONE THING:

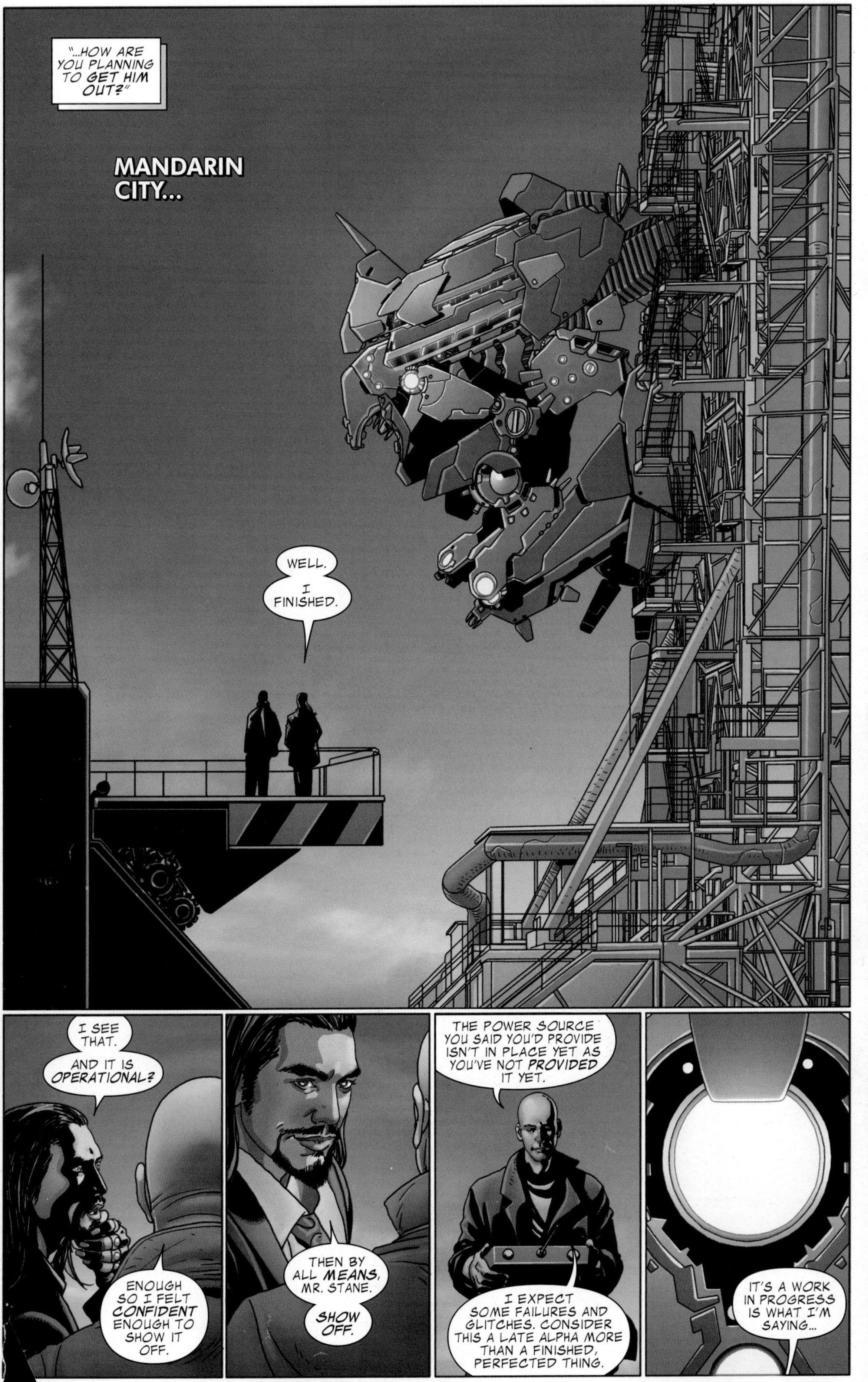
"...HOW ARE YOU PLANNING TO GET HIM OUT?"
MANDARIN CITY...
WELL. I FINISHED.
I SEE THAT.
AND IT IS OPERATIONAL?
ENOUGH SO I FELT CONFIDENT ENOUGH TO SHOW IT OFF.
THEN BY ALL MEANS, MR. STANE.
SHOW OFF.
THE POWER SOURCE YOU SAID YOU'D PROVIDE ISN'T IN PLACE YET AS YOU'VE NOT PROVIDED IT YET.
I EXPECT SOME FAILURES AND GLITCHES. CONSIDER THIS A LATE ALPHA MORE THAN A FINISHED, PERFECTED THING.
IT'S A WORK IN PROGRESS IS WHAT I'M SAYING...

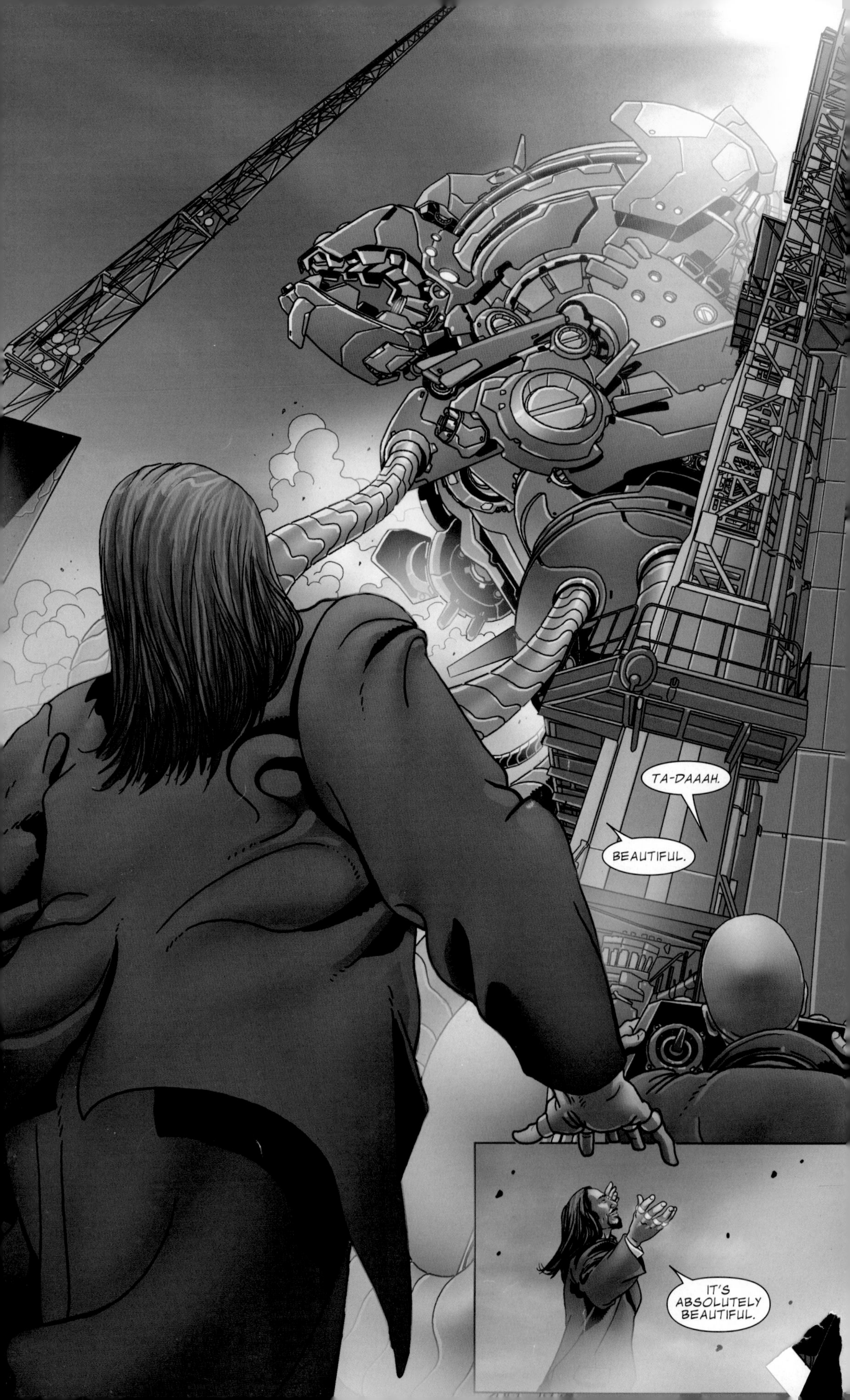
TA-DAAAH.
BEAUTIFUL.
IT'S ABSOLUTELY BEAUTIFUL.

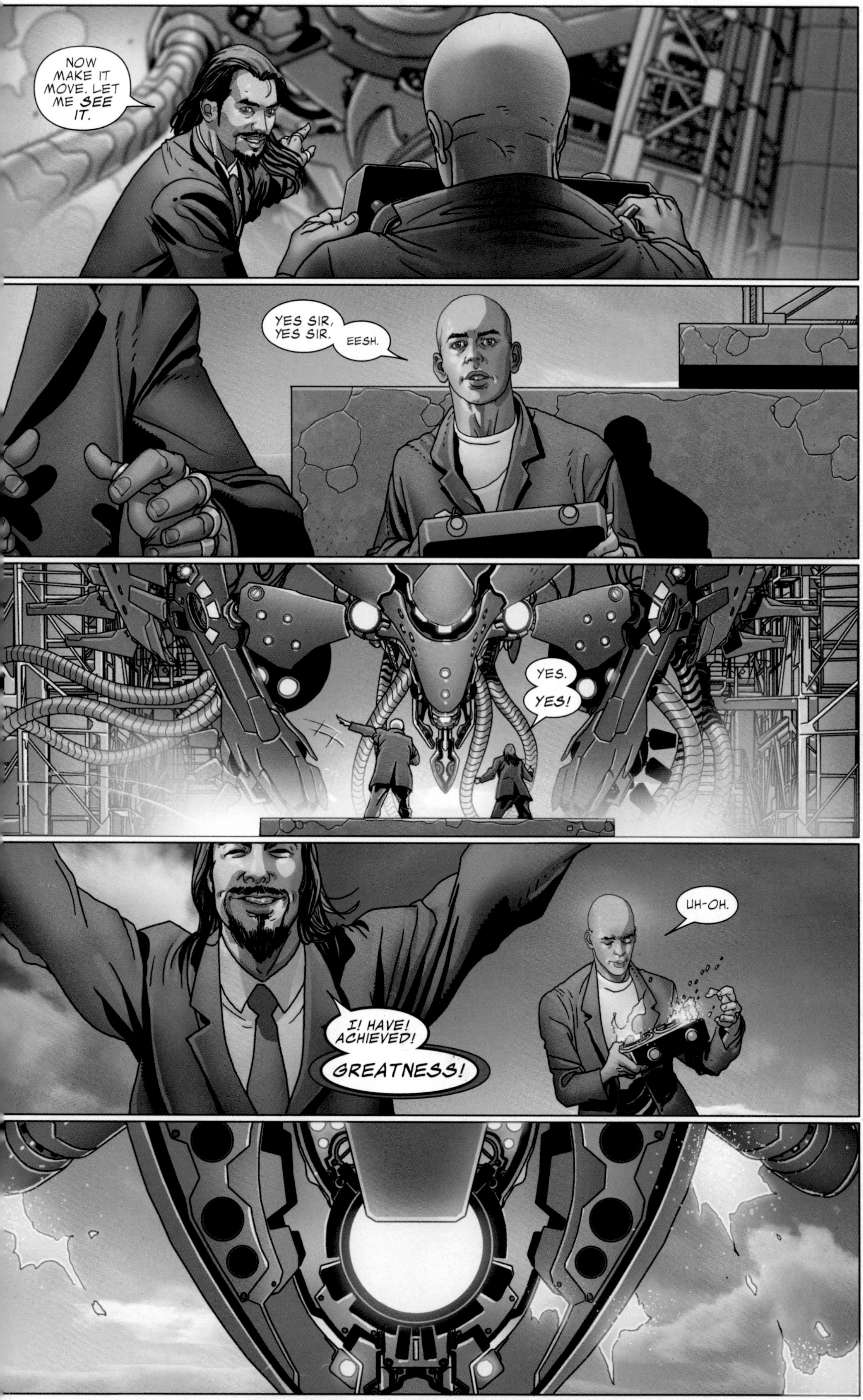
NOW MAKE IT MOVE. LET ME SEE IT.
YES SIR, YES SIR.
EESH.
YES.
YES!
UH-OH.
I! HAVE! ACHIEVED!
GREATNESS!

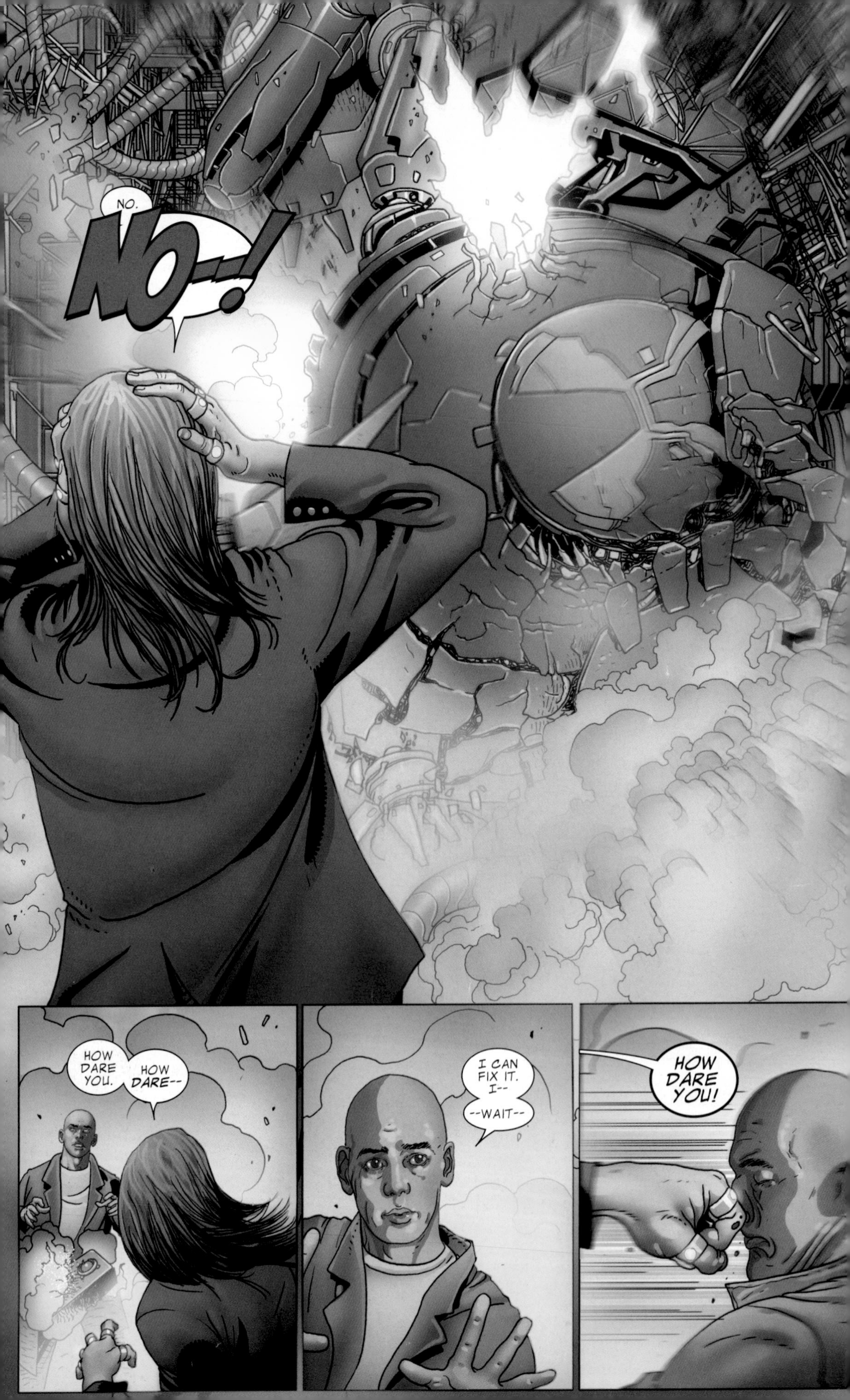
NO.
NO--!
HOW DARE YOU.
HOW DARE--
I CAN FIX IT. I--
--WAIT--
HOW DARE YOU!

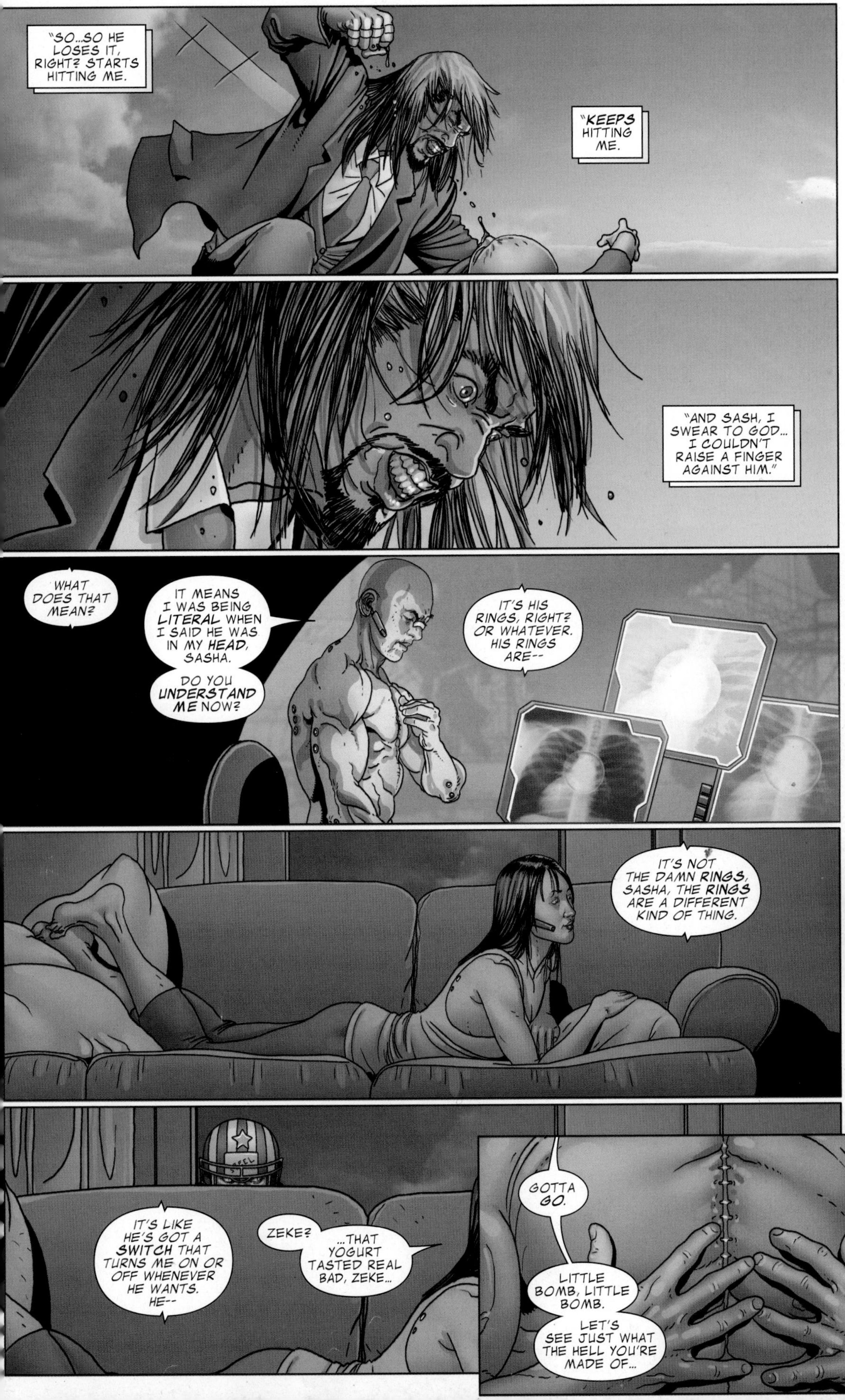
"SO...SO HE LOSES IT, RIGHT? STARTS HITTING ME.
"KEEPS HITTING ME.
"AND SASH, I SWEAR TO GOD... I COULDN'T RAISE A FINGER AGAINST HIM."
WHAT DOES THAT MEAN?
IT MEANS I WAS BEING LITERAL WHEN I SAID HE WAS IN MY HEAD, SASHA.
DO YOU UNDERSTAND ME NOW?
IT'S HIS RINGS, RIGHT? OR WHATEVER. HIS RINGS ARE--
IT'S NOT THE DAMN RINGS, SASHA, THE RINGS ARE A DIFFERENT KIND OF THING.
IT'S LIKE HE'S GOT A SWITCH THAT TURNS ME ON OR OFF WHENEVER HE WANTS. HE--
ZEKE?
...THAT YOGURT TASTED REAL BAD, ZEKE...
GOTTA GO.
LITTLE BOMB, LITTLE BOMB.
LET'S SEE JUST WHAT THE HELL YOU'RE MADE OF...

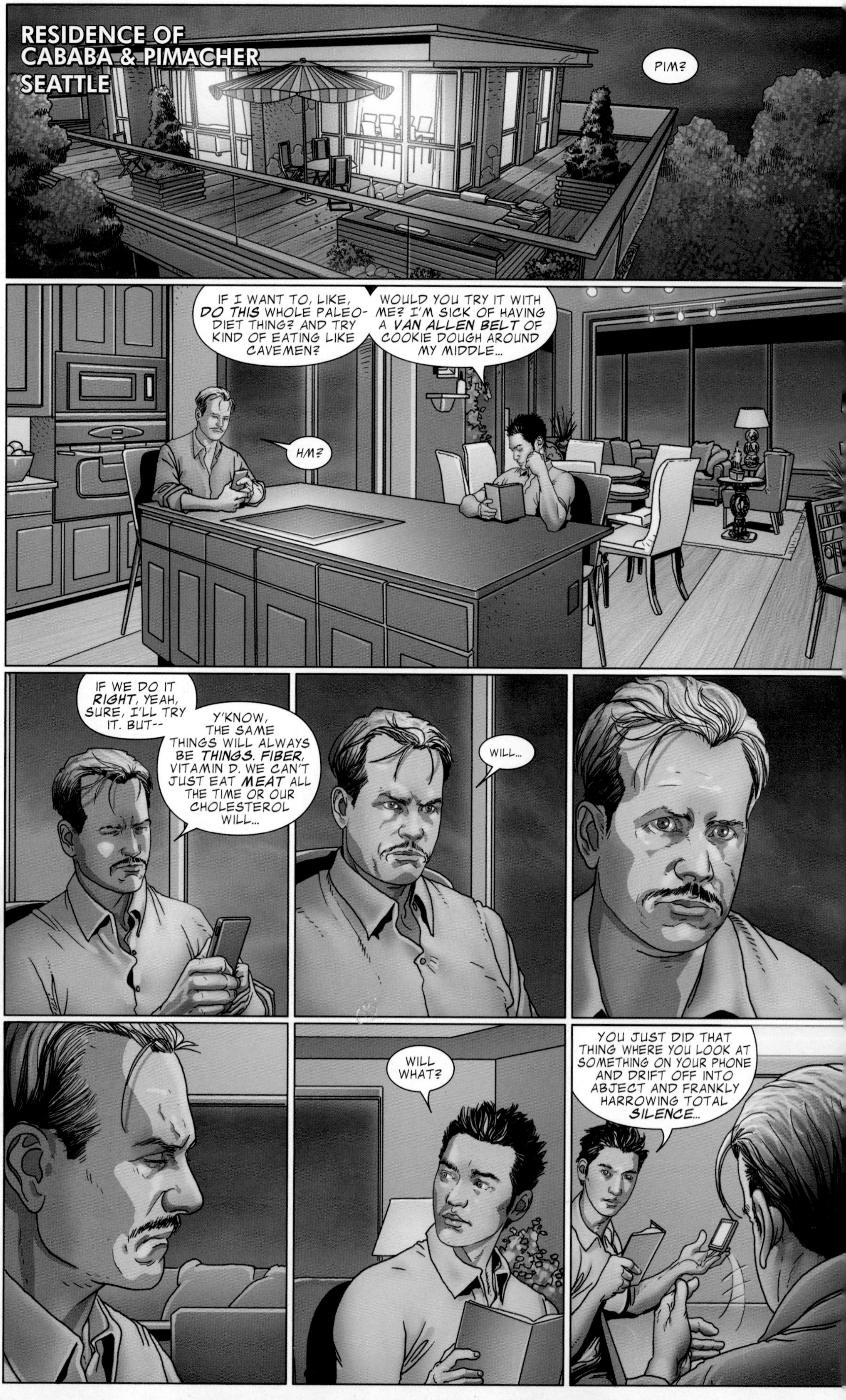
RESIDENCE OF CABABA & PIMACHER SEATTLE
PIM?
IF I WANT TO, LIKE, DO THIS WHOLE PALEO-DIET THING? AND TRY KIND OF EATING LIKE CAVEMEN?
WOULD YOU TRY IT WITH ME? I'M SICK OF HAVING A VAN ALLEN BELT OF COOKIE DOUGH AROUND MY MIDDLE...
HM?
IF WE DO IT RIGHT, YEAH, SURE, I'LL TRY IT. BUT--
Y'KNOW, THE SAME THINGS WILL ALWAYS BE THINGS. FIBER, VITAMIN D. WE CAN'T JUST EAT MEAT ALL THE TIME OR OUR CHOLESTEROL WILL...
WILL...
WILL WHAT?
YOU JUST DID THAT THING WHERE YOU LOOK AT SOMETHING ON YOUR PHONE AND DRIFT OFF INTO ABJECT AND FRANKLY HARROWING TOTAL SILENCE...

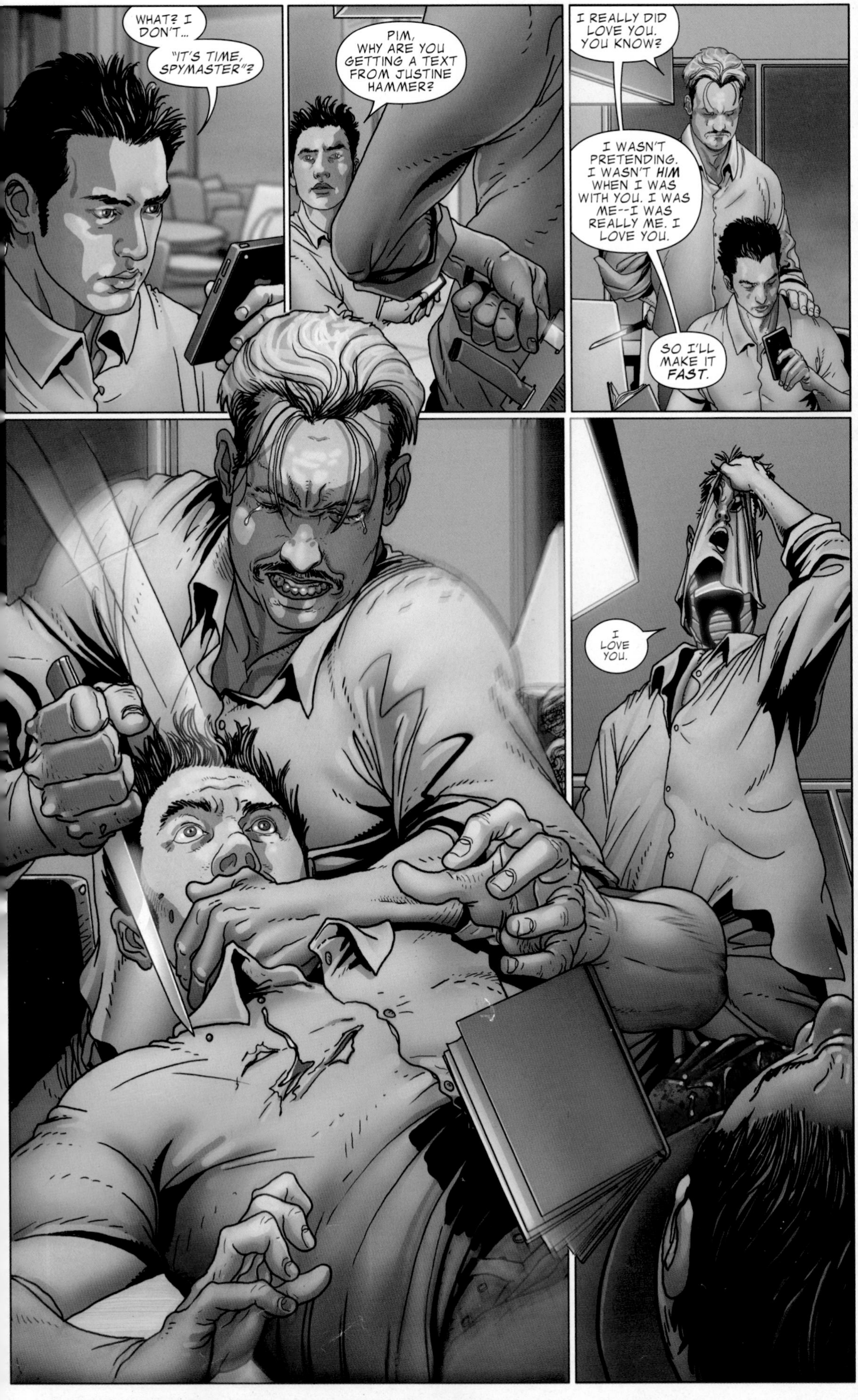
WHAT? I DON'T...
"IT'S TIME, SPYMASTER"?
PIM, WHY ARE YOU GETTING A TEXT FROM JUSTINE HAMMER?
I REALLY DID LOVE YOU. YOU KNOW?
I WASN'T PRETENDING. I WASN'T HIM WHEN I WAS WITH YOU. I WAS ME--I WAS REALLY ME. I LOVE YOU.
SO I'LL MAKE IT FAST.
I LOVE YOU.

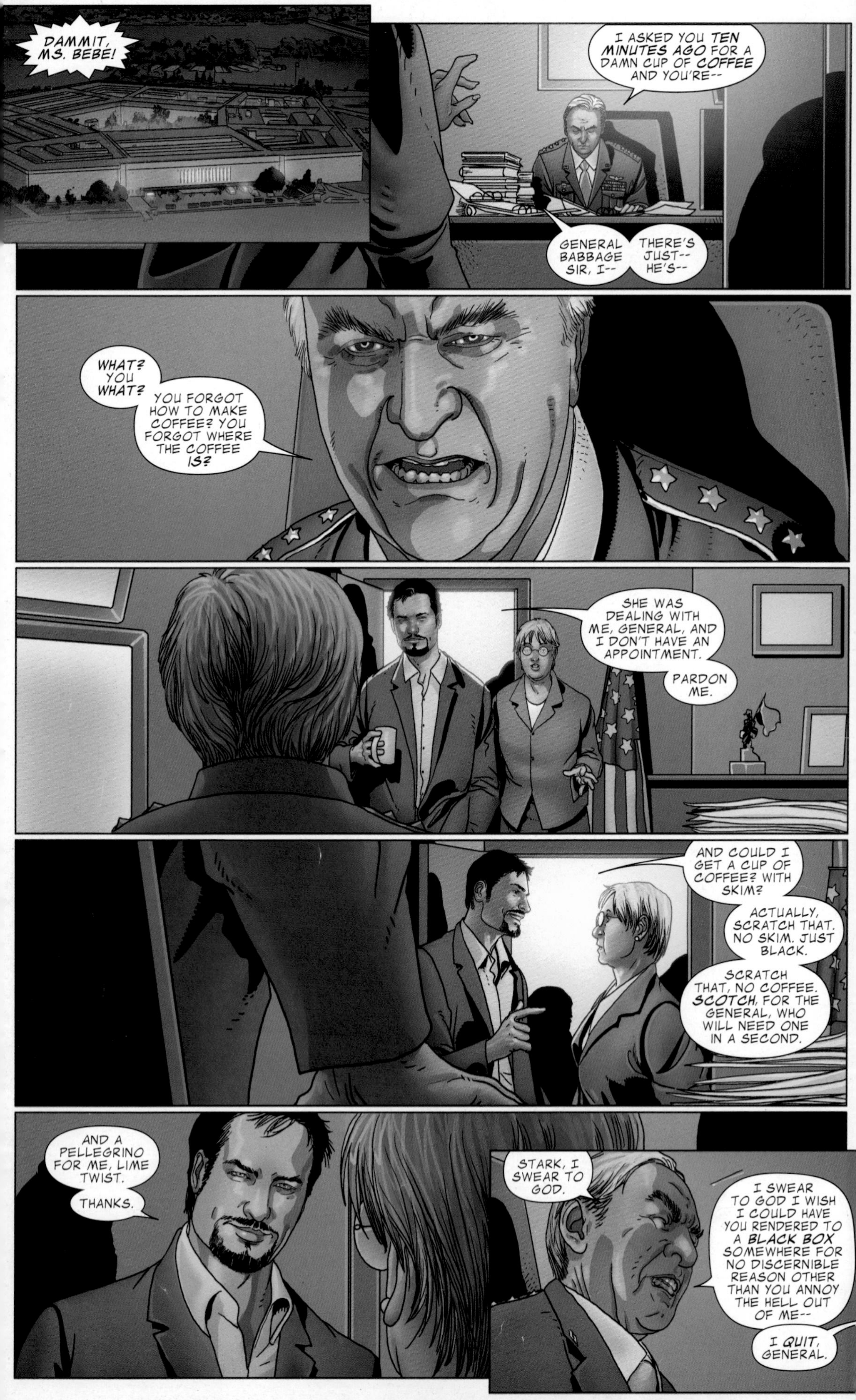
DAMMIT, MS. BEBE!
I ASKED YOU TEN MINUTES AGO FOR A DAMN CUP OF COFFEE AND YOU'RE--
GENERAL BABBAGE SIR, I--
THERE'S JUST-- HE'S--
WHAT? YOU WHAT?
YOU FORGOT HOW TO MAKE COFFEE? YOU FORGOT WHERE THE COFFEE IS?
SHE WAS DEALING WITH ME, GENERAL, AND I DON'T HAVE AN APPOINTMENT.
PARDON ME.
AND COULD I GET A CUP OF COFFEE? WITH SKIM?
ACTUALLY, SCRATCH THAT. NO SKIM. JUST BLACK.
SCRATCH THAT, NO COFFEE. SCOTCH, FOR THE GENERAL, WHO WILL NEED ONE IN A SECOND.
AND A PELLEGRINO FOR ME, LIME TWIST.
THANKS.
STARK, I SWEAR TO GOD.
I SWEAR TO GOD I WISH I COULD HAVE YOU RENDERED TO A BLACK BOX SOMEWHERE FOR NO DISCERNIBLE REASON OTHER THAN YOU ANNOY THE HELL OUT OF ME--
I QUIT, GENERAL.

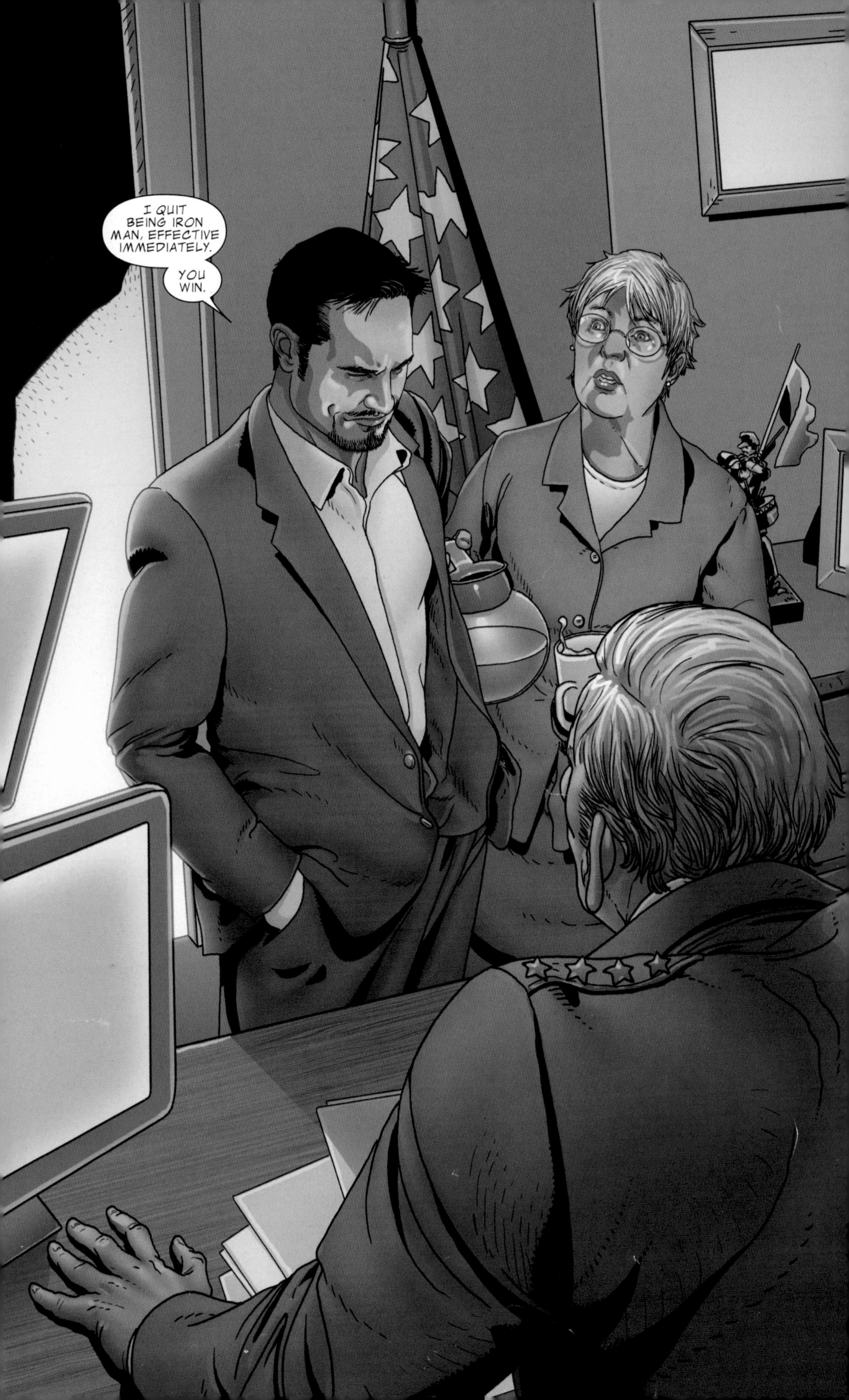
I QUIT BEING IRON MAN, EFFECTIVE IMMEDIATELY.
YOU WIN.

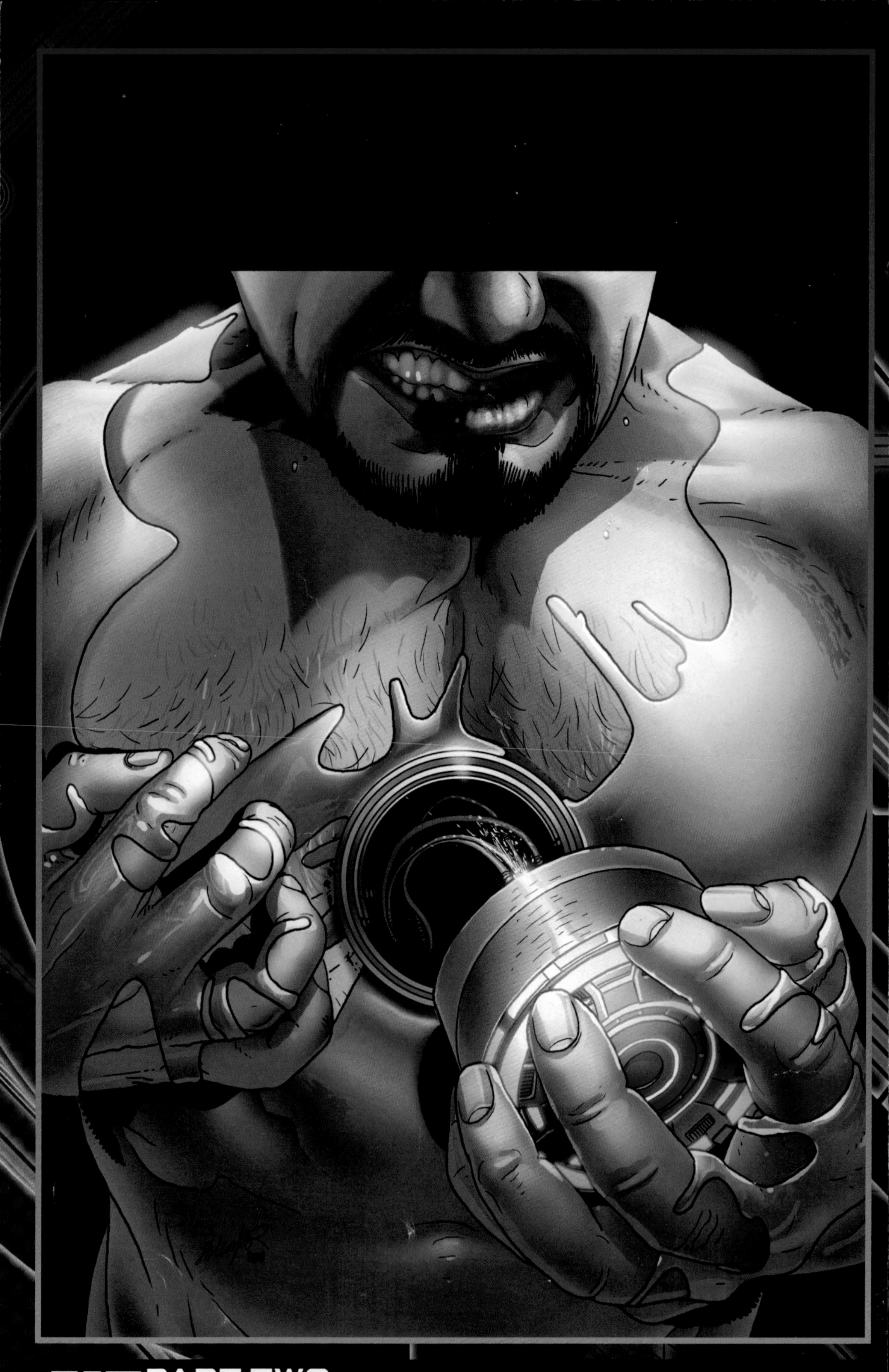

517 PART TWO: HOW TO MAKE A MADMAN

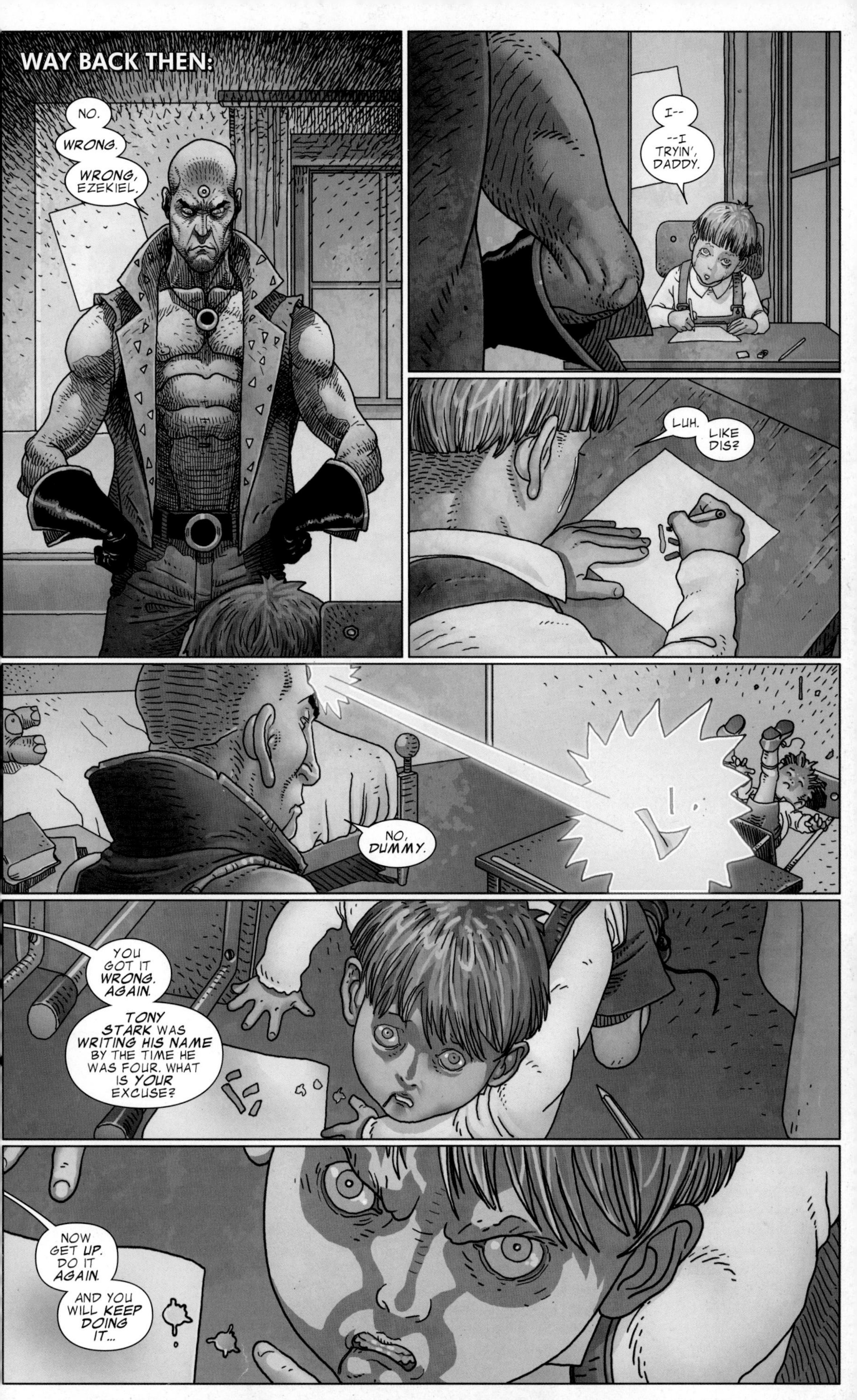
WAY BACK THEN:
NO.
WRONG.
WRONG, EZEKIEL.
I--
--I TRYIN', DADDY.
LUH.
LIKE DIS?
NO, DUMMY.
YOU GOT IT WRONG. AGAIN.
TONY STARK WAS WRITING HIS NAME BY THE TIME HE WAS FOUR. WHAT IS YOUR EXCUSE?
NOW GET UP. DO IT AGAIN.
AND YOU WILL KEEP DOING IT...

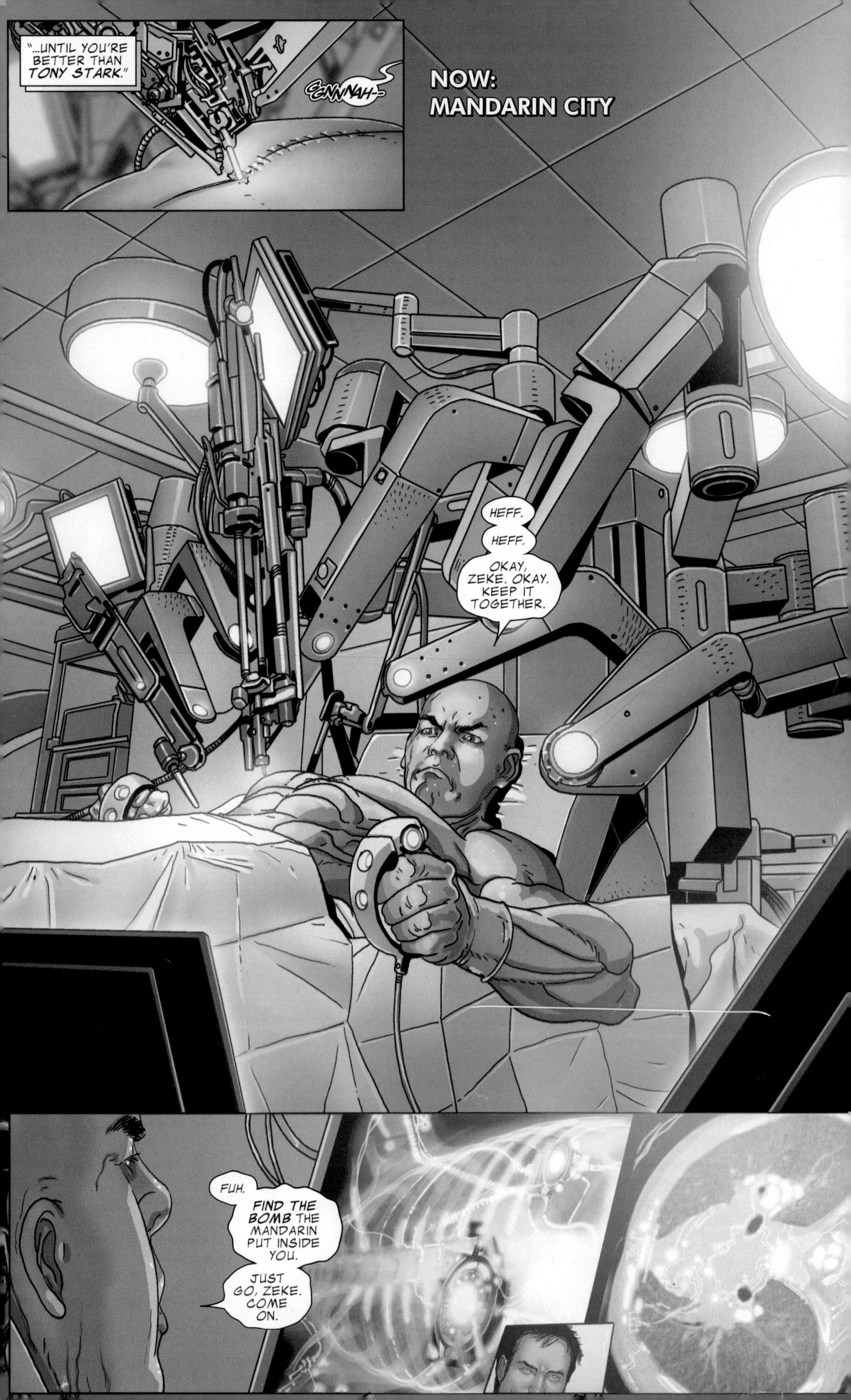
"...UNTIL YOU'RE BETTER THAN *TONY STARK.*"
GNNNAH--
NOW: MANDARIN CITY
HEFF.
HEFF.
OKAY, ZEKE. OKAY. KEEP IT TOGETHER.
FUH.
FIND THE BOMB THE MANDARIN PUT INSIDE YOU.
JUST GO, ZEKE. COME ON.

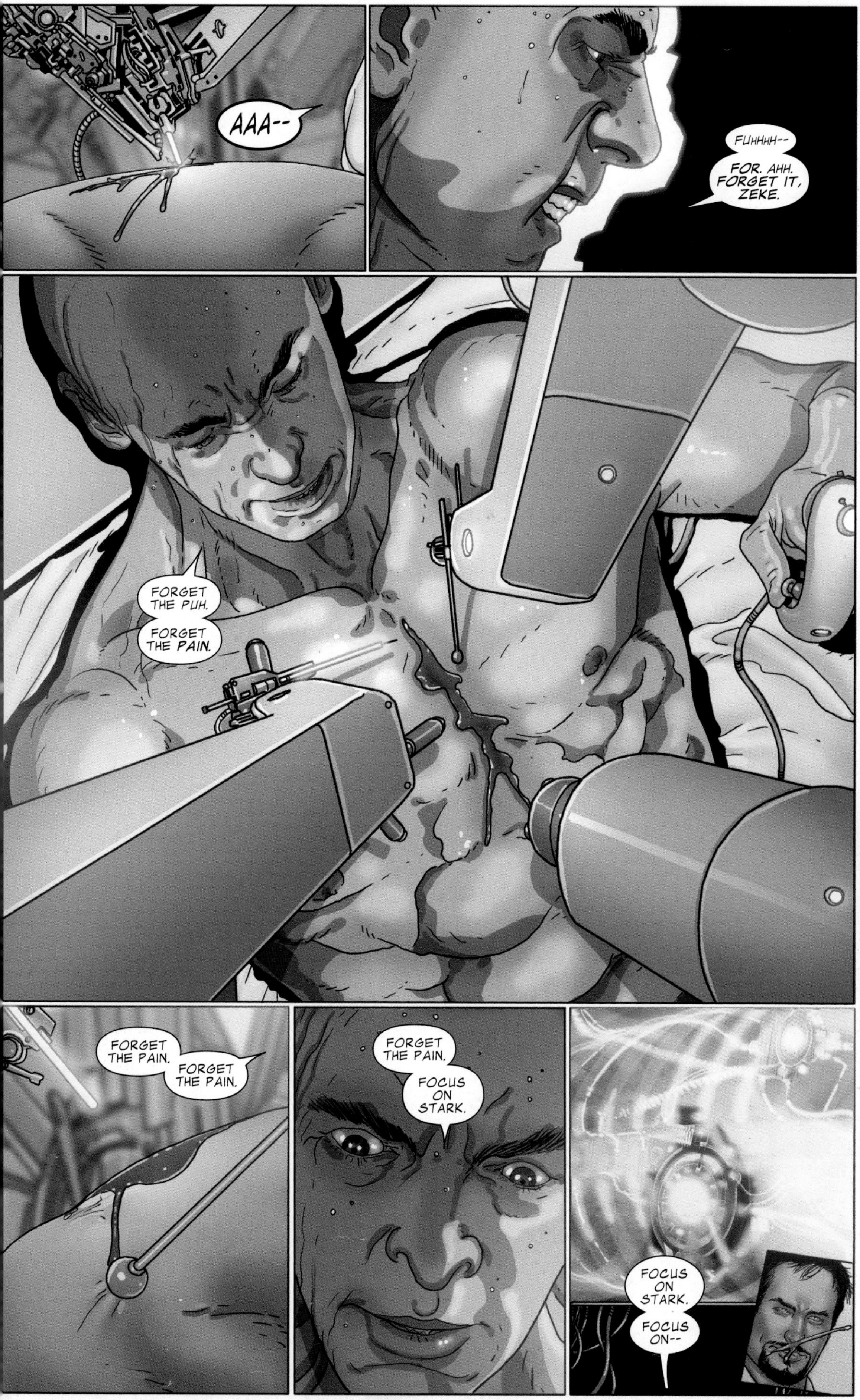
AAA--
FUHHHH--
FOR. AHH. FORGET IT, ZEKE.
FORGET THE PUH.
FORGET THE PAIN.
FORGET THE PAIN.
FORGET THE PAIN.
FORGET THE PAIN.
FOCUS ON STARK.
FOCUS ON STARK.
FOCUS ON--

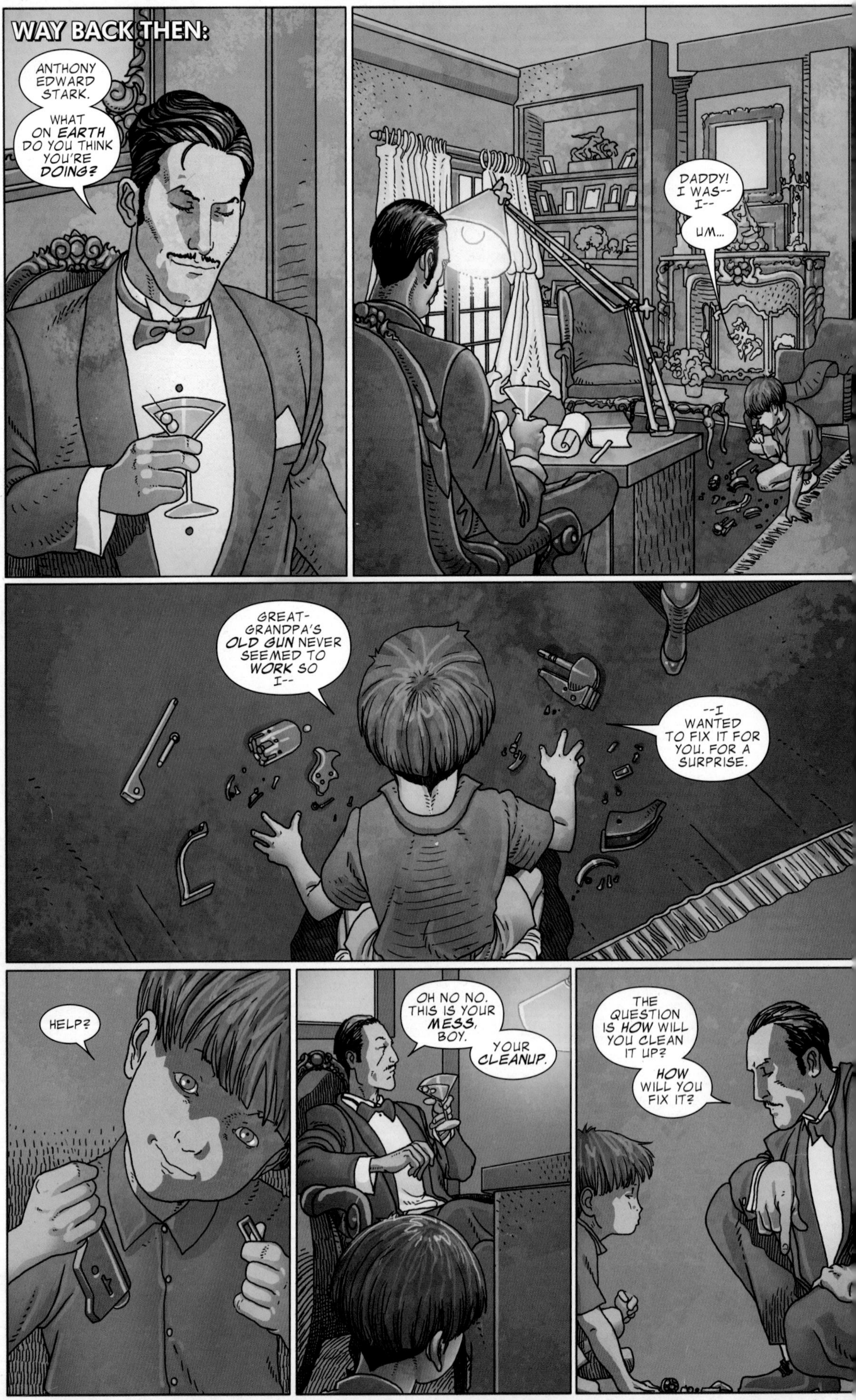
WAY BACK THEN:
ANTHONY EDWARD STARK.
WHAT ON EARTH DO YOU THINK YOU'RE DOING?
DADDY! I WAS-- I--
UM...
GREAT-GRANDPA'S OLD GUN NEVER SEEMED TO WORK SO I--
--I WANTED TO FIX IT FOR YOU. FOR A SURPRISE.
HELP?
OH NO NO. THIS IS YOUR MESS, BOY.
YOUR CLEANUP.
THE QUESTION IS HOW WILL YOU CLEAN IT UP?
HOW WILL YOU FIX IT?

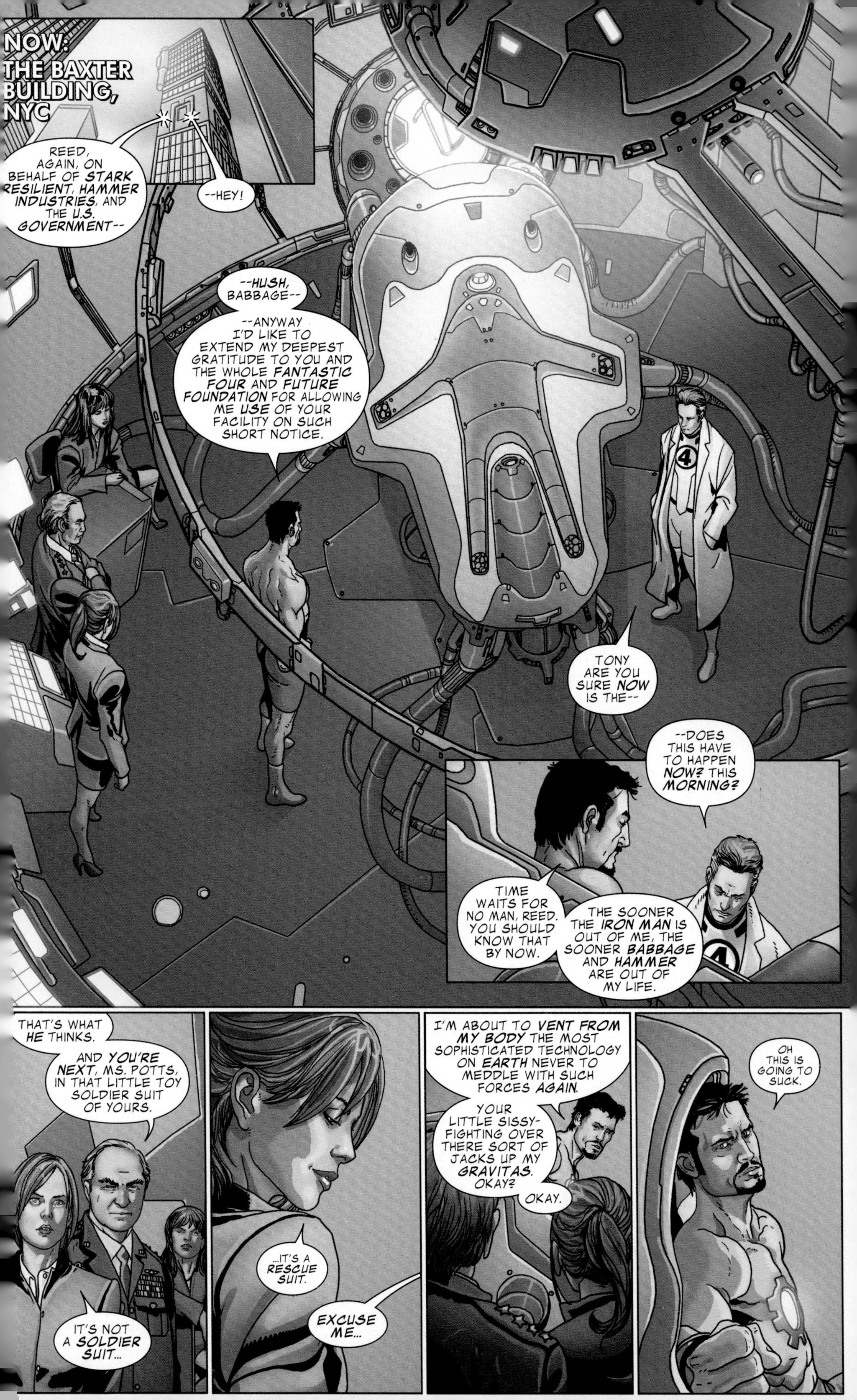
NOW: THE BAXTER BUILDING, NYC
REED, AGAIN, ON BEHALF OF STARK RESILIENT, HAMMER INDUSTRIES, AND THE U.S. GOVERNMENT--
--HEY!
--HUSH, BABBAGE--
--ANYWAY I'D LIKE TO EXTEND MY DEEPEST GRATITUDE TO YOU AND THE WHOLE FANTASTIC FOUR AND FUTURE FOUNDATION FOR ALLOWING ME USE OF YOUR FACILITY ON SUCH SHORT NOTICE.
TONY ARE YOU SURE NOW IS THE--
--DOES THIS HAVE TO HAPPEN NOW? THIS MORNING?
TIME WAITS FOR NO MAN, REED. YOU SHOULD KNOW THAT BY NOW.
THE SOONER THE IRON MAN IS OUT OF ME, THE SOONER BABBAGE AND HAMMER ARE OUT OF MY LIFE.
THAT'S WHAT HE THINKS.
AND YOU'RE NEXT, MS. POTTS, IN THAT LITTLE TOY SOLDIER SUIT OF YOURS.
IT'S NOT A SOLDIER SUIT...
...IT'S A RESCUE SUIT.
EXCUSE ME...
I'M ABOUT TO VENT FROM MY BODY THE MOST SOPHISTICATED TECHNOLOGY ON EARTH NEVER TO MEDDLE WITH SUCH FORCES AGAIN.
YOUR LITTLE SISSY-FIGHTING OVER THERE SORT OF JACKS UP MY GRAVITAS. OKAY?
OKAY.
OH THIS IS GOING TO SUCK.

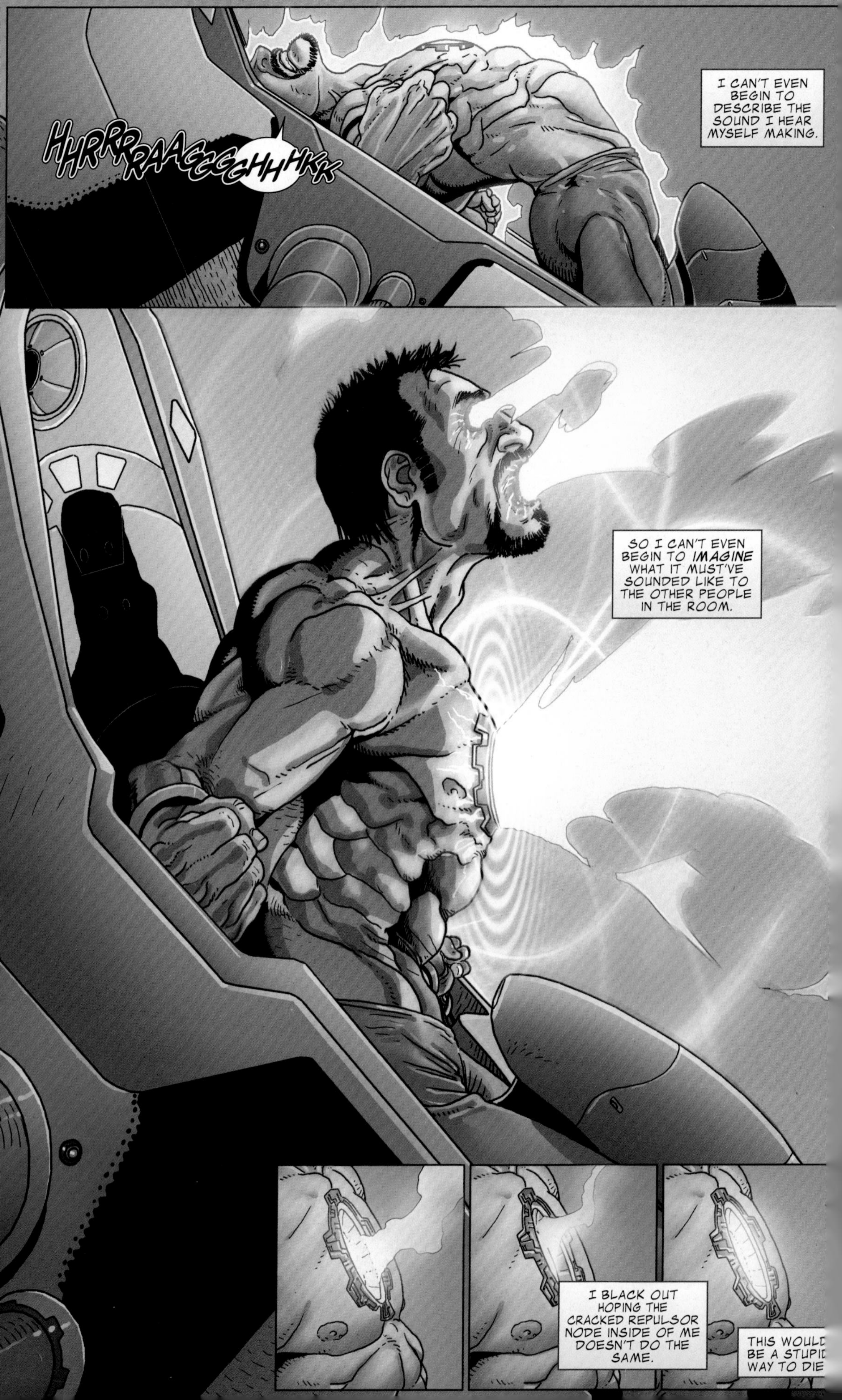
I CAN'T EVEN BEGIN TO DESCRIBE THE SOUND I HEAR MYSELF MAKING.
HHRRRRAAGGGGHHHKKK
SO I CAN'T EVEN BEGIN TO IMAGINE WHAT IT MUST'VE SOUNDED LIKE TO THE OTHER PEOPLE IN THE ROOM.
I BLACK OUT HOPING THE CRACKED REPULSOR NODE INSIDE OF ME DOESN'T DO THE SAME.
THIS WOULD BE A STUPID WAY TO DIE

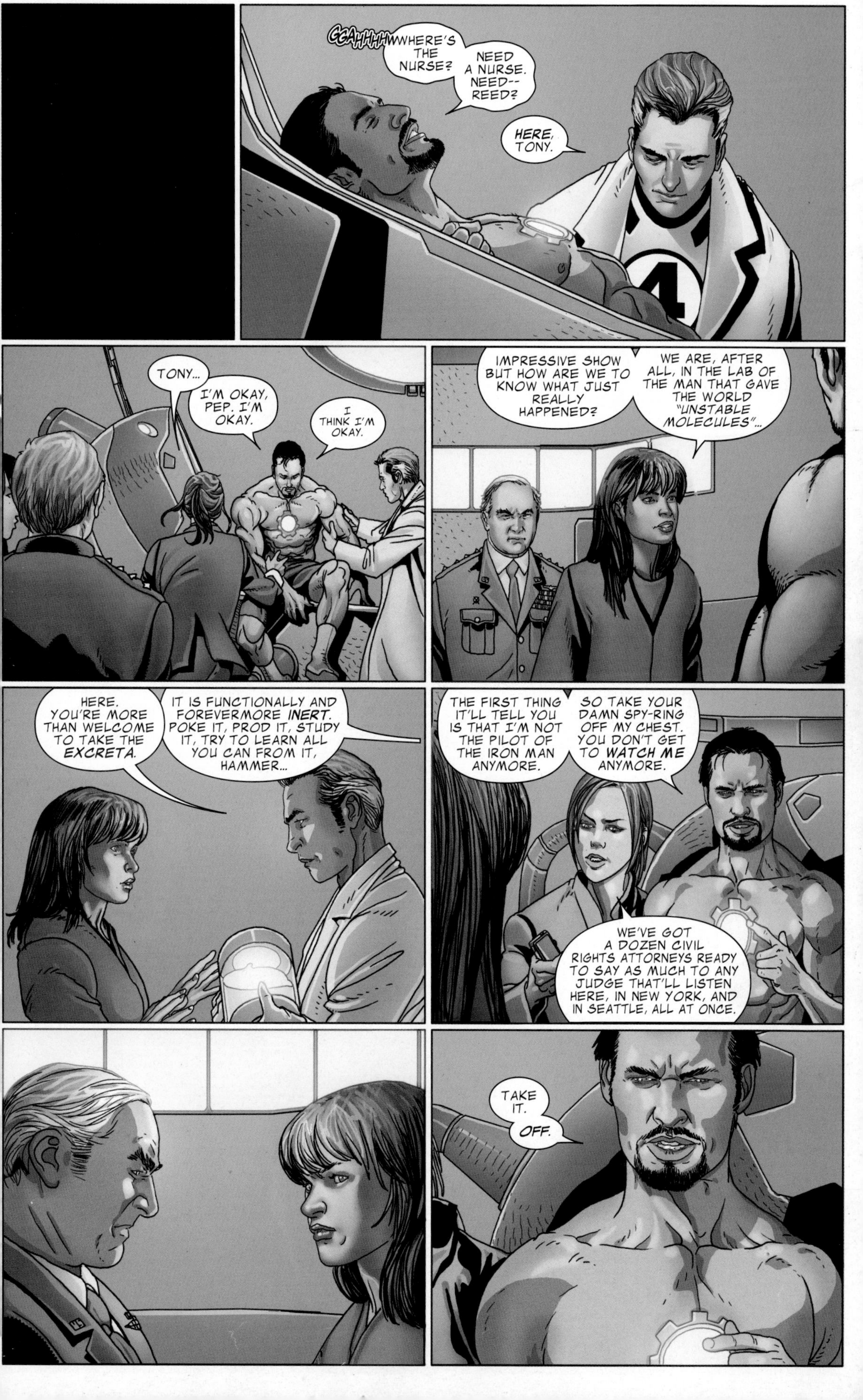
GGAHHHH
WHERE'S THE NURSE?
NEED A NURSE. NEED-- REED?
HERE, TONY.
TONY...
I'M OKAY, PEP. I'M OKAY.
I THINK I'M OKAY.
IMPRESSIVE SHOW BUT HOW ARE WE TO KNOW WHAT JUST REALLY HAPPENED?
WE ARE, AFTER ALL, IN THE LAB OF THE MAN THAT GAVE THE WORLD "UNSTABLE MOLECULES"...
HERE. YOU'RE MORE THAN WELCOME TO TAKE THE EXCRETA.
IT IS FUNCTIONALLY AND FOREVERMORE INERT. POKE IT, PROD IT, STUDY IT, TRY TO LEARN ALL YOU CAN FROM IT, HAMMER...
THE FIRST THING IT'LL TELL YOU IS THAT I'M NOT THE PILOT OF THE IRON MAN ANYMORE.
SO TAKE YOUR DAMN SPY-RING OFF MY CHEST. YOU DON'T GET TO WATCH ME ANYMORE.
WE'VE GOT A DOZEN CIVIL RIGHTS ATTORNEYS READY TO SAY AS MUCH TO ANY JUDGE THAT'LL LISTEN HERE, IN NEW YORK, AND IN SEATTLE, ALL AT ONCE.
TAKE IT. OFF.

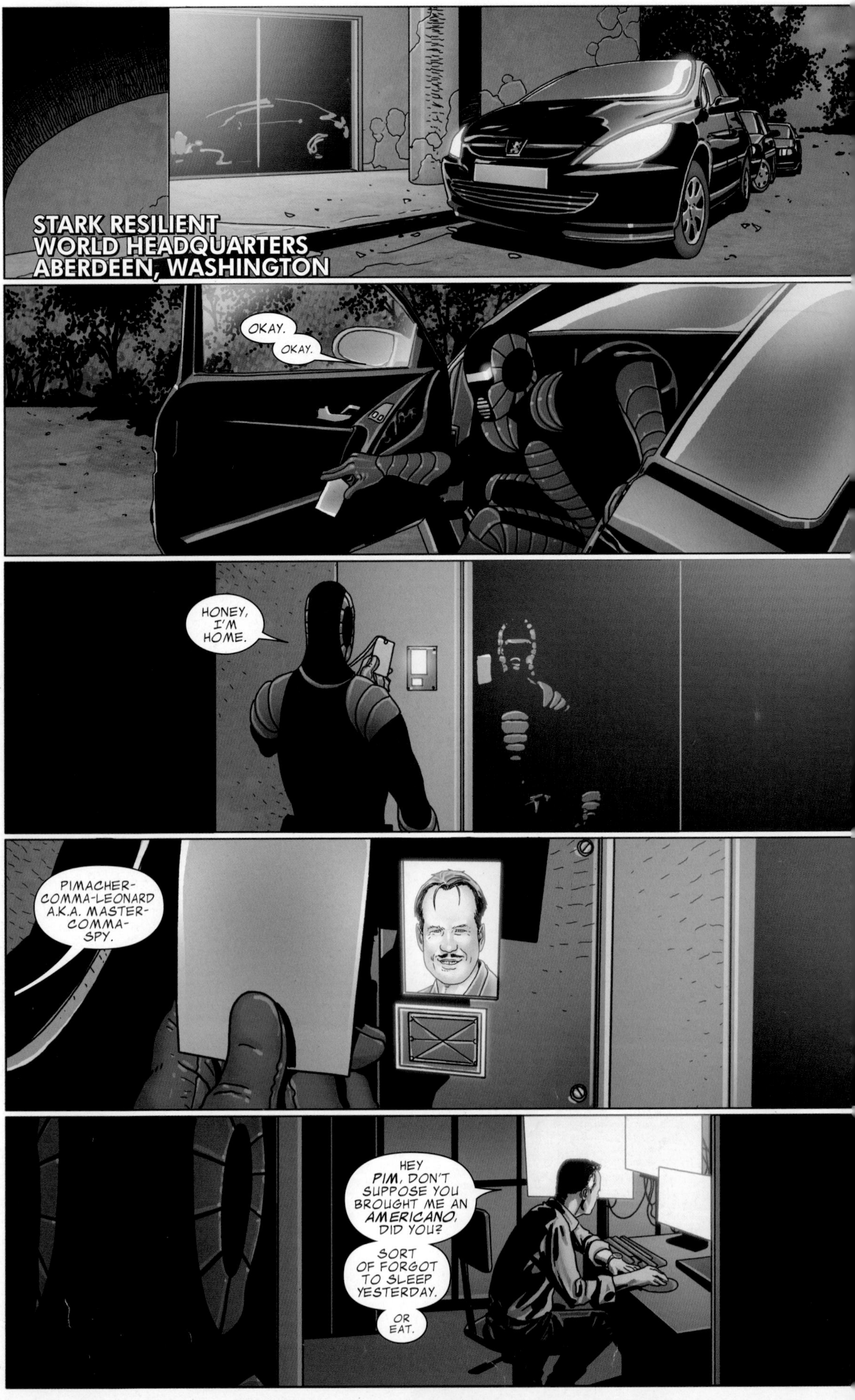
STARK RESILIENT
WORLD HEADQUARTERS
ABERDEEN, WASHINGTON
OKAY.
OKAY.
HONEY, I'M HOME.
PIMACHER-COMMA-LEONARD A.K.A. MASTER-COMMA-SPY.
HEY PIM, DON'T SUPPOSE YOU BROUGHT ME AN AMERICANO, DID YOU?
SORT OF FORGOT TO SLEEP YESTERDAY.
OR EAT.

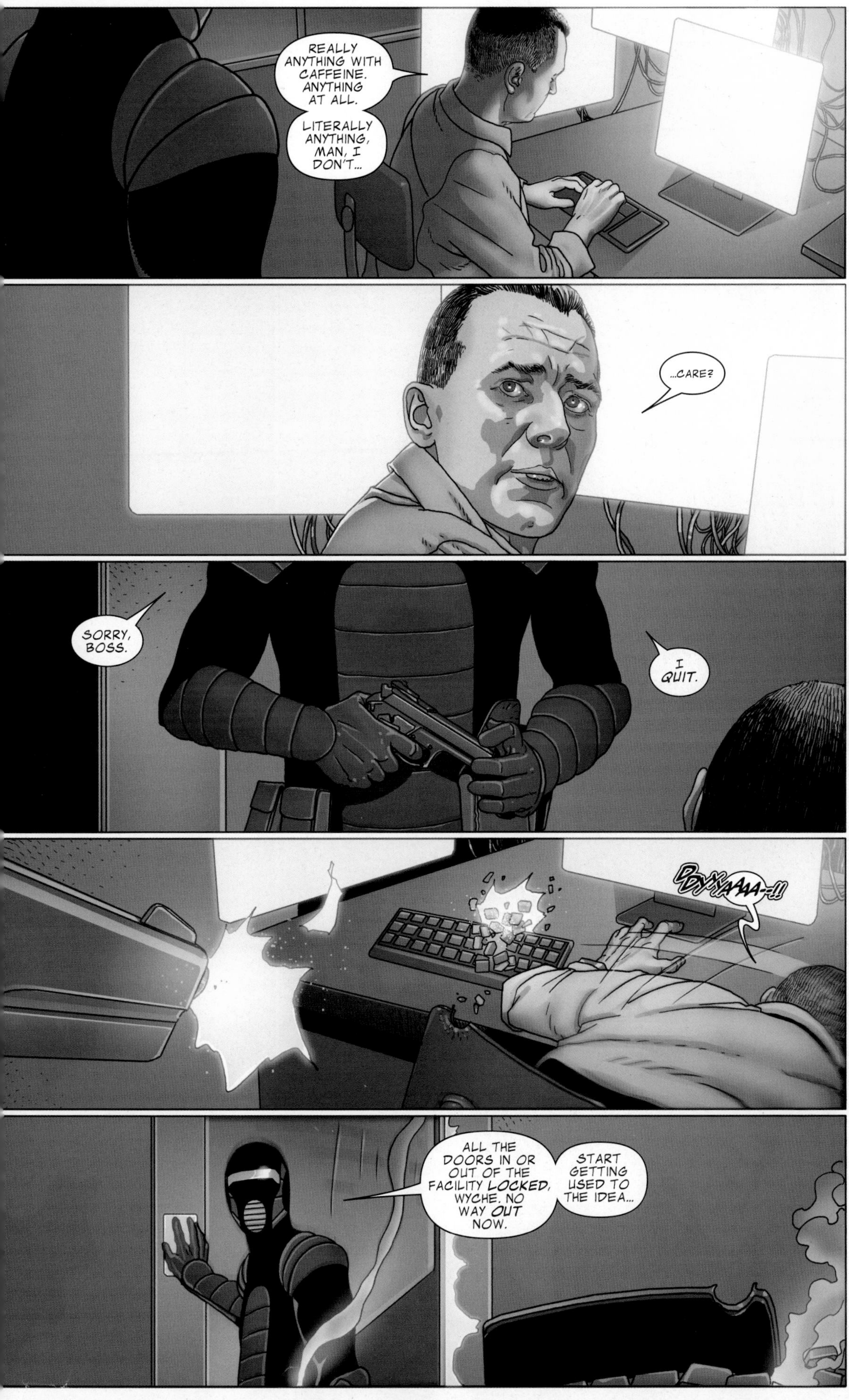
REALLY ANYTHING WITH CAFFEINE. ANYTHING AT ALL.
LITERALLY ANYTHING, MAN, I DON'T...
...CARE?
SORRY, BOSS.
I QUIT.
BDYXYAAAA--!!
ALL THE DOORS IN OR OUT OF THE FACILITY LOCKED, WYCHE. NO WAY OUT NOW.
START GETTING USED TO THE IDEA...

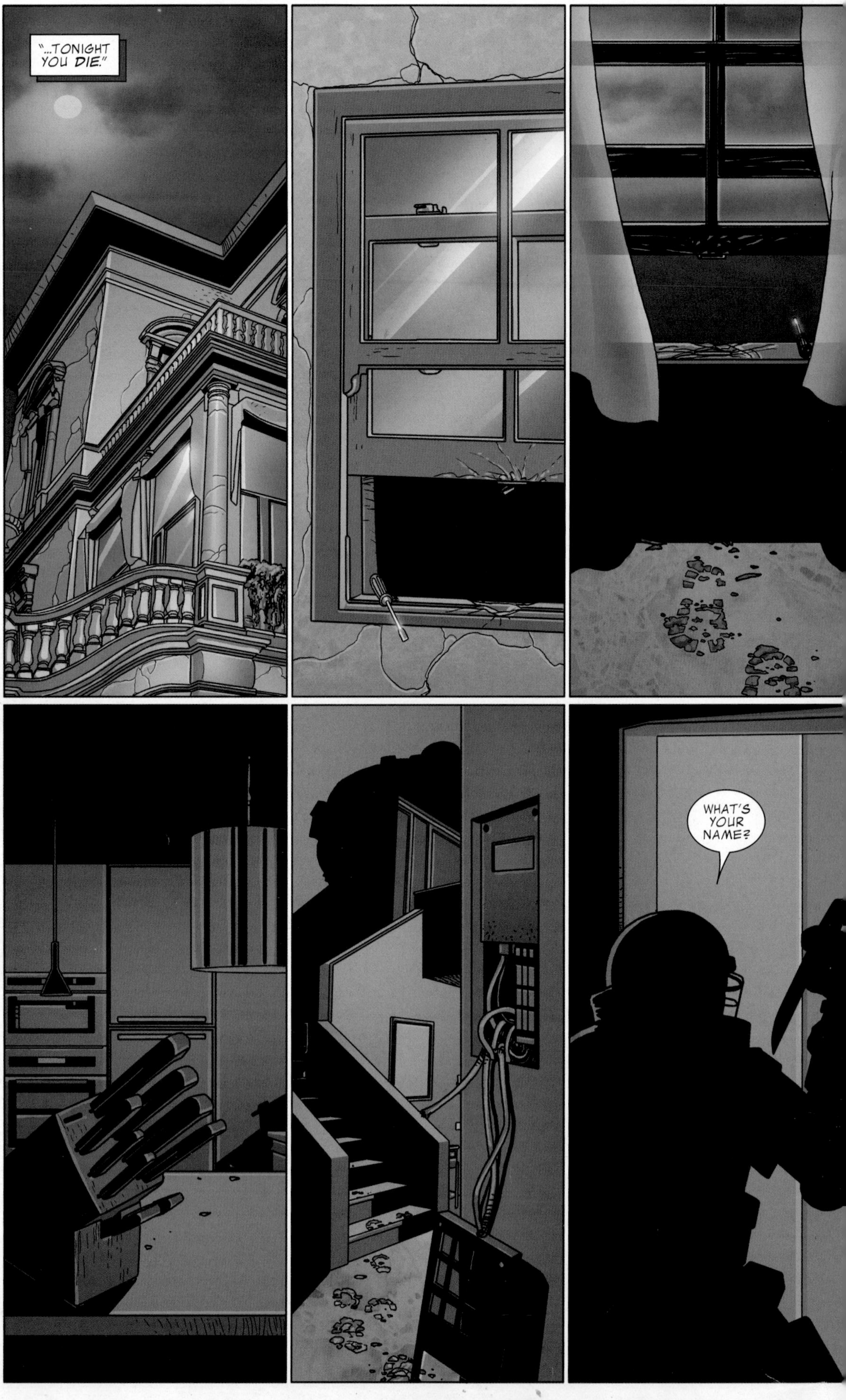
"...TONIGHT YOU DIE."
WHAT'S YOUR NAME?

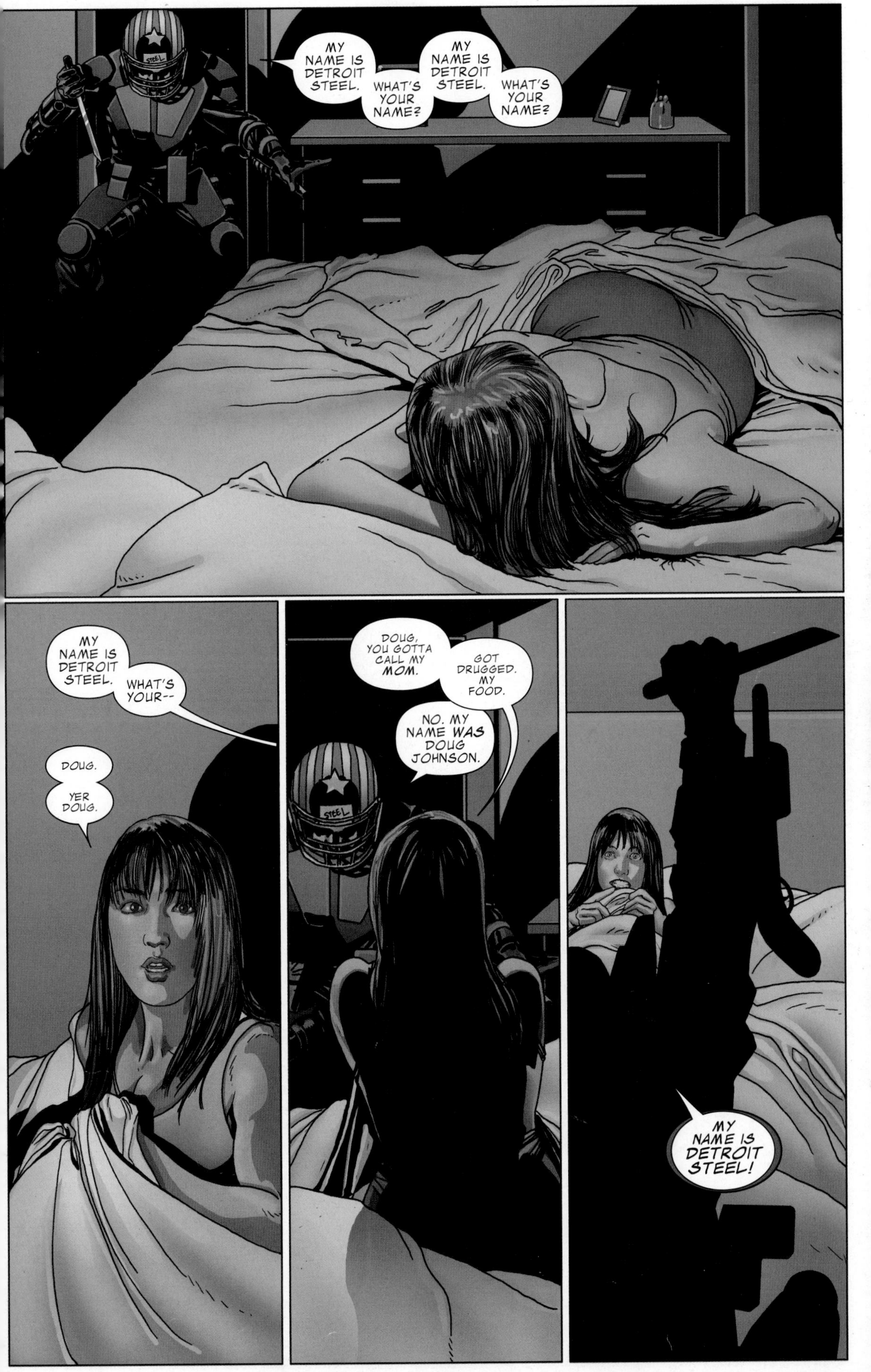
MY NAME IS DETROIT STEEL.
WHAT'S YOUR NAME?
MY NAME IS DETROIT STEEL.
WHAT'S YOUR NAME?
MY NAME IS DETROIT STEEL.
WHAT'S YOUR--
DOUG.
YER DOUG.
DOUG, YOU GOTTA CALL MY MOM.
GOT DRUGGED. MY FOOD.
NO. MY NAME WAS DOUG JOHNSON.
MY NAME IS DETROIT STEEL!

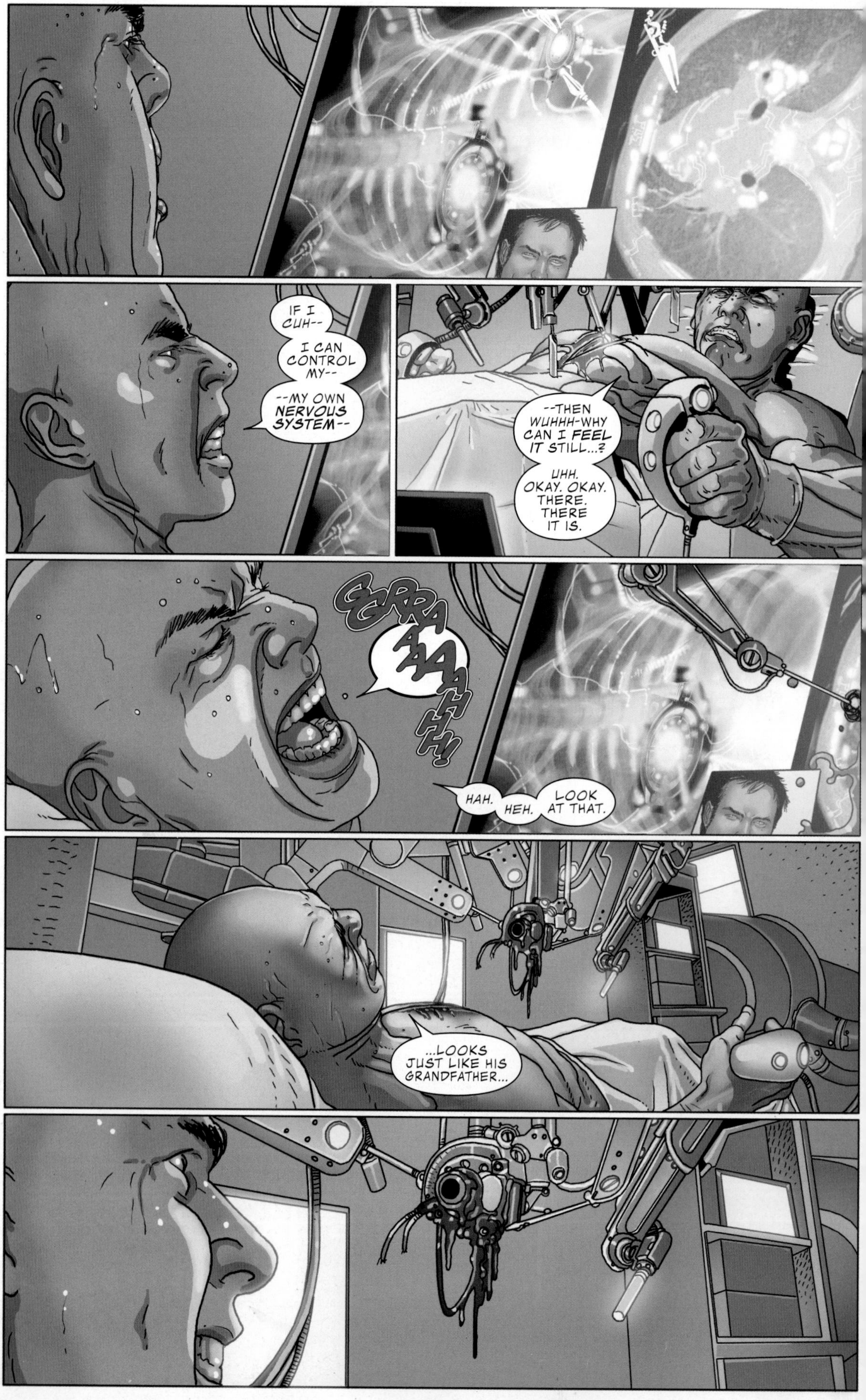
IF I CUH--
I CAN CONTROL MY--
--MY OWN NERVOUS SYSTEM--
--THEN WUHHH-WHY CAN I FEEL IT STILL...?
UHH. OKAY. OKAY. THERE. THERE IT IS.
GGRRAAAAAHHHH!
HAH.
HEH.
LOOK AT THAT.
...LOOKS JUST LIKE HIS GRANDFATHER...

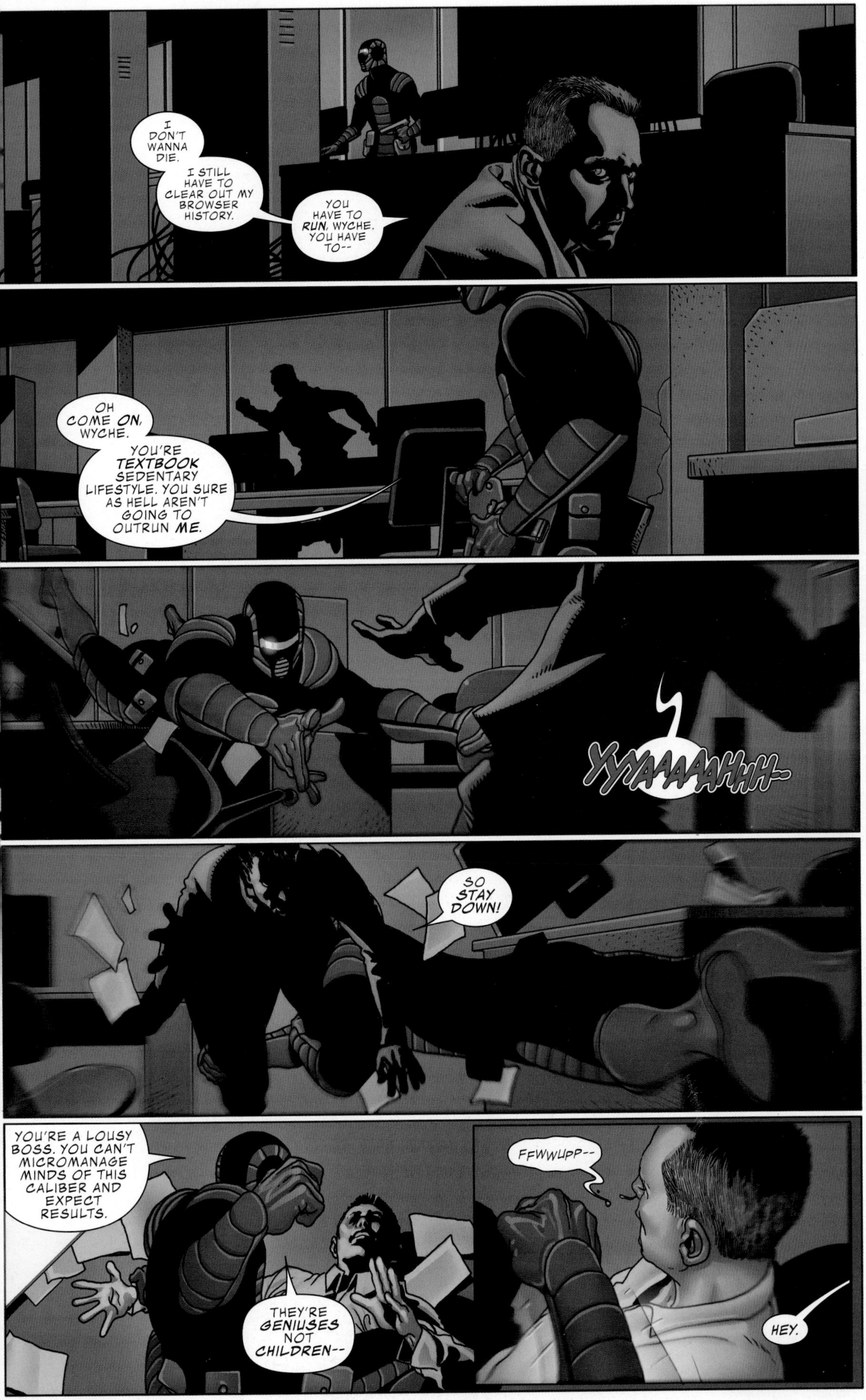
I DON'T WANNA DIE.
I STILL HAVE TO CLEAR OUT MY BROWSER HISTORY.
YOU HAVE TO RUN, WYCHE. YOU HAVE TO--
OH COME ON, WYCHE.
YOU'RE TEXTBOOK SEDENTARY LIFESTYLE. YOU SURE AS HELL AREN'T GOING TO OUTRUN ME.
YYYAAAAAHHH--
SO STAY DOWN!
YOU'RE A LOUSY BOSS. YOU CAN'T MICROMANAGE MINDS OF THIS CALIBER AND EXPECT RESULTS.
THEY'RE GENIUSES NOT CHILDREN--
FFWWUPP--
HEY.

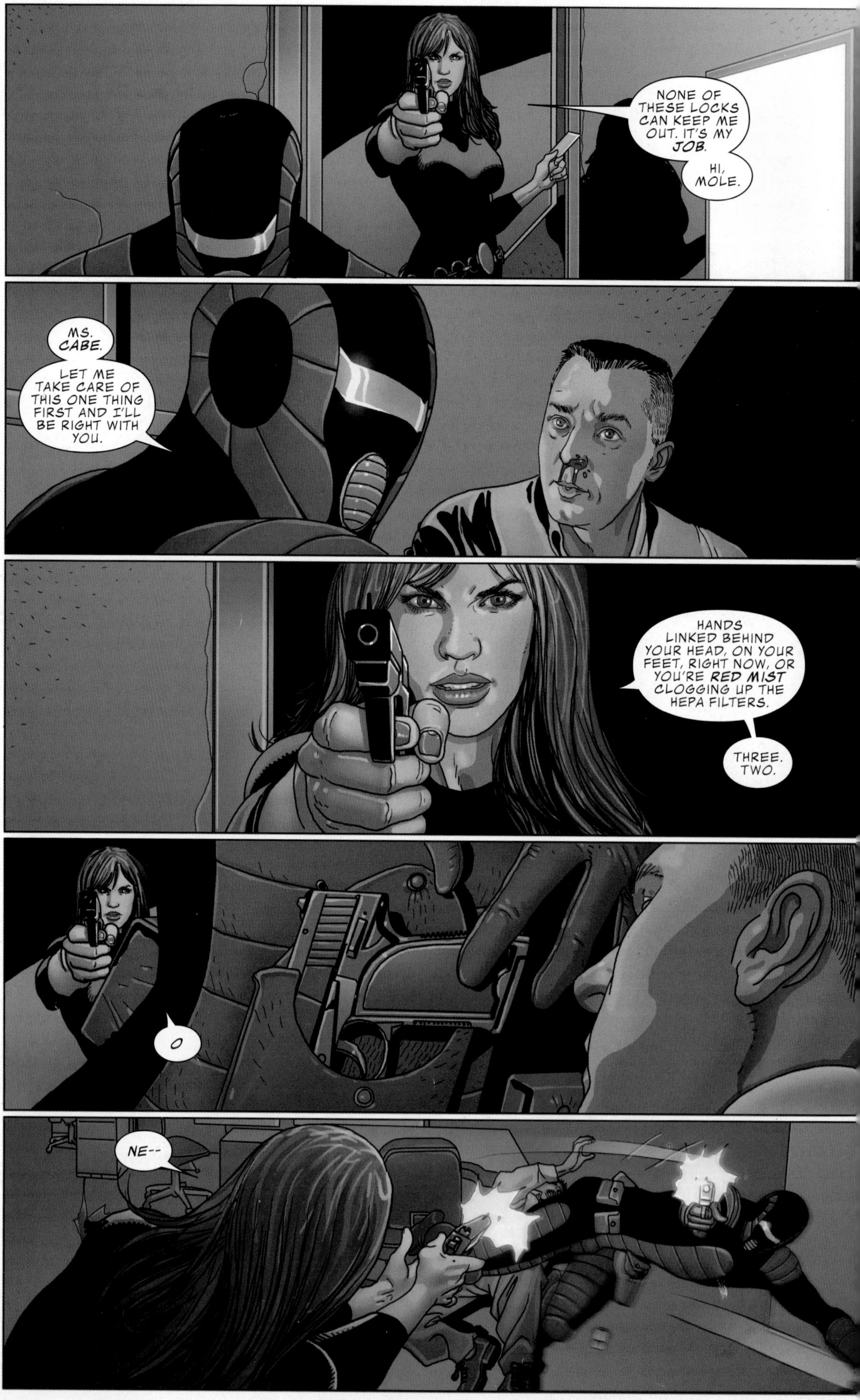
NONE OF THESE LOCKS CAN KEEP ME OUT. IT'S MY JOB.
HI, MOLE.
MS. CABE.
LET ME TAKE CARE OF THIS ONE THING FIRST AND I'LL BE RIGHT WITH YOU.
HANDS LINKED BEHIND YOUR HEAD, ON YOUR FEET, RIGHT NOW, OR YOU'RE RED MIST CLOGGING UP THE HEPA FILTERS.
THREE. TWO.
O
NE--

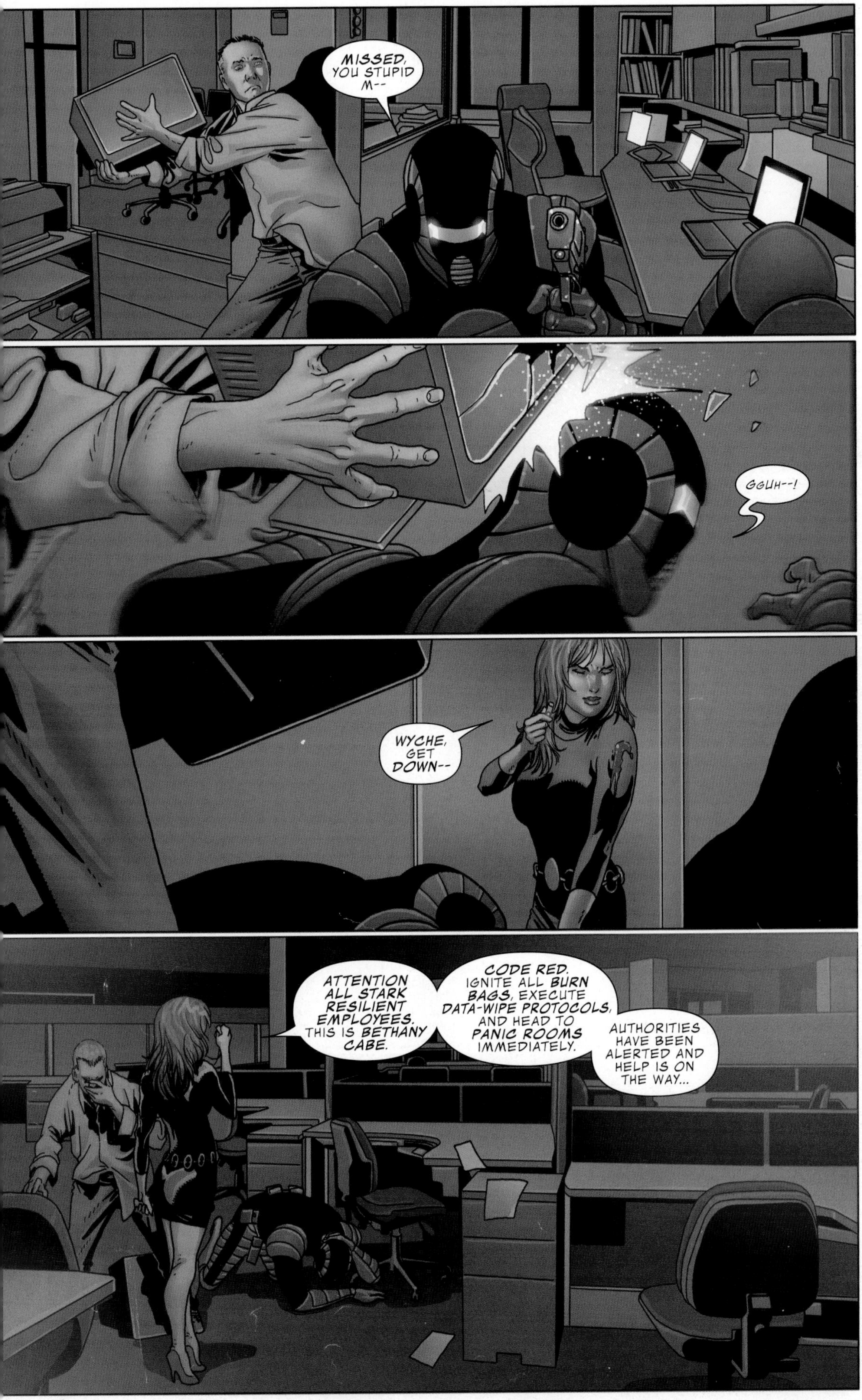
MISSED, YOU STUPID M--
GGUH--!
WYCHE, GET DOWN--
ATTENTION ALL STARK RESILIENT EMPLOYEES. THIS IS BETHANY CABE.
CODE RED. IGNITE ALL BURN BAGS, EXECUTE DATA-WIPE PROTOCOLS, AND HEAD TO PANIC ROOMS IMMEDIATELY.
AUTHORITIES HAVE BEEN ALERTED AND HELP IS ON THE WAY...

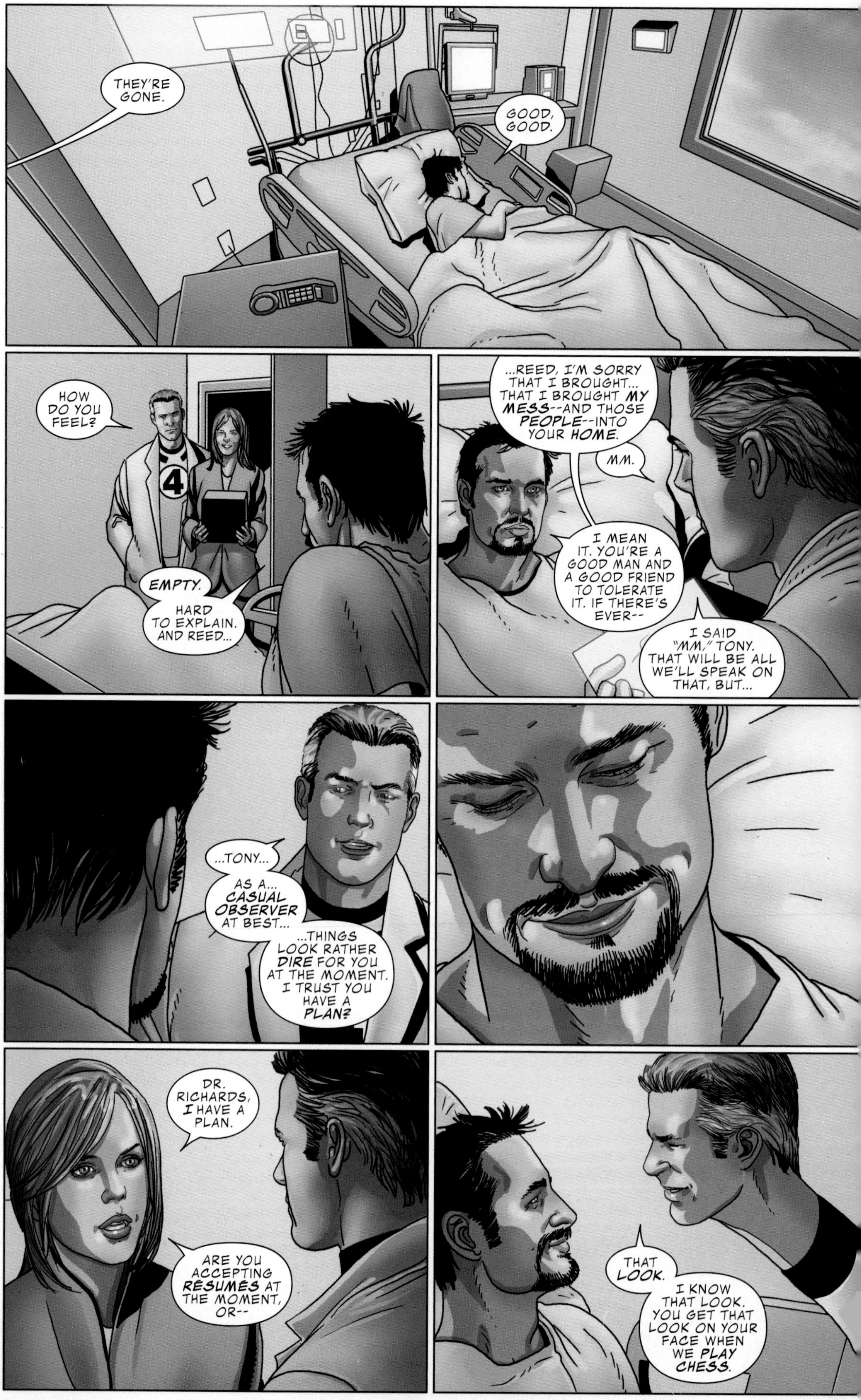
THEY'RE GONE.
GOOD, GOOD.
HOW DO YOU FEEL?
EMPTY.
HARD TO EXPLAIN. AND REED...
...REED, I'M SORRY THAT I BROUGHT... THAT I BROUGHT MY MESS--AND THOSE PEOPLE--INTO YOUR HOME.
MM.
I MEAN IT. YOU'RE A GOOD MAN AND A GOOD FRIEND TO TOLERATE IT. IF THERE'S EVER--
I SAID "MM," TONY. THAT WILL BE ALL WE'LL SPEAK ON THAT, BUT...
...TONY...
AS A... CASUAL OBSERVER AT BEST...
...THINGS LOOK RATHER DIRE FOR YOU AT THE MOMENT. I TRUST YOU HAVE A PLAN?
DR. RICHARDS, I HAVE A PLAN.
ARE YOU ACCEPTING RESUMES AT THE MOMENT, OR--
THAT LOOK.
I KNOW THAT LOOK. YOU GET THAT LOOK ON YOUR FACE WHEN WE PLAY CHESS.

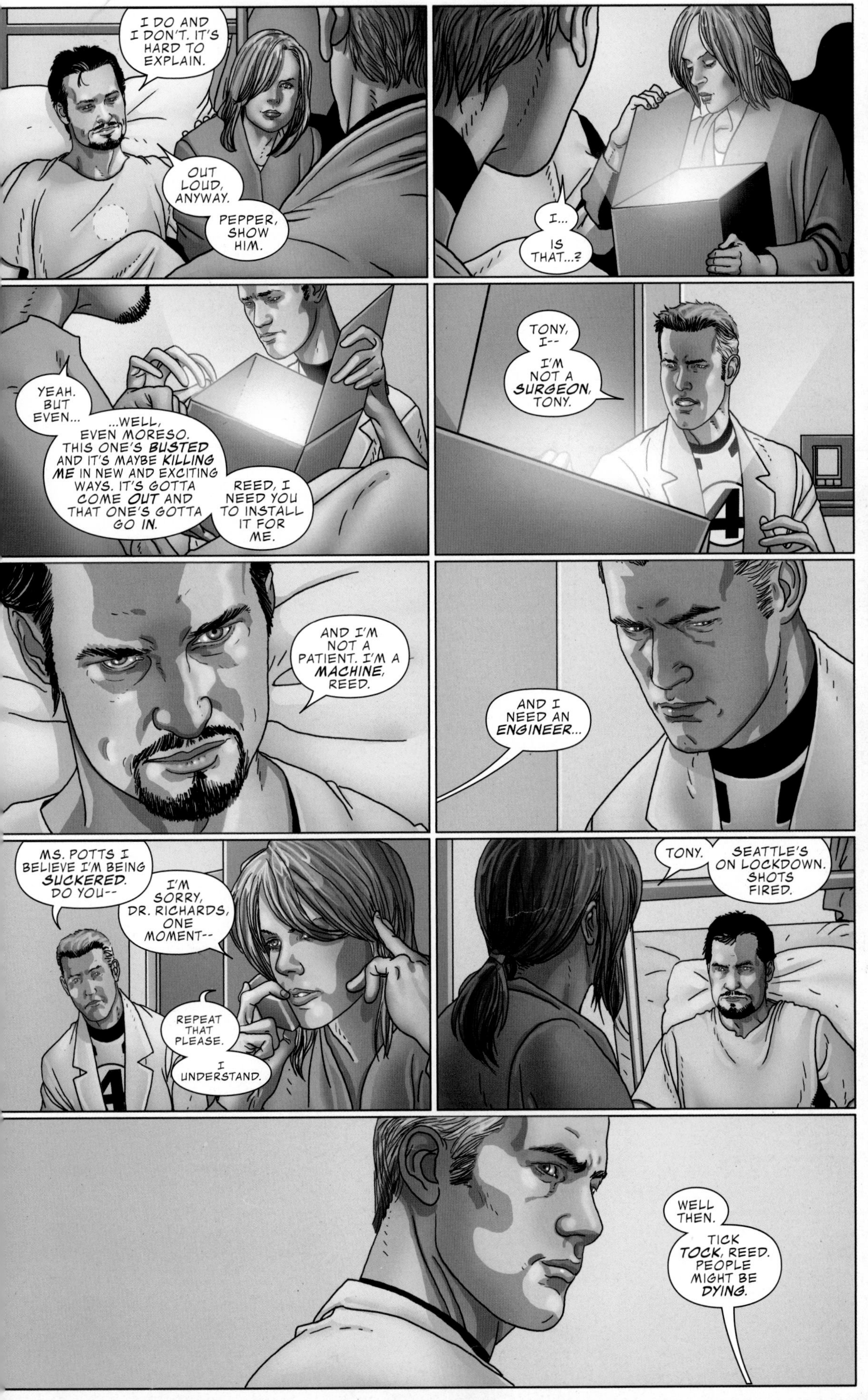
I DO AND I DON'T. IT'S HARD TO EXPLAIN.
OUT LOUD, ANYWAY.
PEPPER, SHOW HIM.
I...
IS THAT...?
YEAH. BUT EVEN...
...WELL, EVEN MORESO. THIS ONE'S BUSTED AND IT'S MAYBE KILLING ME IN NEW AND EXCITING WAYS. IT'S GOTTA COME OUT AND THAT ONE'S GOTTA GO IN.
REED, I NEED YOU TO INSTALL IT FOR ME.
TONY, I--
I'M NOT A SURGEON, TONY.
AND I'M NOT A PATIENT. I'M A MACHINE, REED.
AND I NEED AN ENGINEER...
MS. POTTS I BELIEVE I'M BEING SUCKERED. DO YOU--
I'M SORRY, DR. RICHARDS, ONE MOMENT--
REPEAT THAT PLEASE.
I UNDERSTAND.
TONY.
SEATTLE'S ON LOCKDOWN. SHOTS FIRED.
WELL THEN.
TICK TOCK, REED. PEOPLE MIGHT BE DYING.

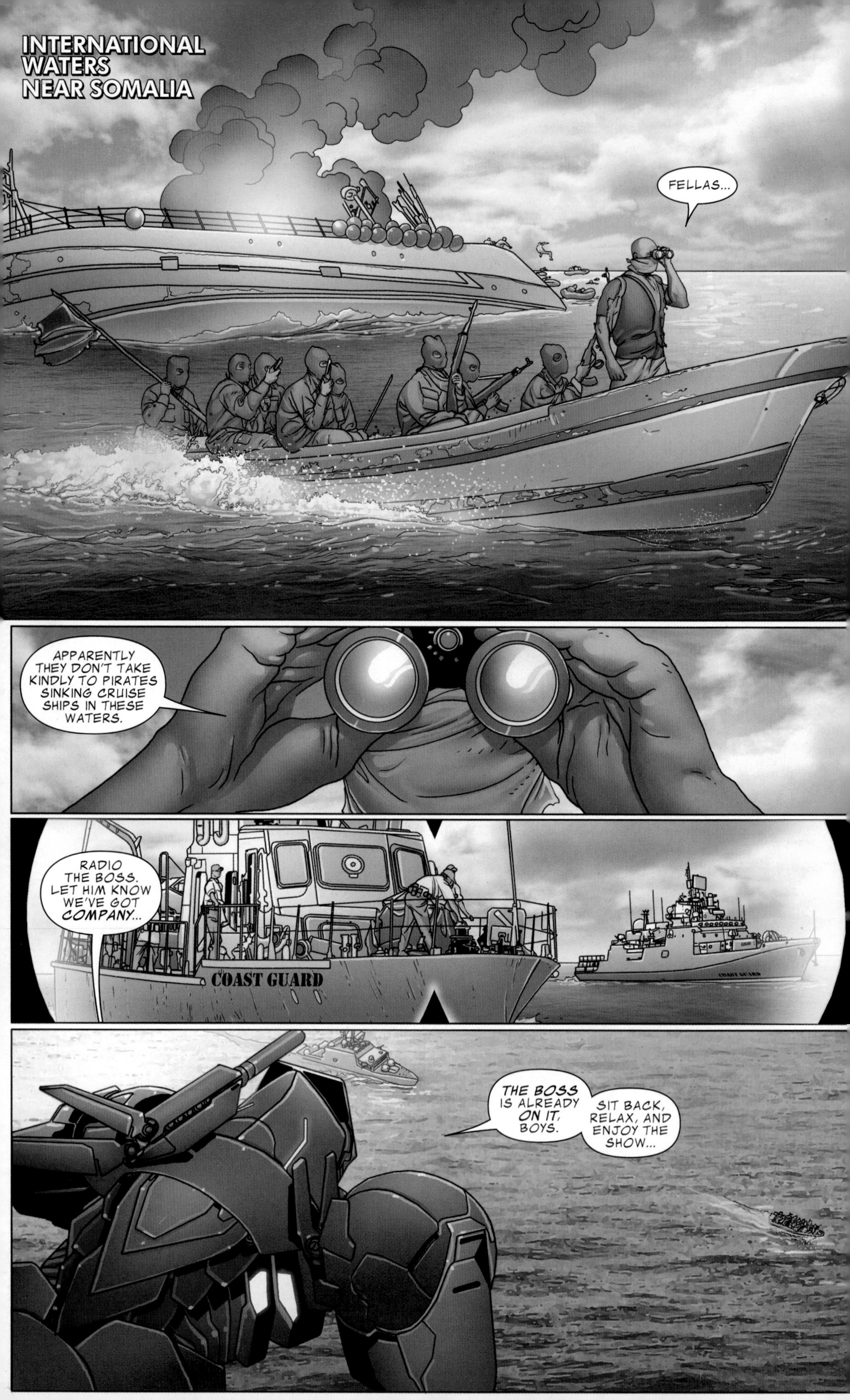
INTERNATIONAL WATERS NEAR SOMALIA
FELLAS...
APPARENTLY THEY DON'T TAKE KINDLY TO PIRATES SINKING CRUISE SHIPS IN THESE WATERS.
RADIO THE BOSS. LET HIM KNOW WE'VE GOT COMPANY...
COAST GUARD
THE BOSS IS ALREADY ON IT, BOYS.
SIT BACK, RELAX, AND ENJOY THE SHOW...

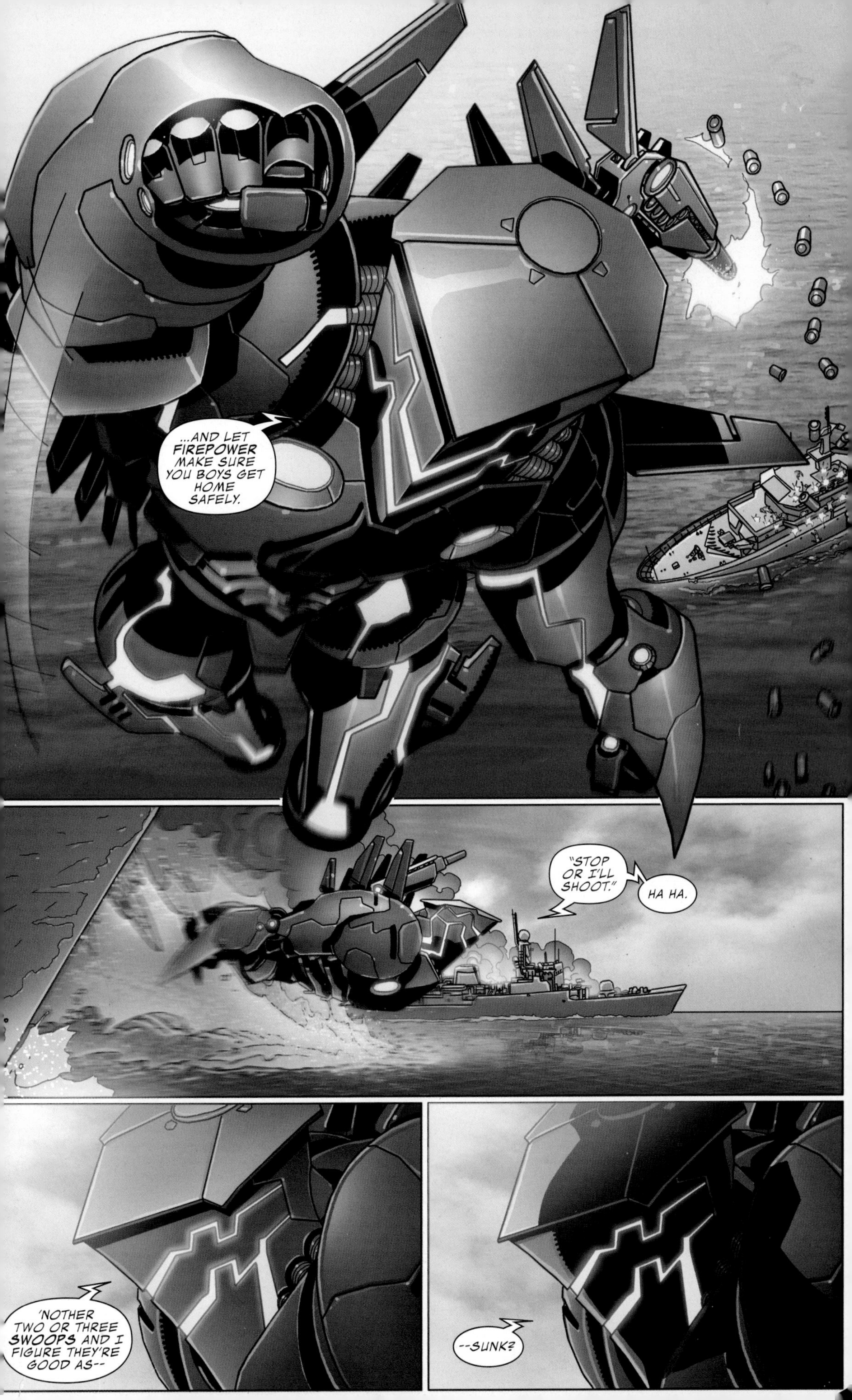
...AND LET FIREPOWER MAKE SURE YOU BOYS GET HOME SAFELY.
"STOP OR I'LL SHOOT."
HA HA.
'NOTHER TWO OR THREE SWOOPS AND I FIGURE THEY'RE GOOD AS--
--SUNK?

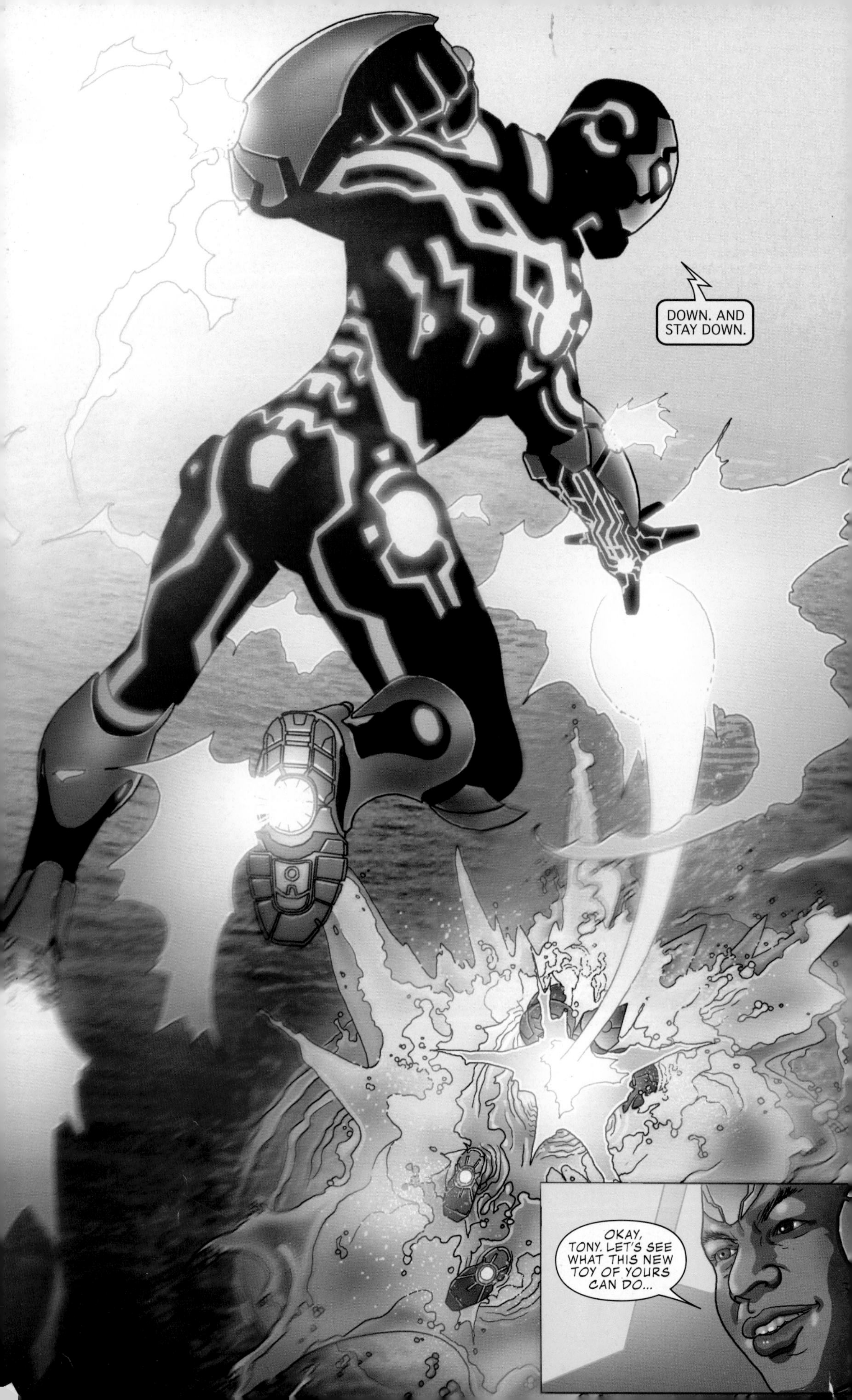
DOWN. AND STAY DOWN.
OKAY, TONY. LET'S SEE WHAT THIS NEW TOY OF YOURS CAN DO...

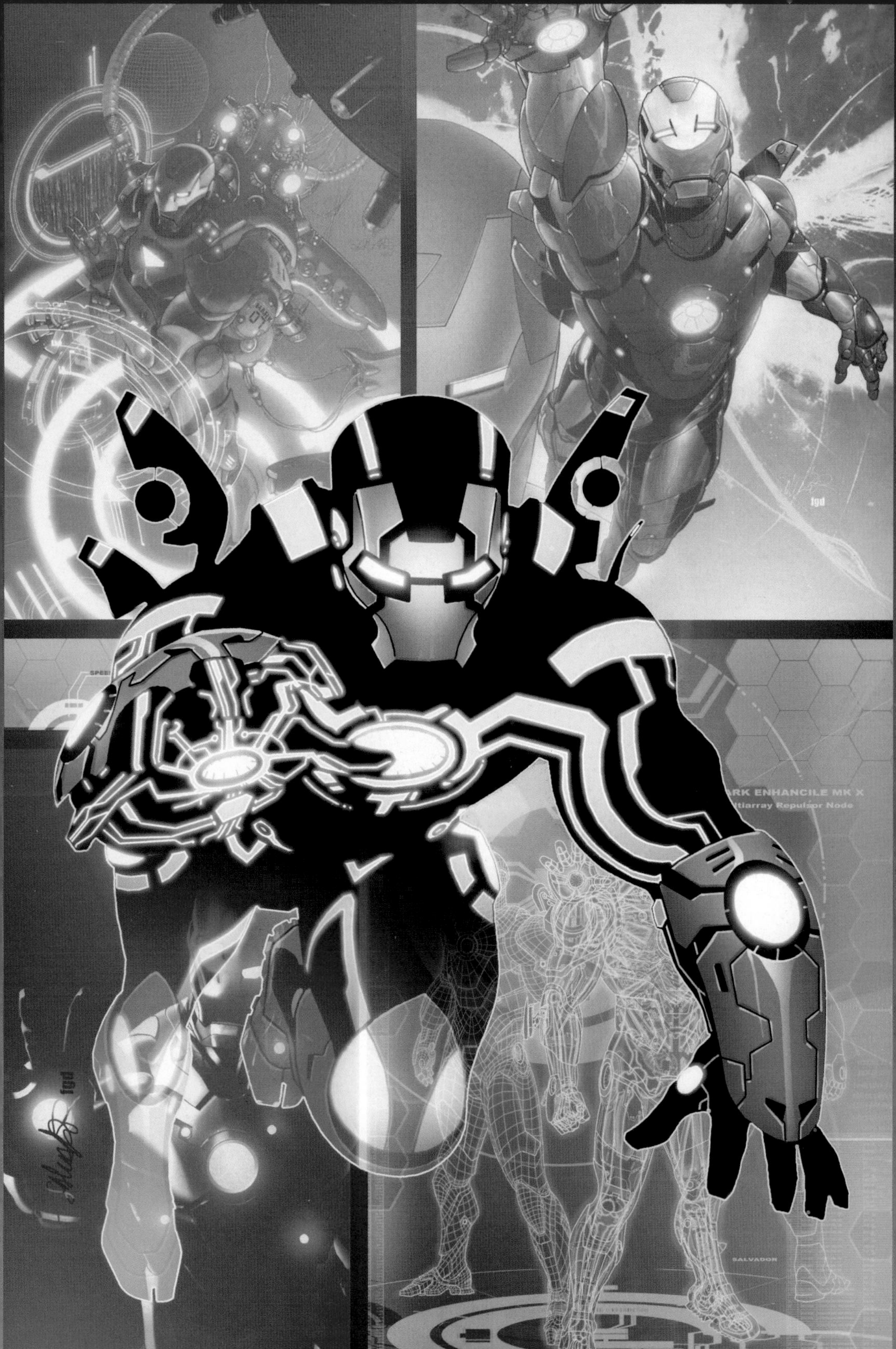
SALVADOR

PART THREE: YOU GHOSTS OF MINE BOTH NEW AND OLD

518

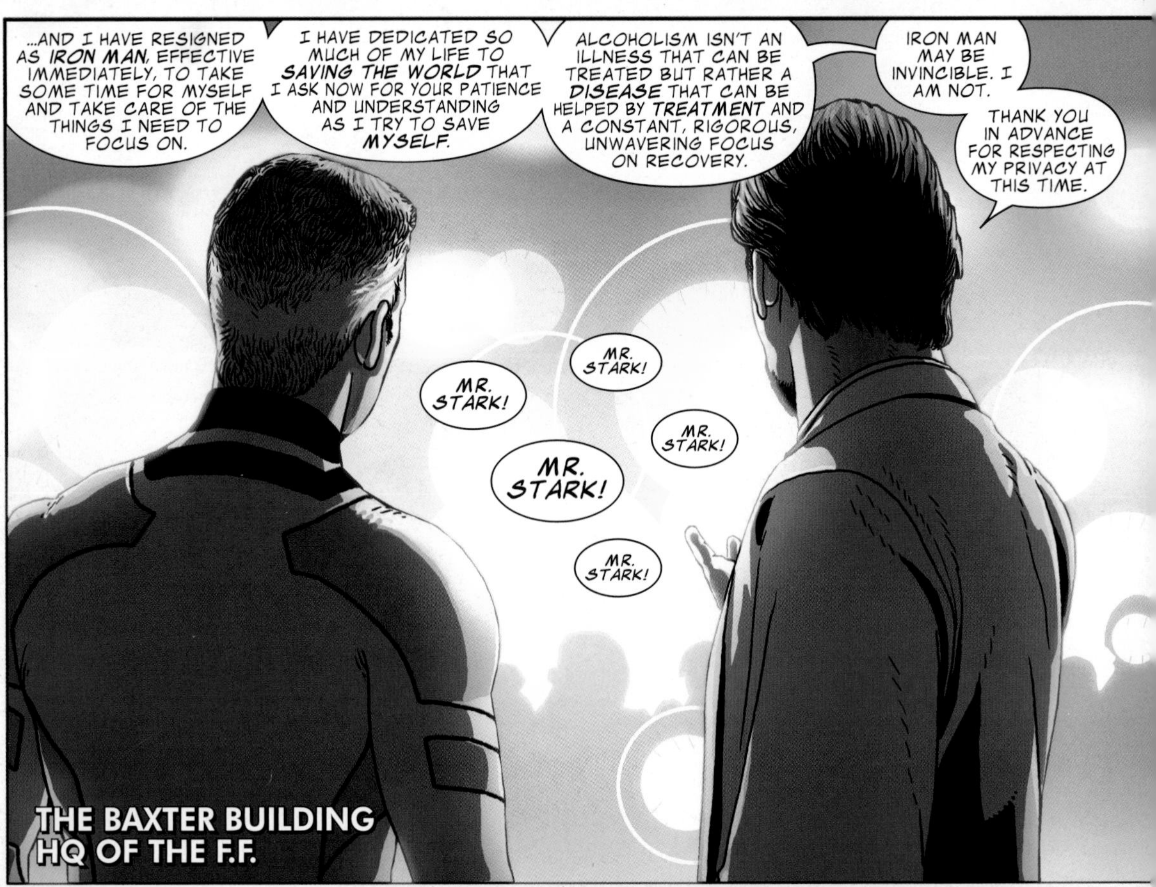
...AND I HAVE RESIGNED AS IRON MAN, EFFECTIVE IMMEDIATELY, TO TAKE SOME TIME FOR MYSELF AND TAKE CARE OF THE THINGS I NEED TO FOCUS ON.
I HAVE DEDICATED SO MUCH OF MY LIFE TO SAVING THE WORLD THAT I ASK NOW FOR YOUR PATIENCE AND UNDERSTANDING AS I TRY TO SAVE MYSELF.
ALCOHOLISM ISN'T AN ILLNESS THAT CAN BE TREATED BUT RATHER A DISEASE THAT CAN BE HELPED BY TREATMENT AND A CONSTANT, RIGOROUS, UNWAVERING FOCUS ON RECOVERY.
IRON MAN MAY BE INVINCIBLE. I AM NOT.
THANK YOU IN ADVANCE FOR RESPECTING MY PRIVACY AT THIS TIME.
MR. STARK!
MR. STARK!
MR. STARK!
MR. STARK!
MR. STARK!
THE BAXTER BUILDING
HQ OF THE F.F.

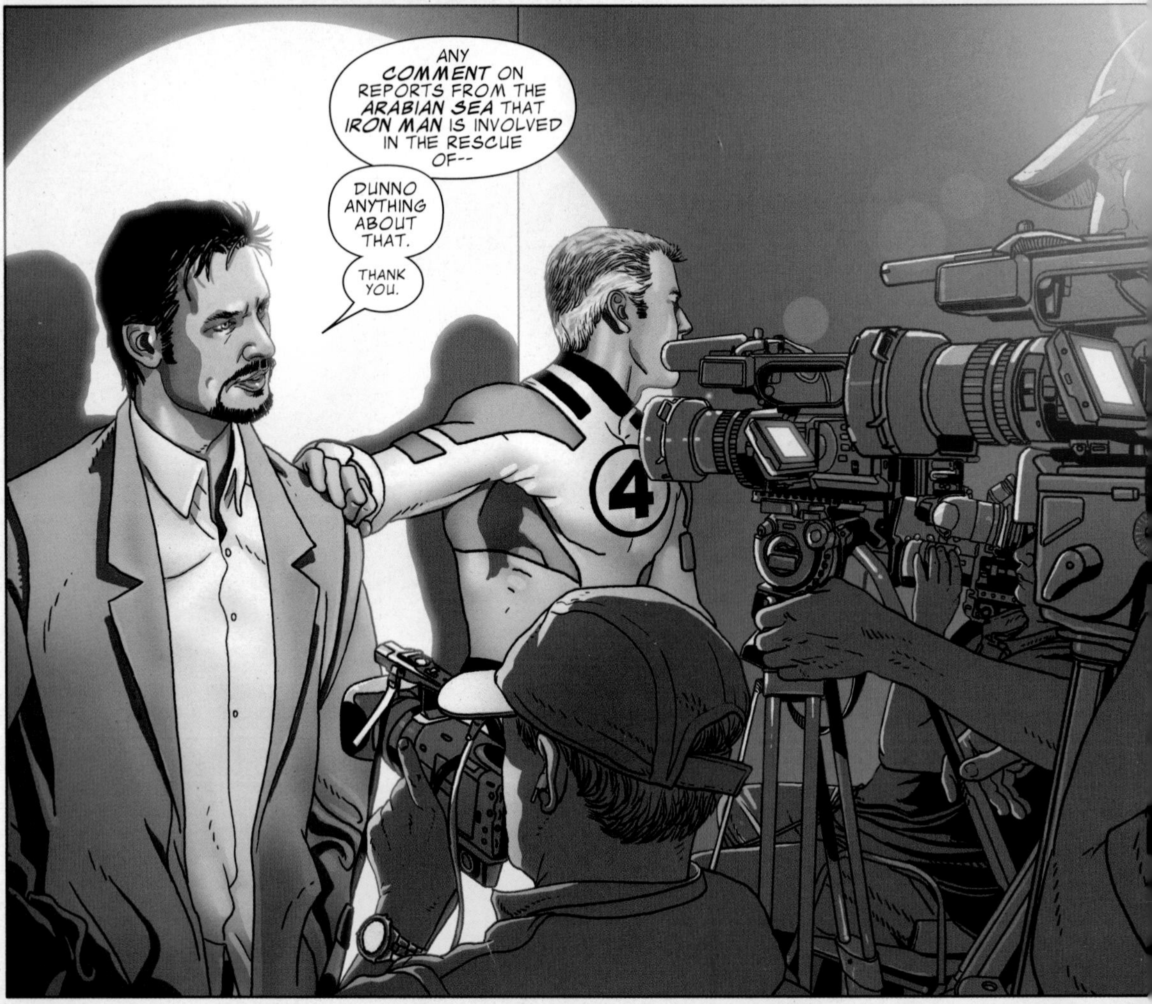
ANY COMMENT ON REPORTS FROM THE ARABIAN SEA THAT IRON MAN IS INVOLVED IN THE RESCUE OF--
DUNNO ANYTHING ABOUT THAT.
THANK YOU.

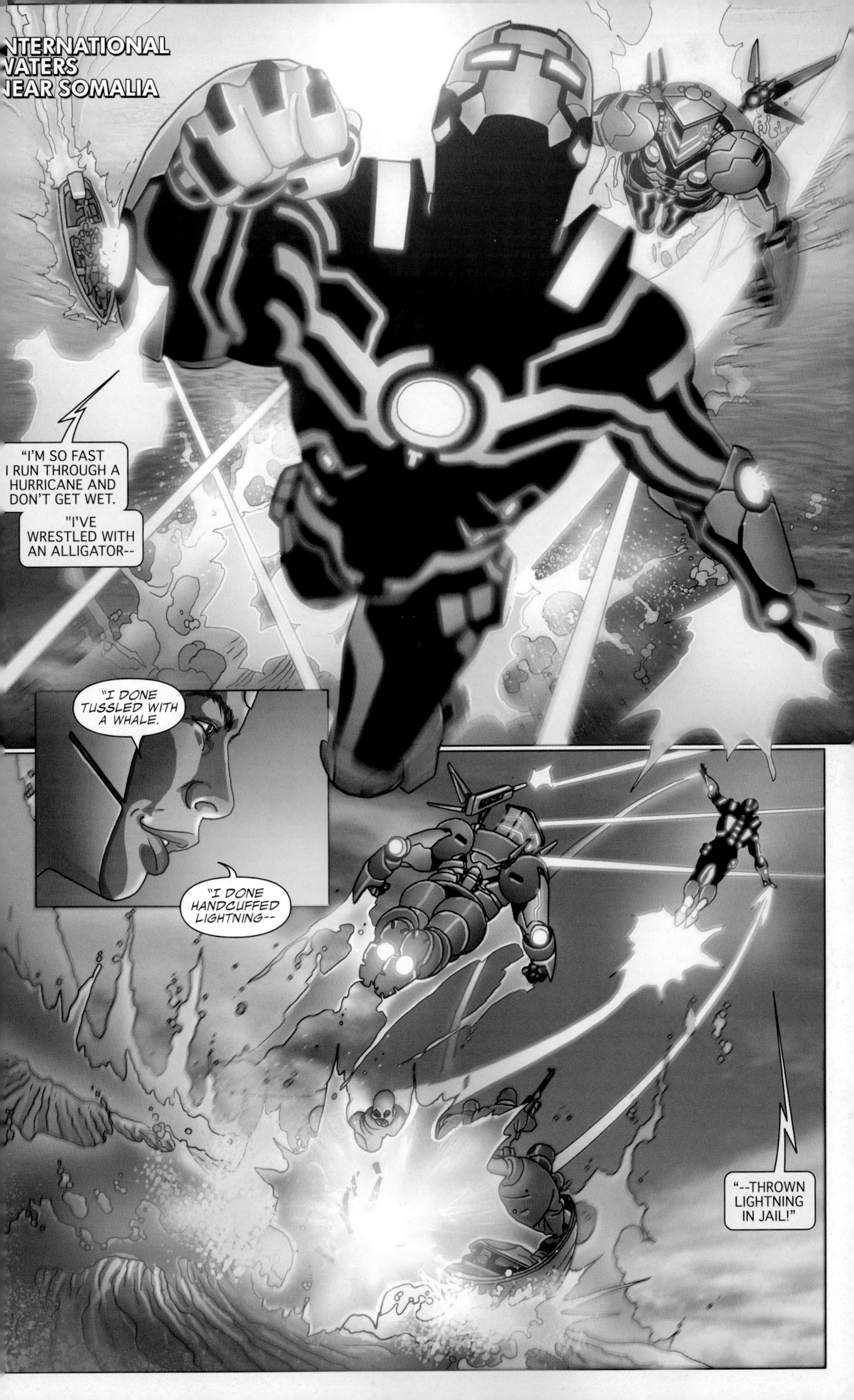
NTERNATIONAL
VATERS
IEAR SOMALIA
"I'M SO FAST I RUN THROUGH A HURRICANE AND DON'T GET WET.
"I'VE WRESTLED WITH AN ALLIGATOR--
"I DONE TUSSLED WITH A WHALE.
"I DONE HANDCUFFED LIGHTNING--
"--THROWN LIGHTNING IN JAIL!"

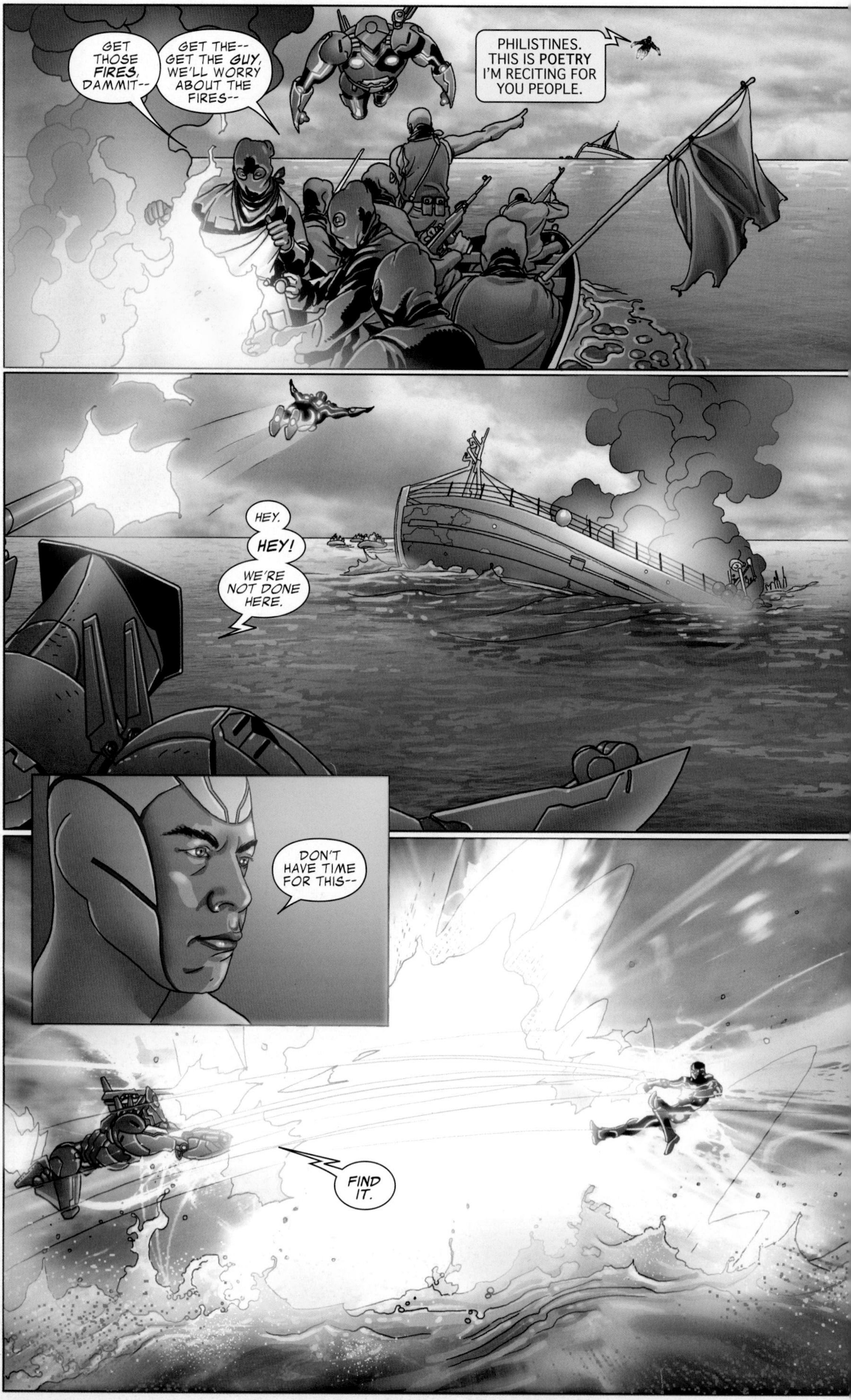
GET THOSE FIRES, DAMMIT--
GET THE-- GET THE GUY, WE'LL WORRY ABOUT THE FIRES--
PHILISTINES. THIS IS POETRY I'M RECITING FOR YOU PEOPLE.
HEY.
HEY!
WE'RE NOT DONE HERE.
DON'T HAVE TIME FOR THIS--
FIND IT.

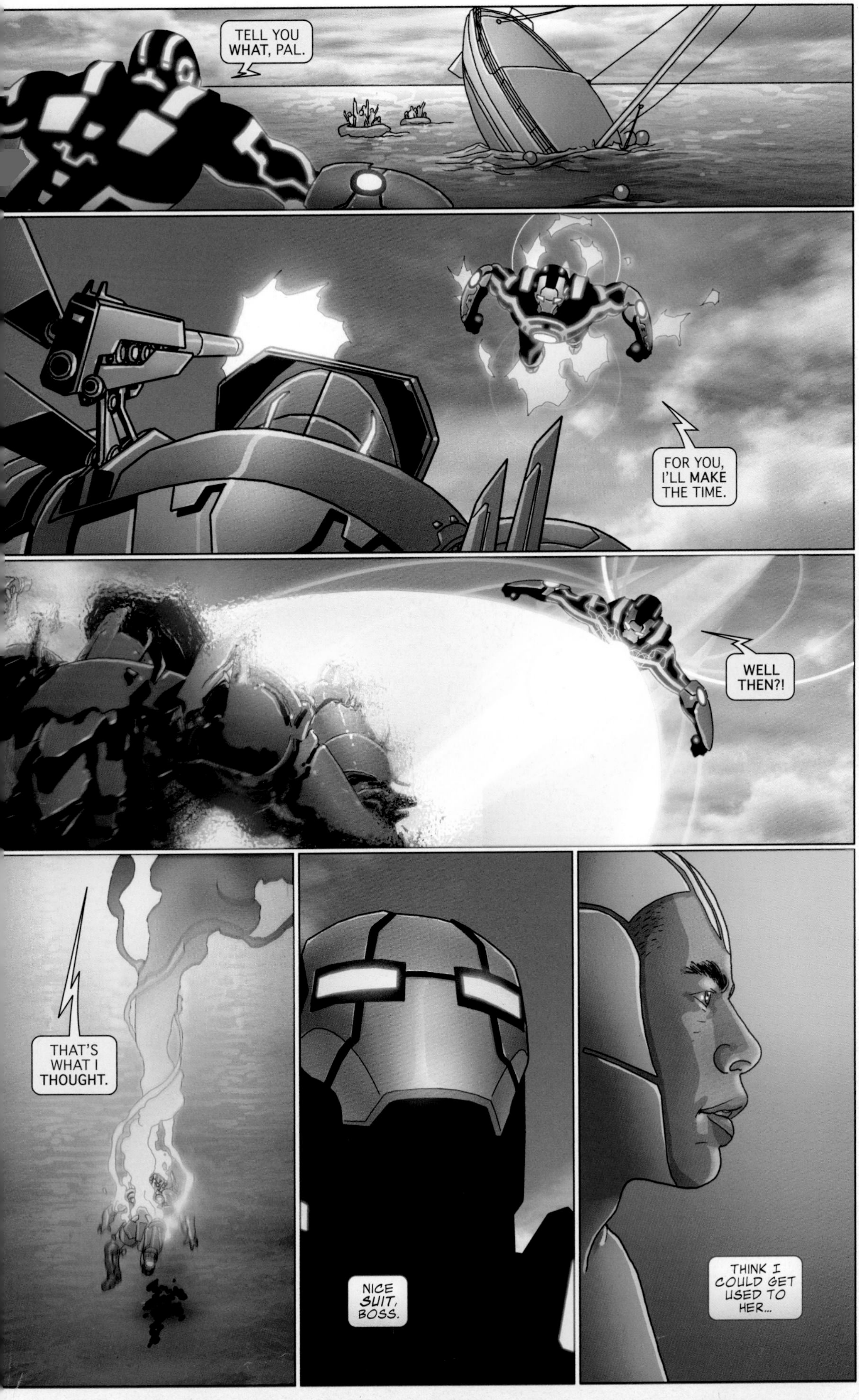
TELL YOU WHAT, PAL.
FOR YOU, I'LL MAKE THE TIME.
WELL THEN?!
THAT'S WHAT I THOUGHT.
NICE SUIT, BOSS.
THINK I COULD GET USED TO HER...

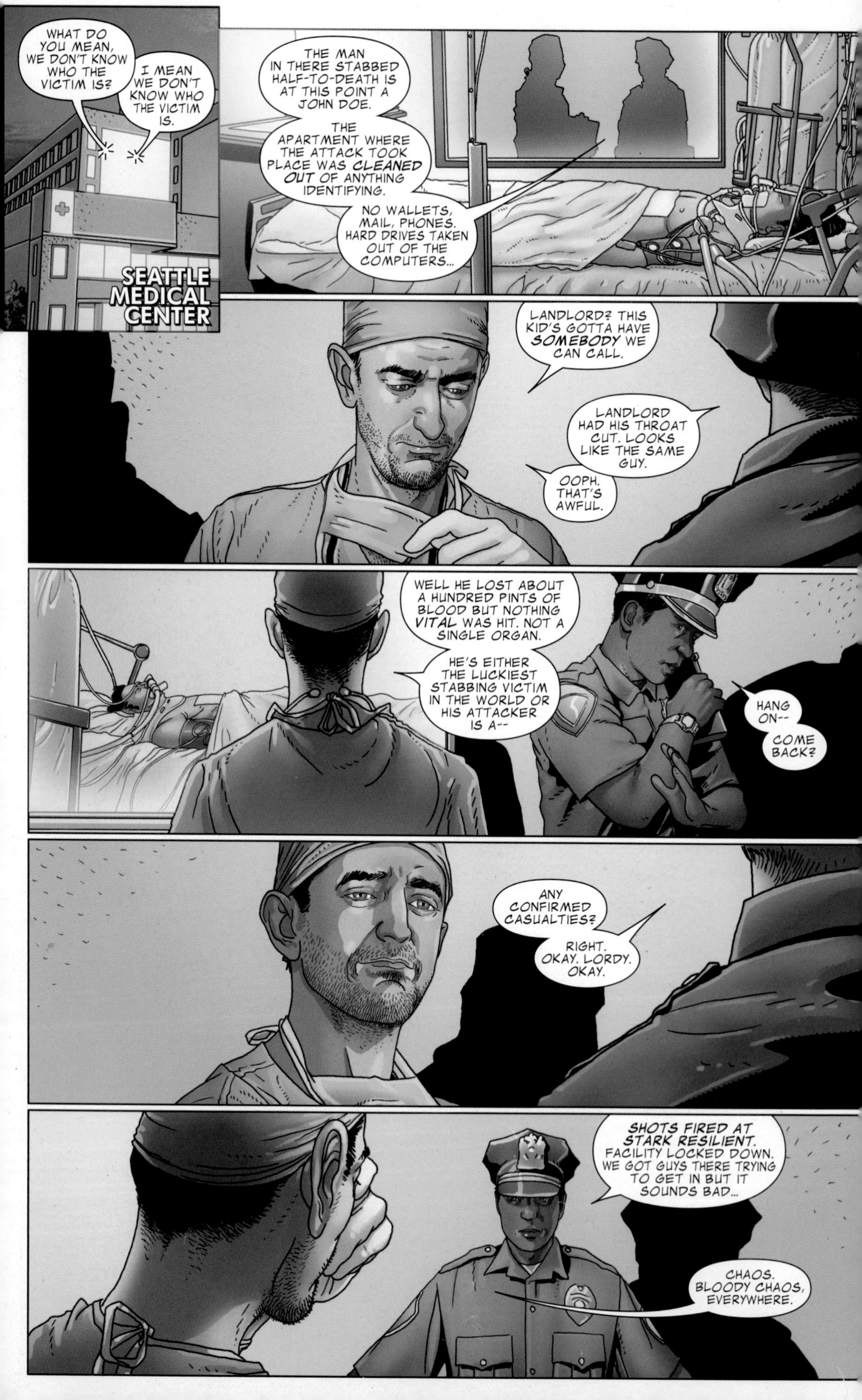
SEATTLE MEDICAL CENTER
WHAT DO YOU MEAN, WE DON'T KNOW WHO THE VICTIM IS?
I MEAN WE DON'T KNOW WHO THE VICTIM IS.
THE MAN IN THERE STABBED HALF-TO-DEATH IS AT THIS POINT A JOHN DOE.
THE APARTMENT WHERE THE ATTACK TOOK PLACE WAS CLEANED OUT OF ANYTHING IDENTIFYING.
NO WALLETS, MAIL, PHONES. HARD DRIVES TAKEN OUT OF THE COMPUTERS...
LANDLORD? THIS KID'S GOTTA HAVE SOMEBODY WE CAN CALL.
LANDLORD HAD HIS THROAT CUT. LOOKS LIKE THE SAME GUY.
OOPH. THAT'S AWFUL.
WELL HE LOST ABOUT A HUNDRED PINTS OF BLOOD BUT NOTHING VITAL WAS HIT. NOT A SINGLE ORGAN.
HE'S EITHER THE LUCKIEST STABBING VICTIM IN THE WORLD OR HIS ATTACKER IS A--
HANG ON--
COME BACK?
ANY CONFIRMED CASUALTIES?
RIGHT. OKAY. LORDY. OKAY.
SHOTS FIRED AT STARK RESILIENT. FACILITY LOCKED DOWN. WE GOT GUYS THERE TRYING TO GET IN BUT IT SOUNDS BAD...
CHAOS. BLOODY CHAOS, EVERYWHERE.

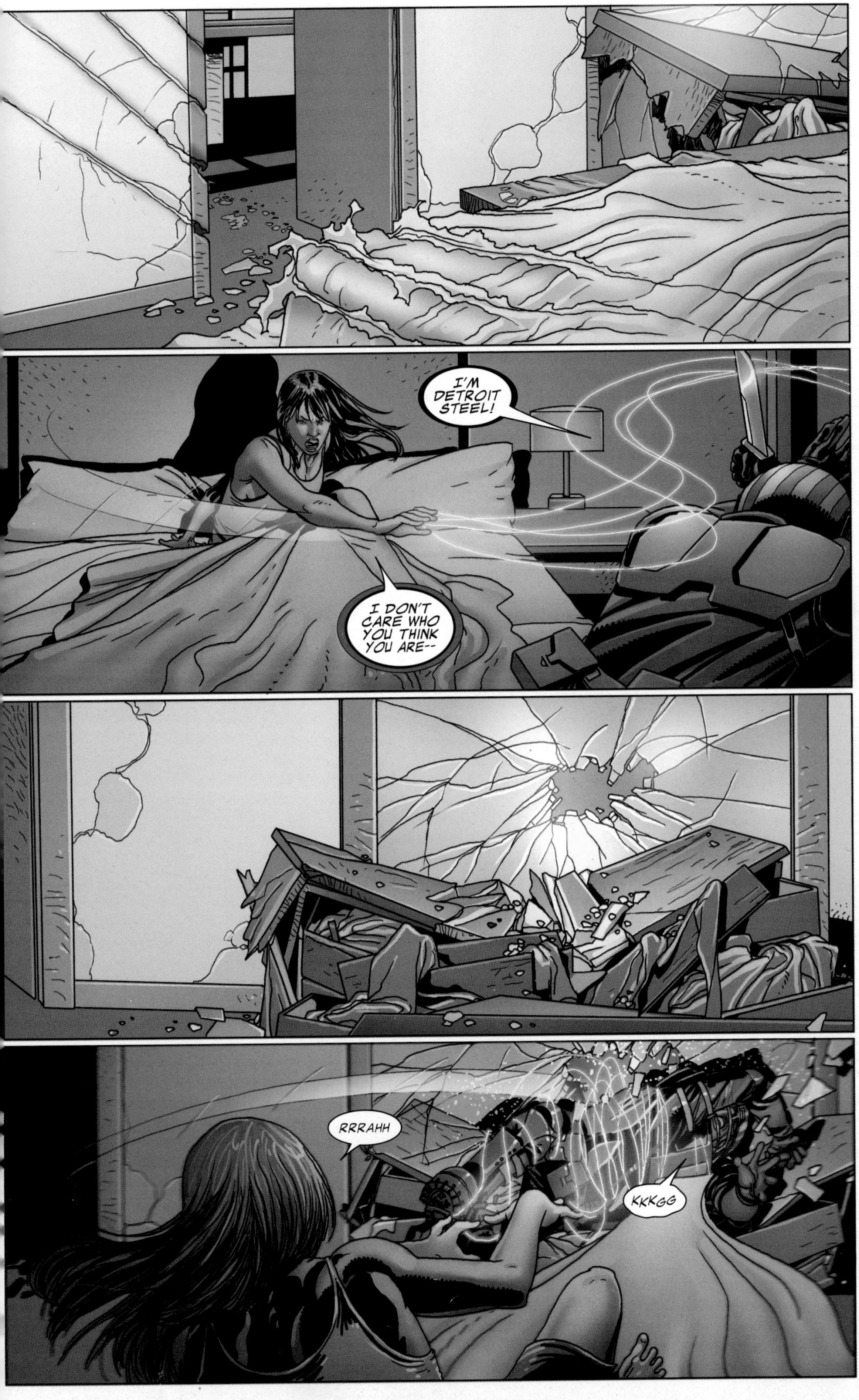
I'M DETROIT STEEL!
I DON'T CARE WHO YOU THINK YOU ARE--
RRRAHH
KKKGG

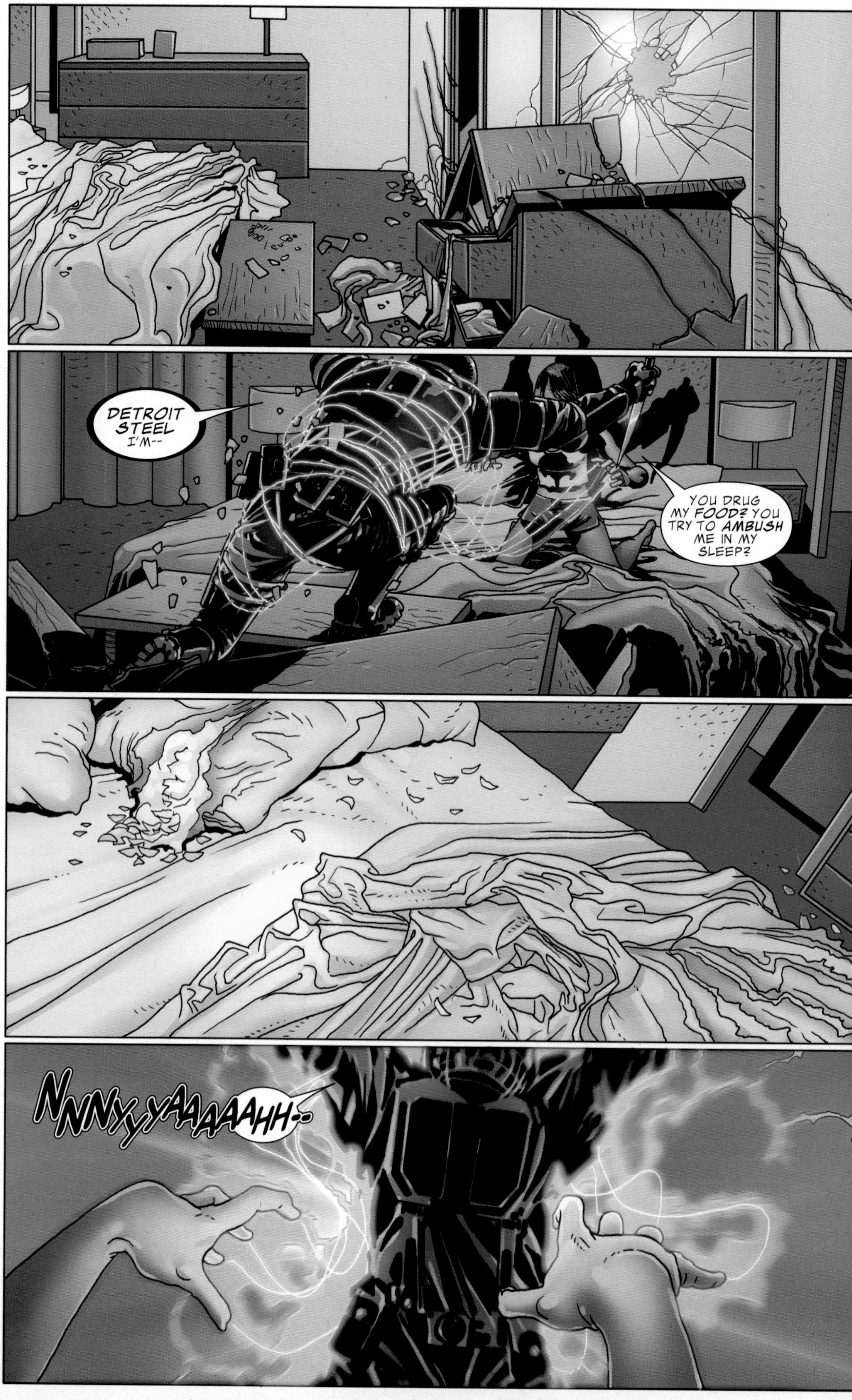
DETROIT STEEL I'M--
YOU DRUG MY FOOD? YOU TRY TO AMBUSH ME IN MY SLEEP?
NNNYYYAAAAAHH--

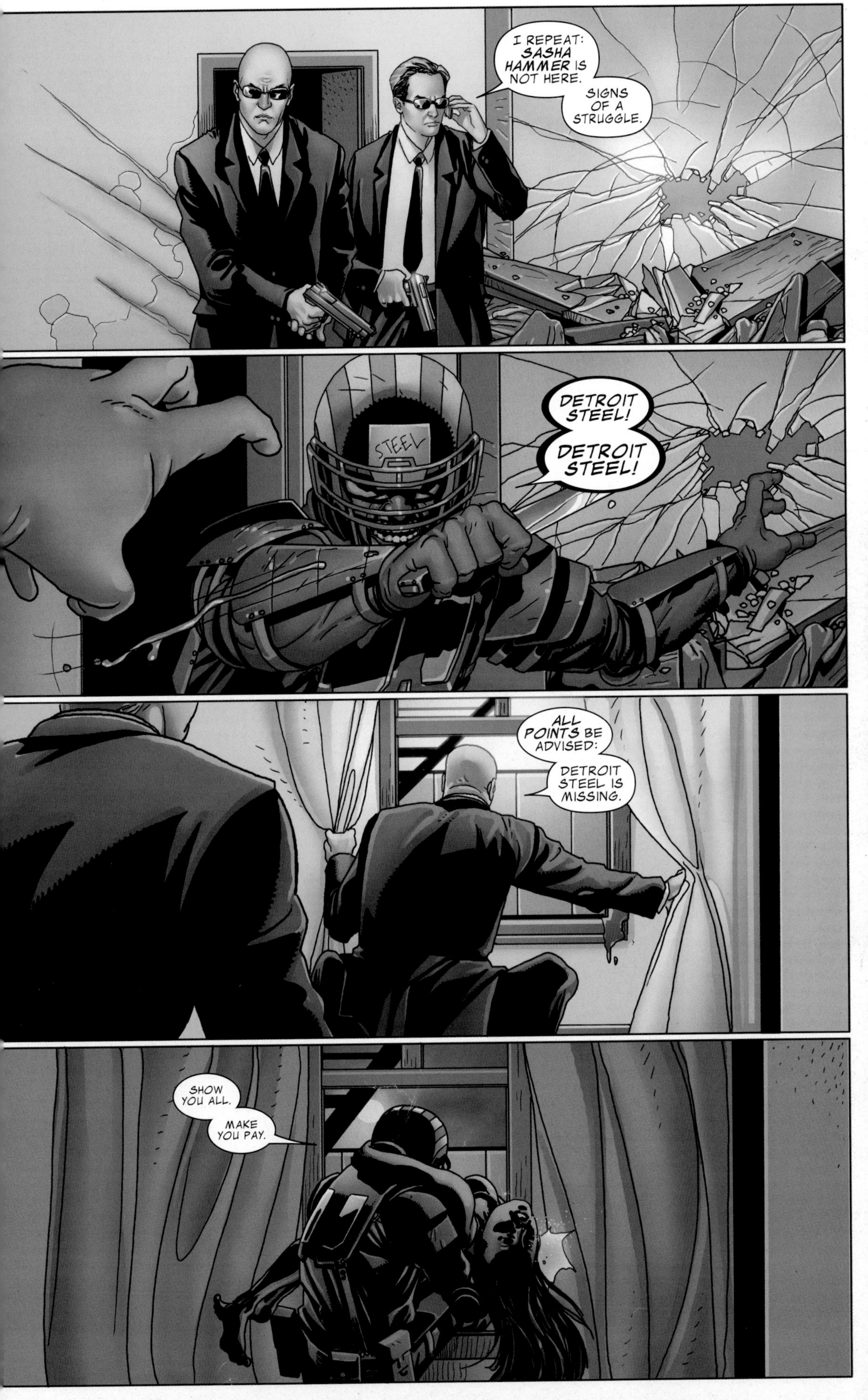
I REPEAT: SASHA HAMMER IS NOT HERE.
SIGNS OF A STRUGGLE.
STEEL
DETROIT STEEL!
DETROIT STEEL!
ALL POINTS BE ADVISED:
DETROIT STEEL IS MISSING.
SHOW YOU ALL.
MAKE YOU PAY.

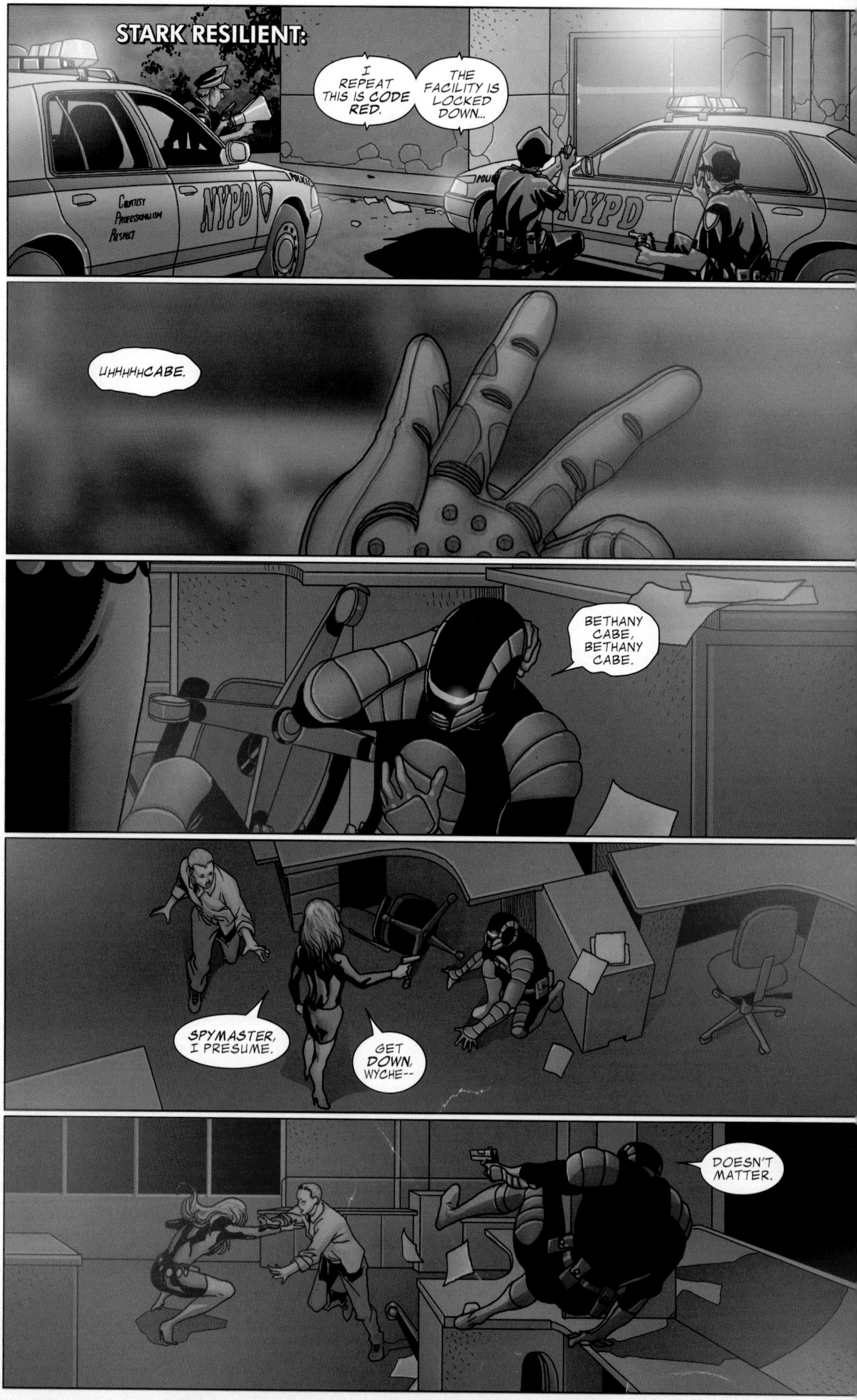
STARK RESILIENT:
I REPEAT THIS IS CODE RED.
THE FACILITY IS LOCKED DOWN...
COURTESY PROFESSIONALISM RESPECT
NYPD
UHHHHHCABE.
BETHANY CABE, BETHANY CABE.
SPYMASTER, I PRESUME.
GET DOWN, WYCHE--
DOESN'T MATTER.

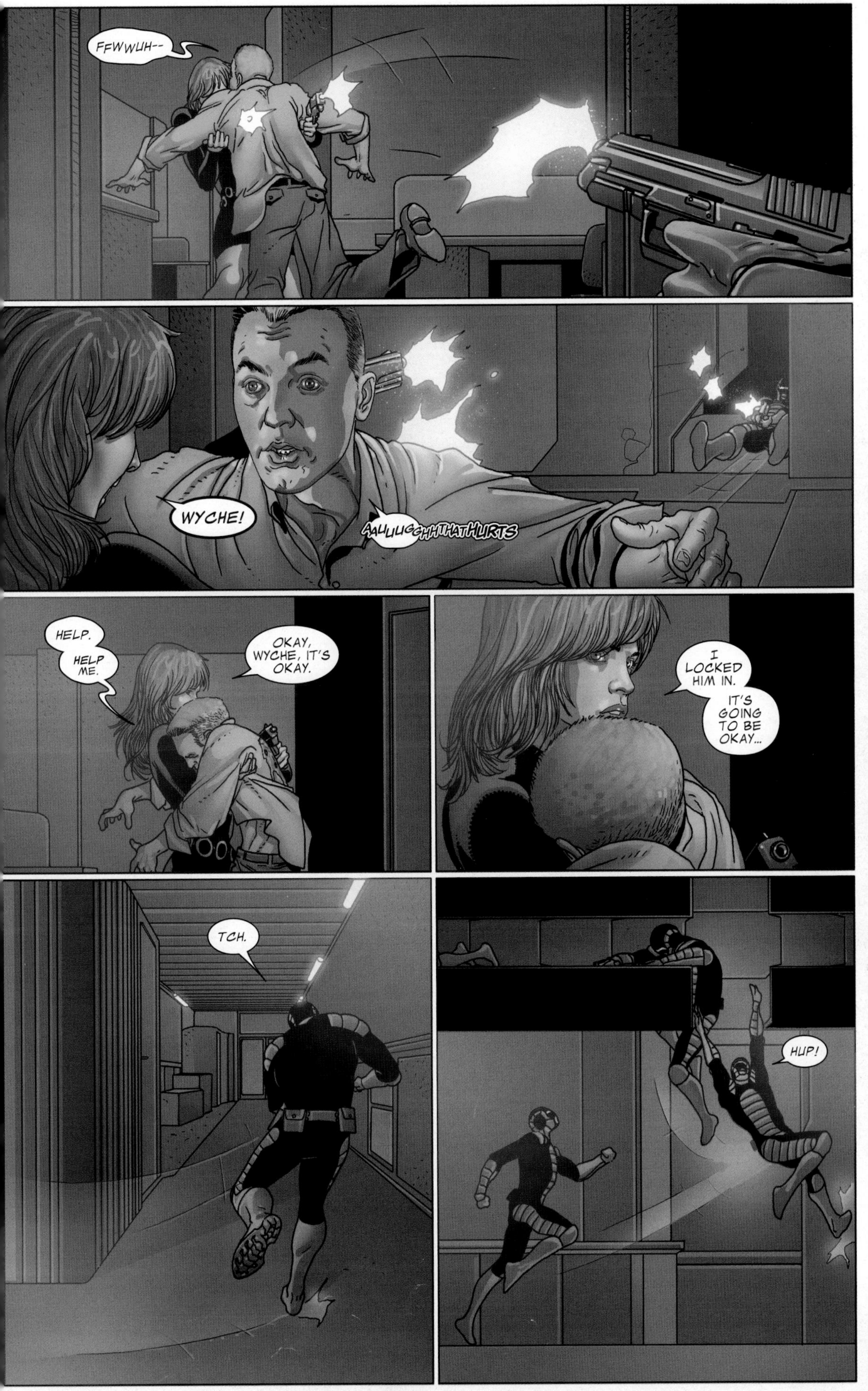
FFWWUH--
WYCHE!
AAUUUGHHTHATHURTS
HELP.
HELP ME.
OKAY, WYCHE, IT'S OKAY.
I LOCKED HIM IN.
IT'S GOING TO BE OKAY...
TCH.
HUP!

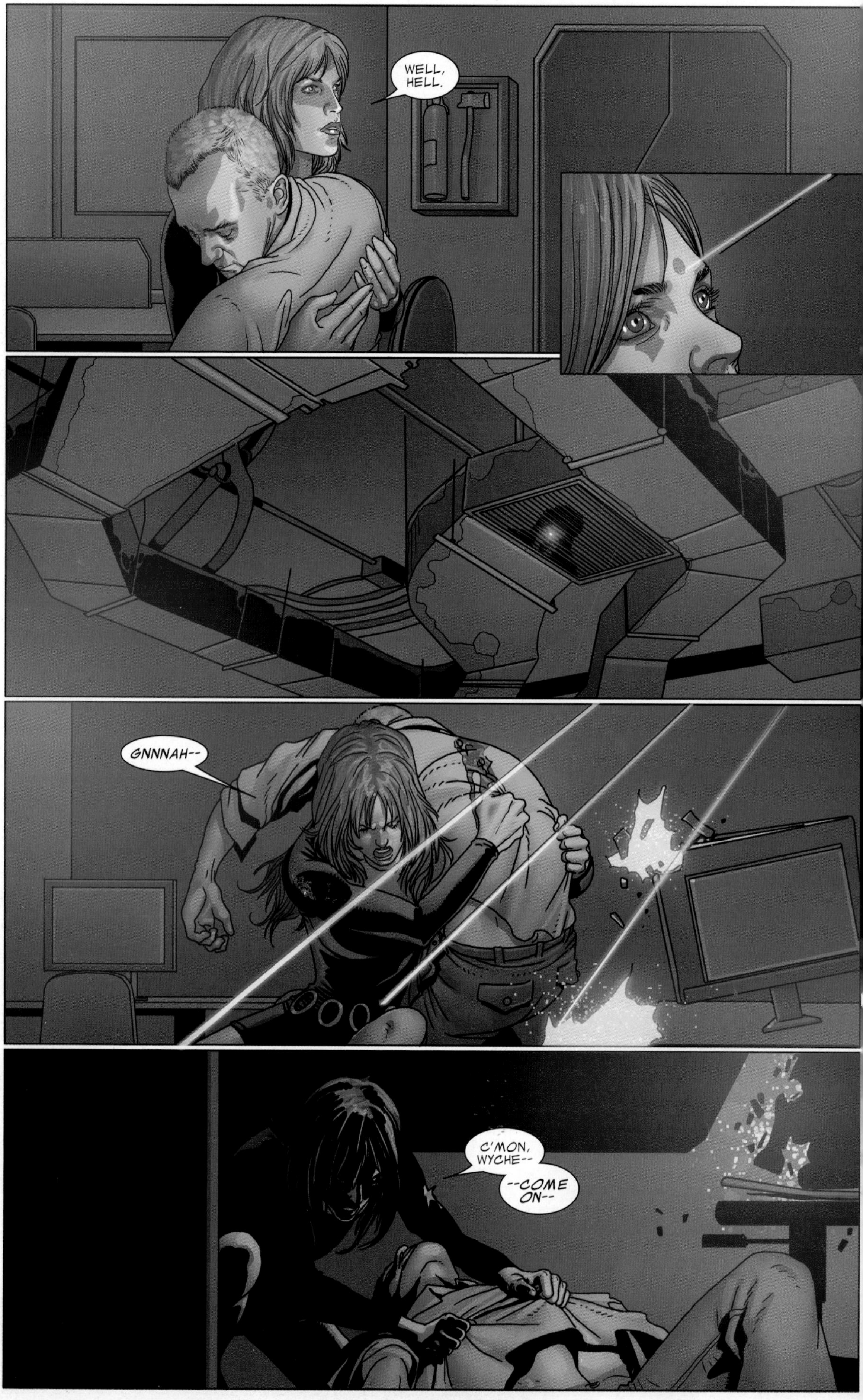
WELL, HELL.
GNNNAH--
C'MON, WYCHE--
--COME ON--

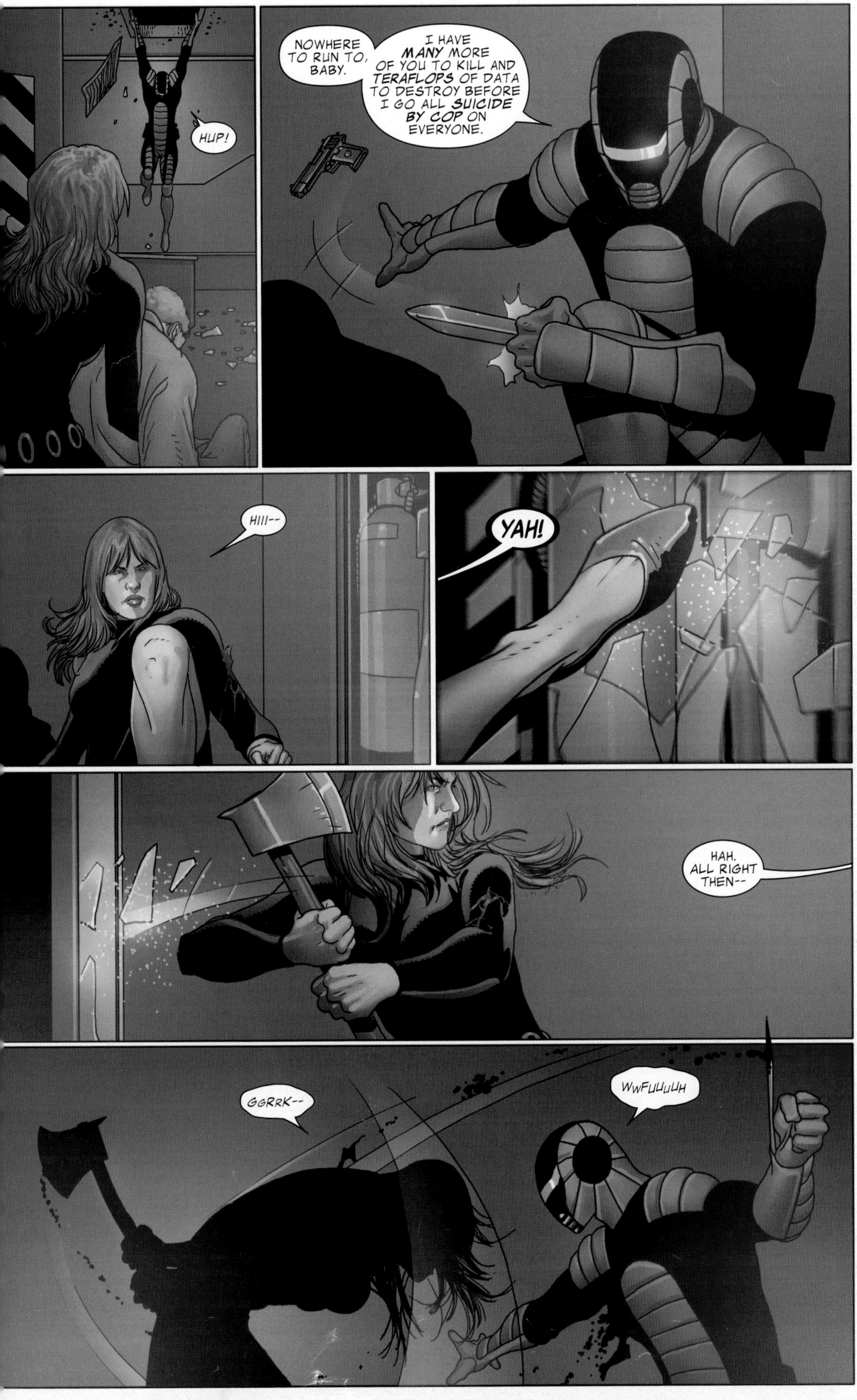
HUP!
NOWHERE TO RUN TO, BABY.
I HAVE MANY MORE OF YOU TO KILL AND TERAFLOPS OF DATA TO DESTROY BEFORE I GO ALL SUICIDE BY COP ON EVERYONE.
HIII--
YAH!
HAH. ALL RIGHT THEN--
GGRRK--
WWFUUUUH

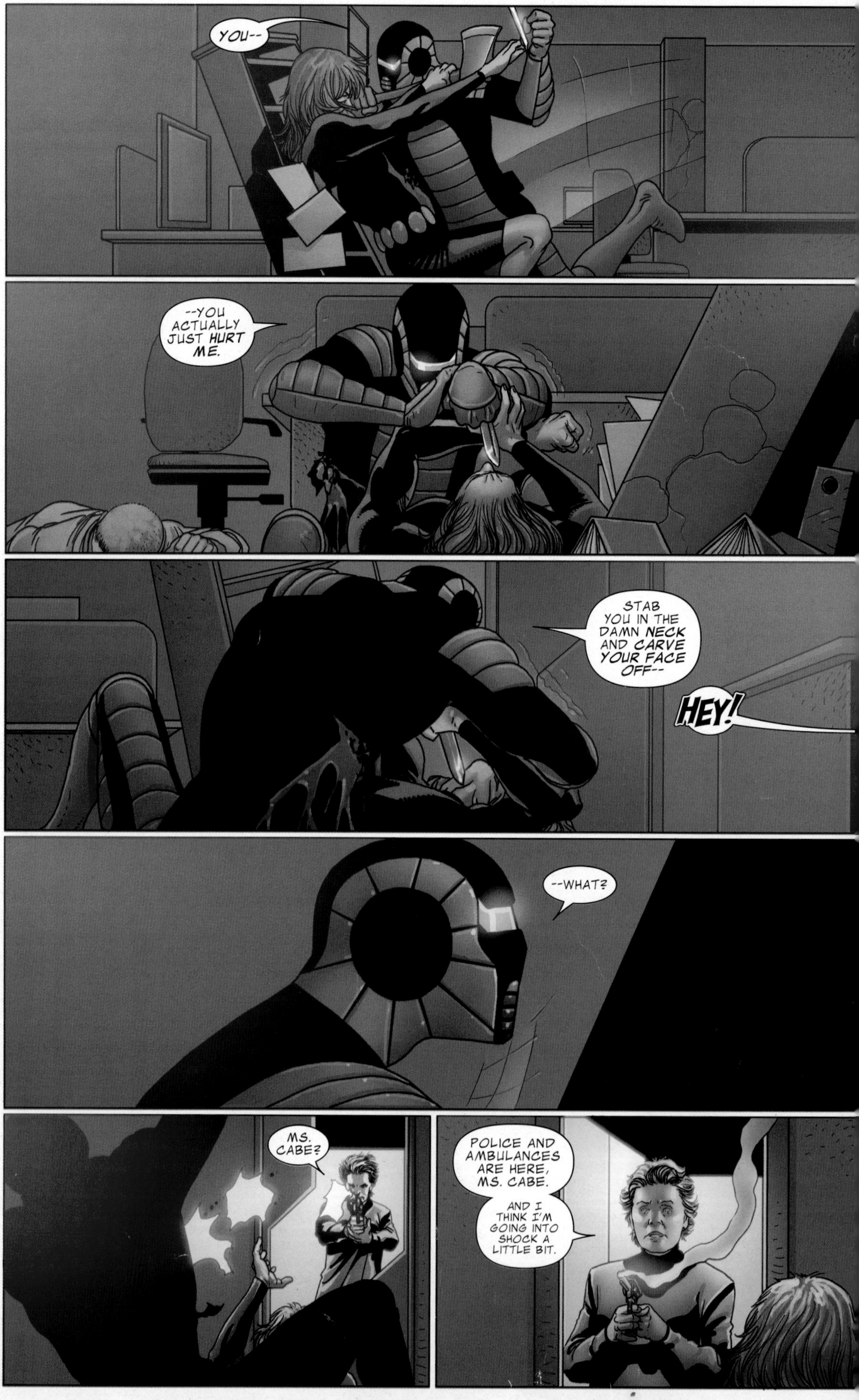
YOU--
--YOU ACTUALLY JUST HURT ME.
STAB YOU IN THE DAMN NECK AND CARVE YOUR FACE OFF--
HEY!
--WHAT?
MS. CABE?
POLICE AND AMBULANCES ARE HERE, MS. CABE.
AND I THINK I'M GOING INTO SHOCK A LITTLE BIT.

TAKE MORE THAN **LIGHTS** AND **ELECTRICITY** TO STOP ME, PUNK.

THE SUIT LIGHTS UP INSIDE A FULL SECOND BEFORE HE FIRES.

ALL LOCKED ON AND GAINING.

MEANWHILE THE SHIP'S STILL SINKING. NEED TO PUT THIS GUY AWAY--

WATCH OUT WATCHOUT--

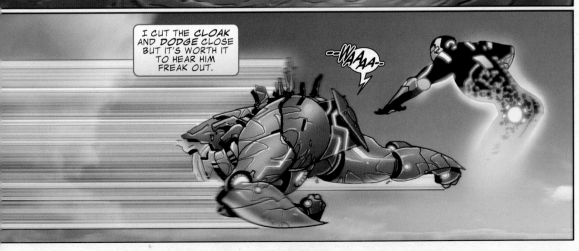

I CUT THE **CLOAK** AND **DODGE** CLOSE BUT IT'S WORTH IT TO HEAR HIM FREAK OUT.

--WAAAA--

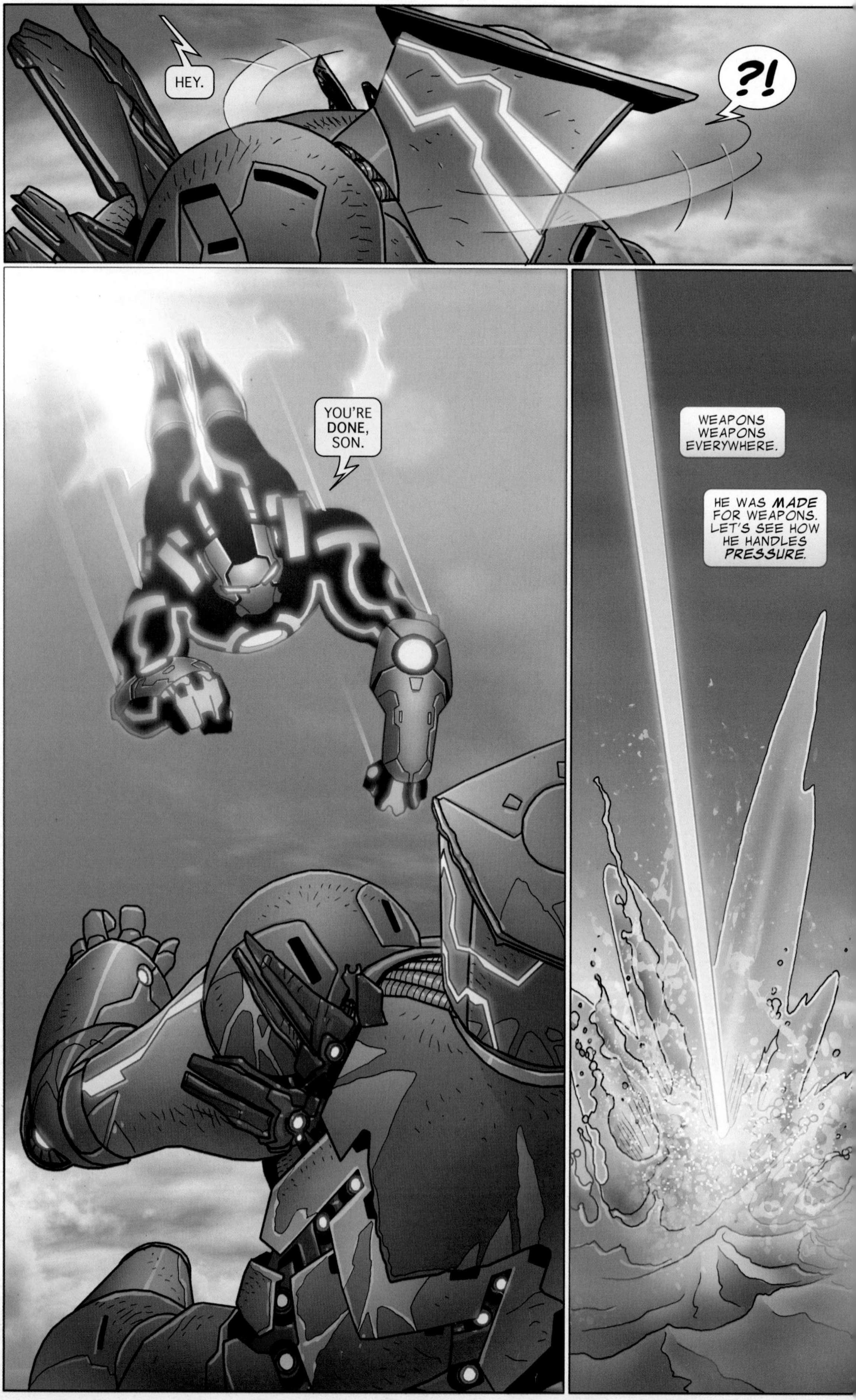
HEY.
?!
YOU'RE DONE, SON.
WEAPONS WEAPONS EVERYWHERE.
HE WAS MADE FOR WEAPONS. LET'S SEE HOW HE HANDLES PRESSURE.

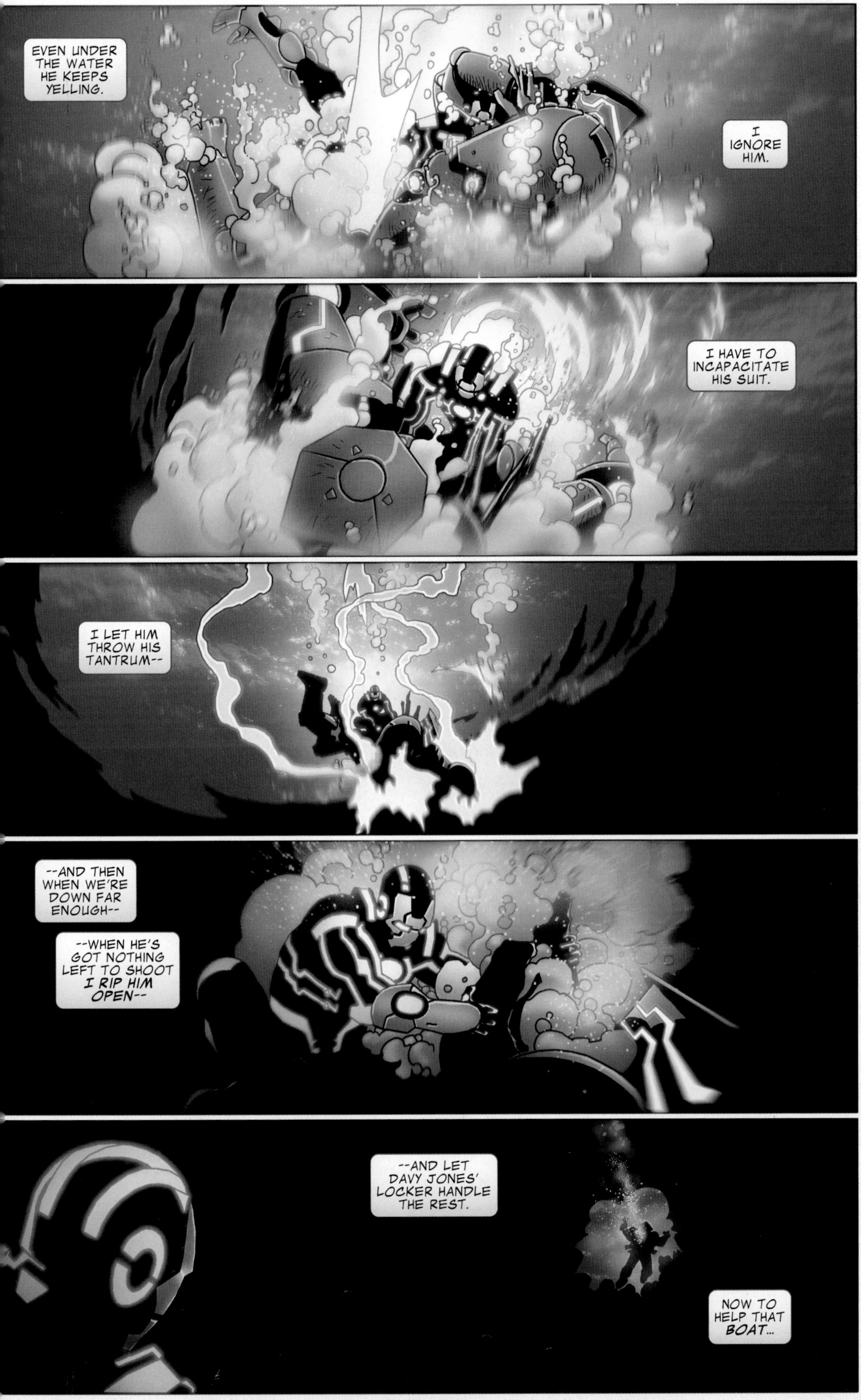
EVEN UNDER THE WATER HE KEEPS YELLING.
I IGNORE HIM.
I HAVE TO INCAPACITATE HIS SUIT.
I LET HIM THROW HIS TANTRUM--
--AND THEN WHEN WE'RE DOWN FAR ENOUGH--
--WHEN HE'S GOT NOTHING LEFT TO SHOOT *I RIP HIM OPEN*--
--AND LET DAVY JONES' LOCKER HANDLE THE REST.
NOW TO HELP THAT *BOAT*...

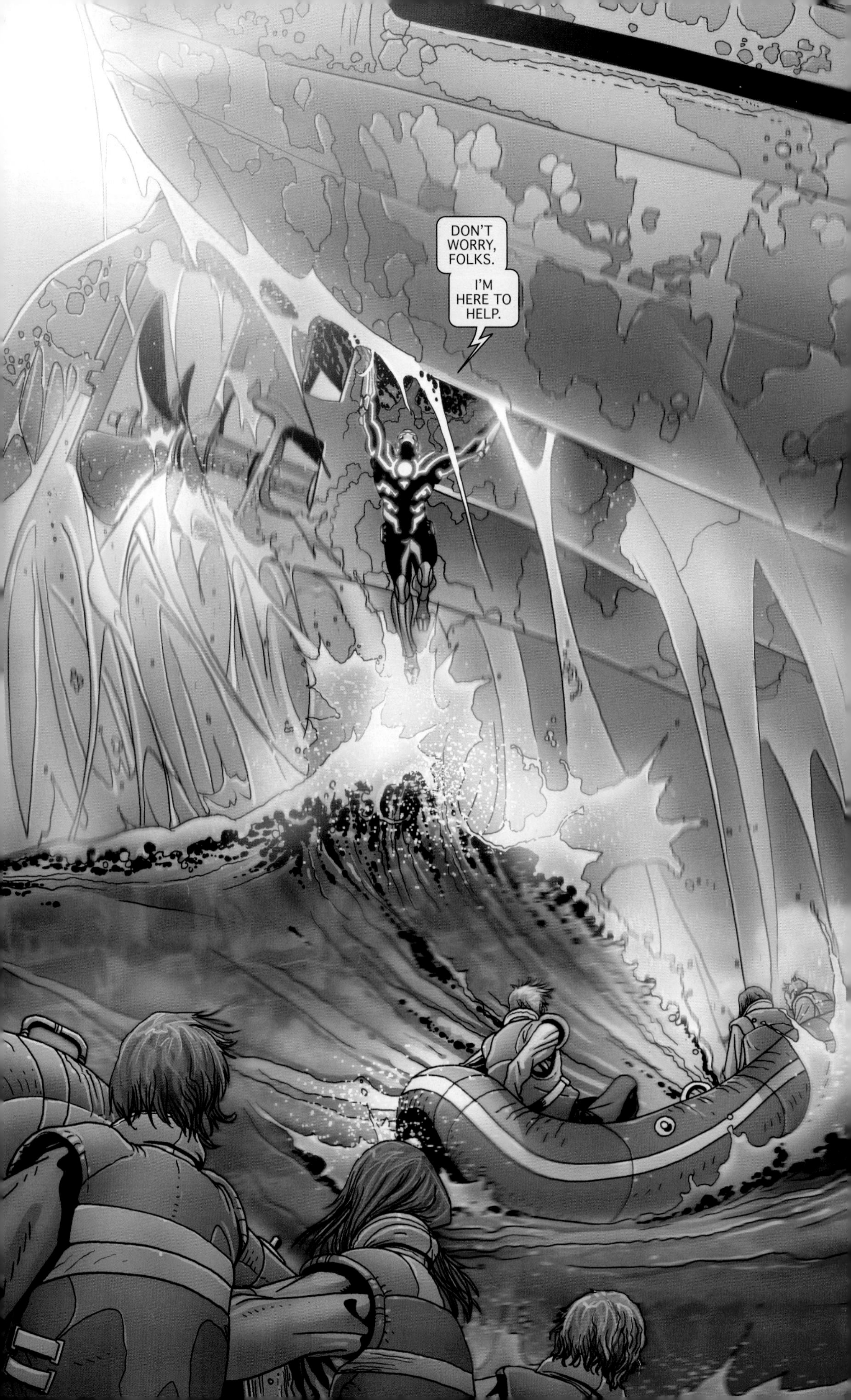
DON'T WORRY, FOLKS.
I'M HERE TO HELP.

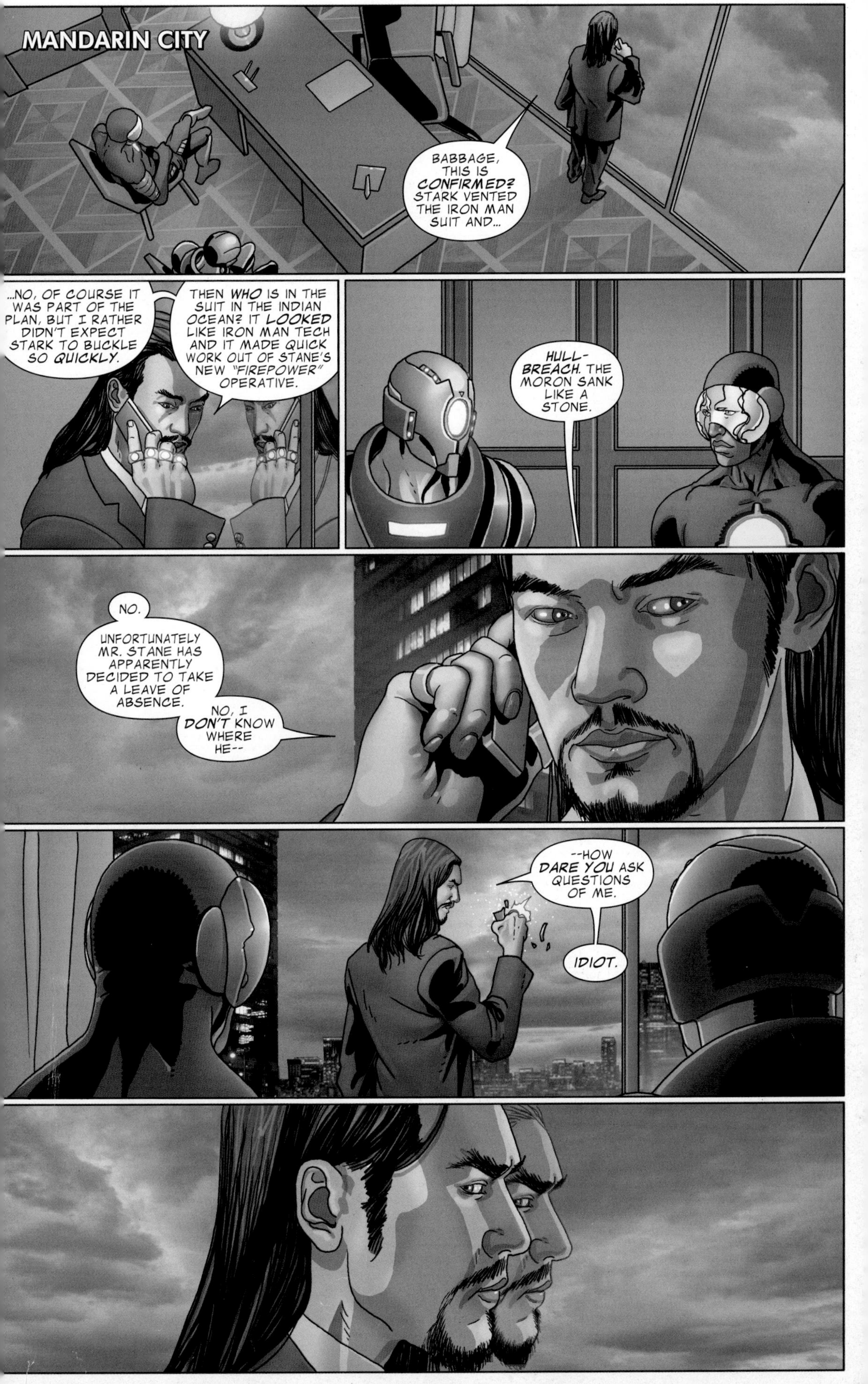
MANDARIN CITY
BABBAGE, THIS IS CONFIRMED? STARK VENTED THE IRON MAN SUIT AND...
...NO, OF COURSE IT WAS PART OF THE PLAN, BUT I RATHER DIDN'T EXPECT STARK TO BUCKLE SO QUICKLY.
THEN WHO IS IN THE SUIT IN THE INDIAN OCEAN? IT LOOKED LIKE IRON MAN TECH AND IT MADE QUICK WORK OUT OF STANE'S NEW "FIREPOWER" OPERATIVE.
HULL-BREACH. THE MORON SANK LIKE A STONE.
NO.
UNFORTUNATELY MR. STANE HAS APPARENTLY DECIDED TO TAKE A LEAVE OF ABSENCE.
NO, I DON'T KNOW WHERE HE--
--HOW DARE YOU ASK QUESTIONS OF ME.
IDIOT.

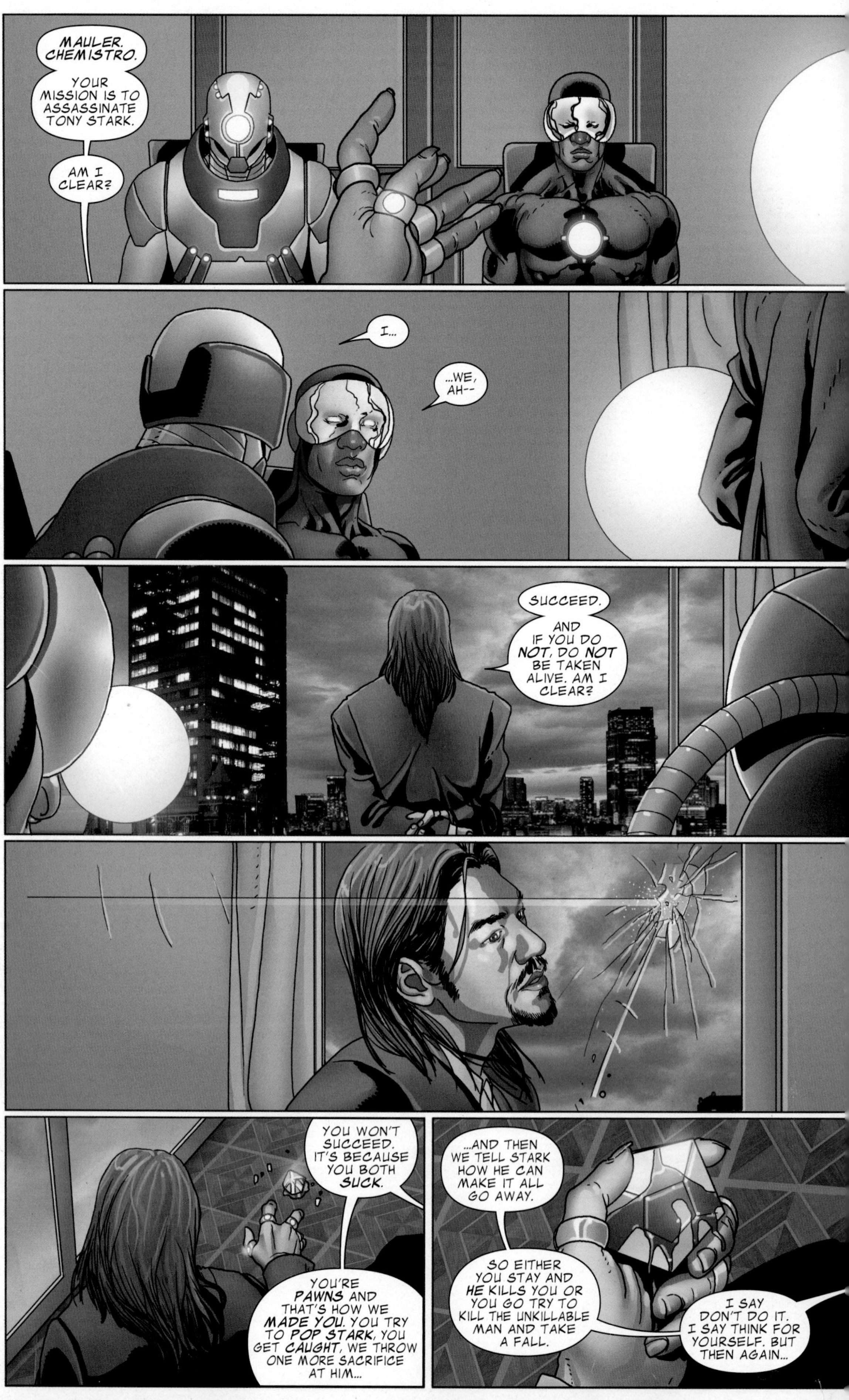
MAULER. CHEMISTRO.
YOUR MISSION IS TO ASSASSINATE TONY STARK.
AM I CLEAR?
I...
...WE, AH--
SUCCEED.
AND IF YOU DO NOT, DO NOT BE TAKEN ALIVE. AM I CLEAR?
YOU WON'T SUCCEED. IT'S BECAUSE YOU BOTH SUCK.
YOU'RE PAWNS AND THAT'S HOW WE MADE YOU. YOU TRY TO POP STARK, YOU GET CAUGHT, WE THROW ONE MORE SACRIFICE AT HIM...
...AND THEN WE TELL STARK HOW HE CAN MAKE IT ALL GO AWAY.
SO EITHER YOU STAY AND HE KILLS YOU OR YOU GO TRY TO KILL THE UNKILLABLE MAN AND TAKE A FALL.
I SAY DON'T DO IT. I SAY THINK FOR YOURSELF. BUT THEN AGAIN...

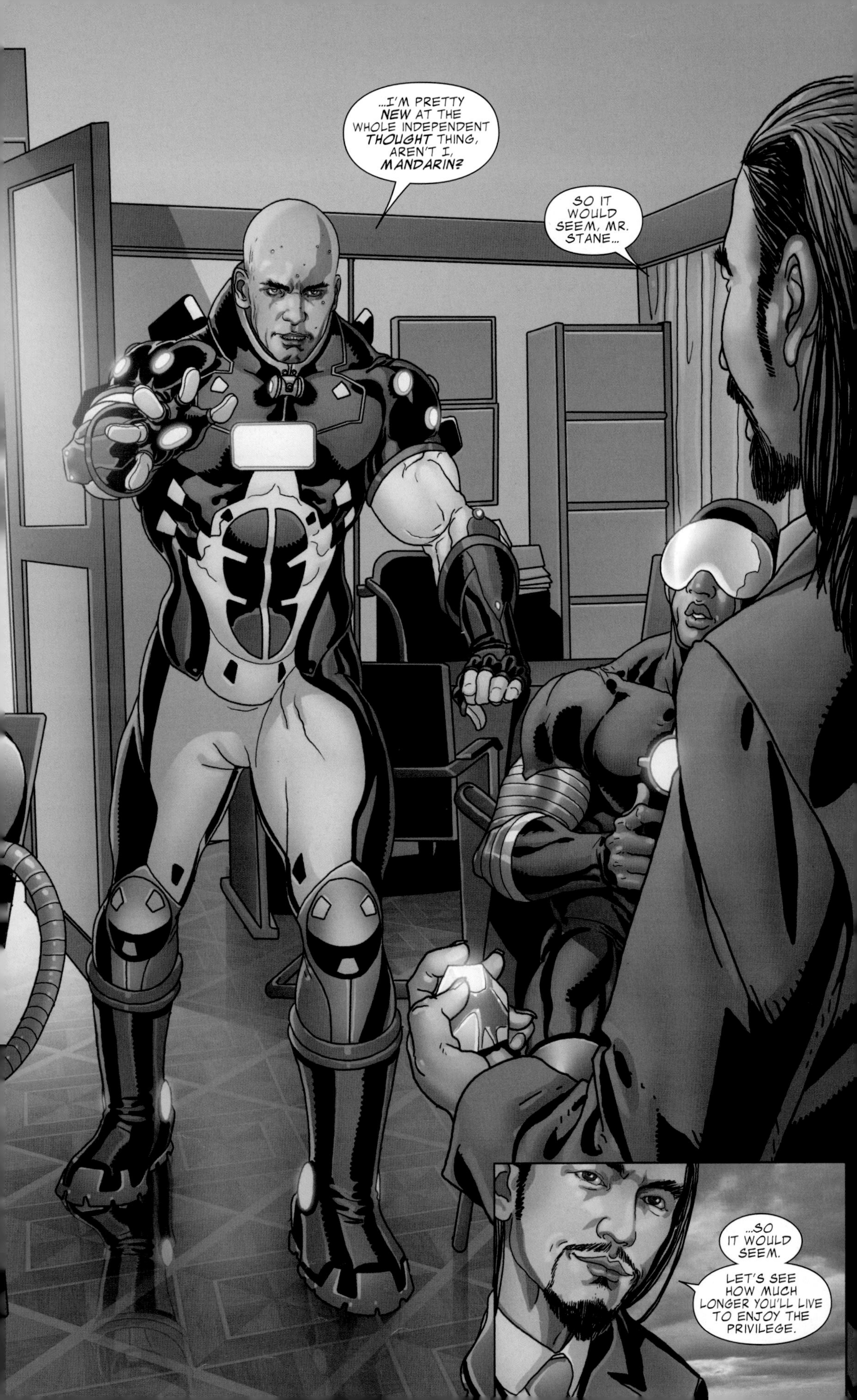
...I'M PRETTY NEW AT THE WHOLE INDEPENDENT THOUGHT THING, AREN'T I, MANDARIN?
SO IT WOULD SEEM, MR. STANE...
...SO IT WOULD SEEM.
LET'S SEE HOW MUCH LONGER YOU'LL LIVE TO ENJOY THE PRIVILEGE.

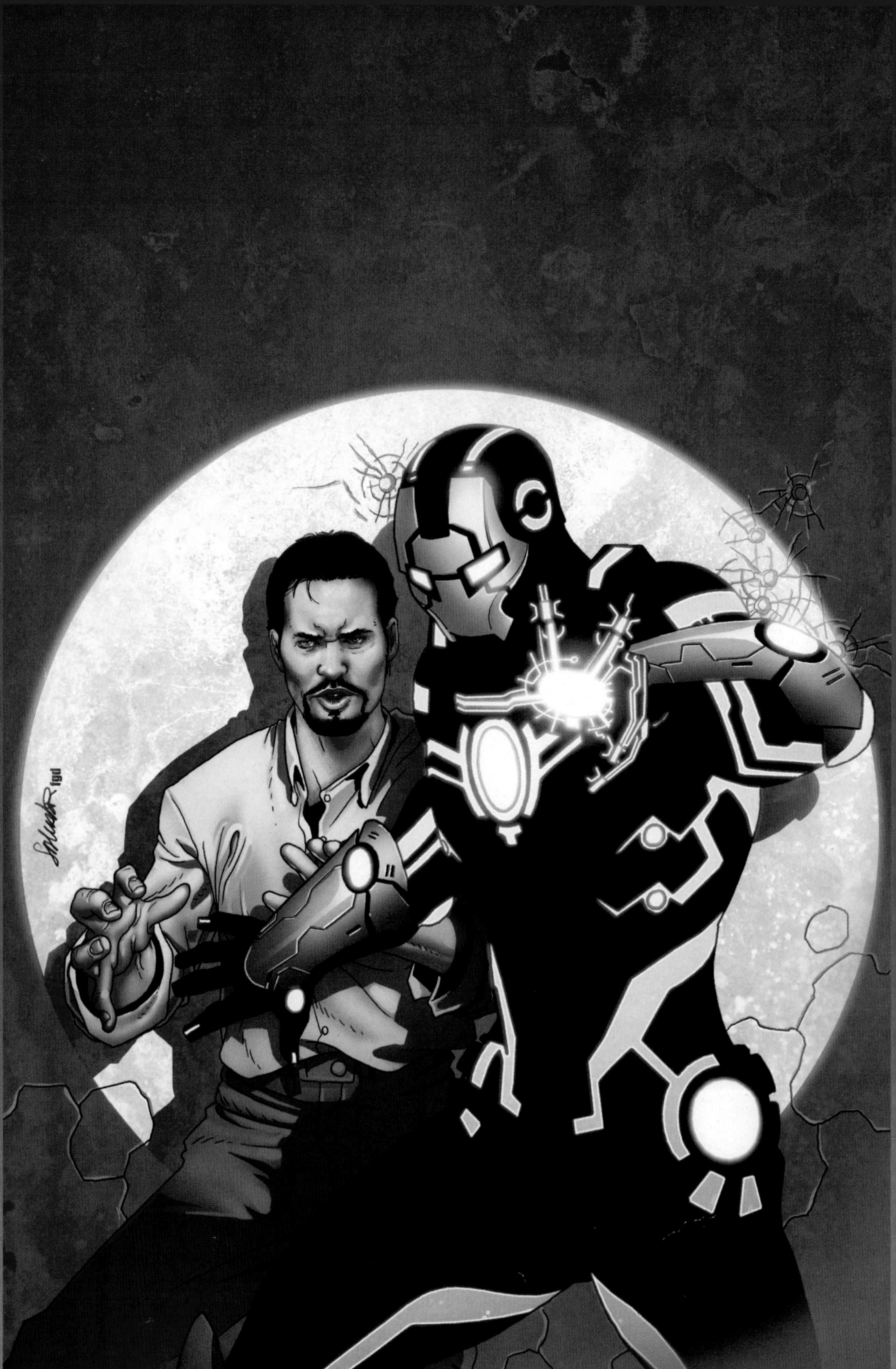

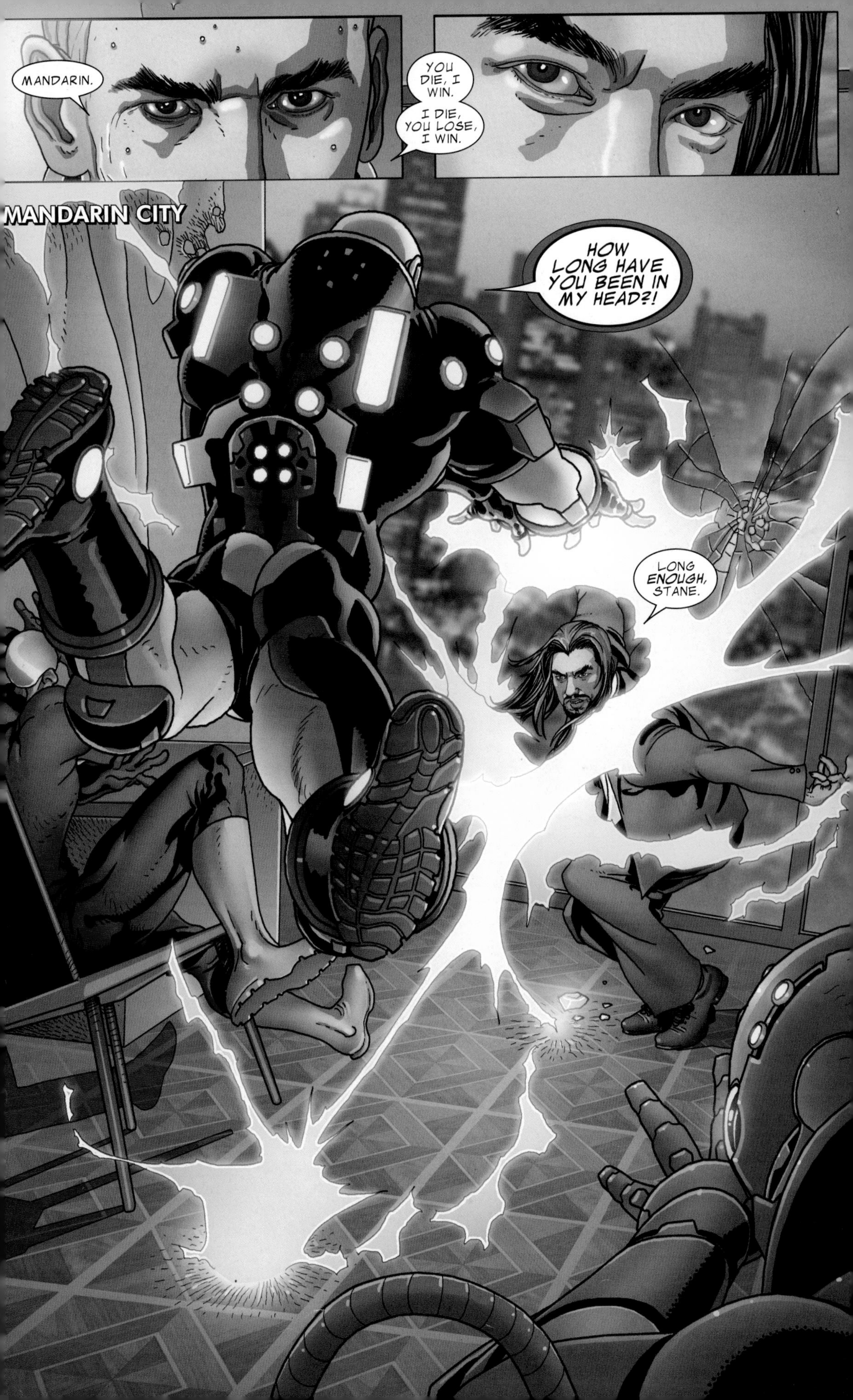
MANDARIN.
YOU DIE, I WIN.
I DIE, YOU LOSE, I WIN.
MANDARIN CITY
HOW LONG HAVE YOU BEEN IN MY HEAD?!
LONG ENOUGH, STANE.

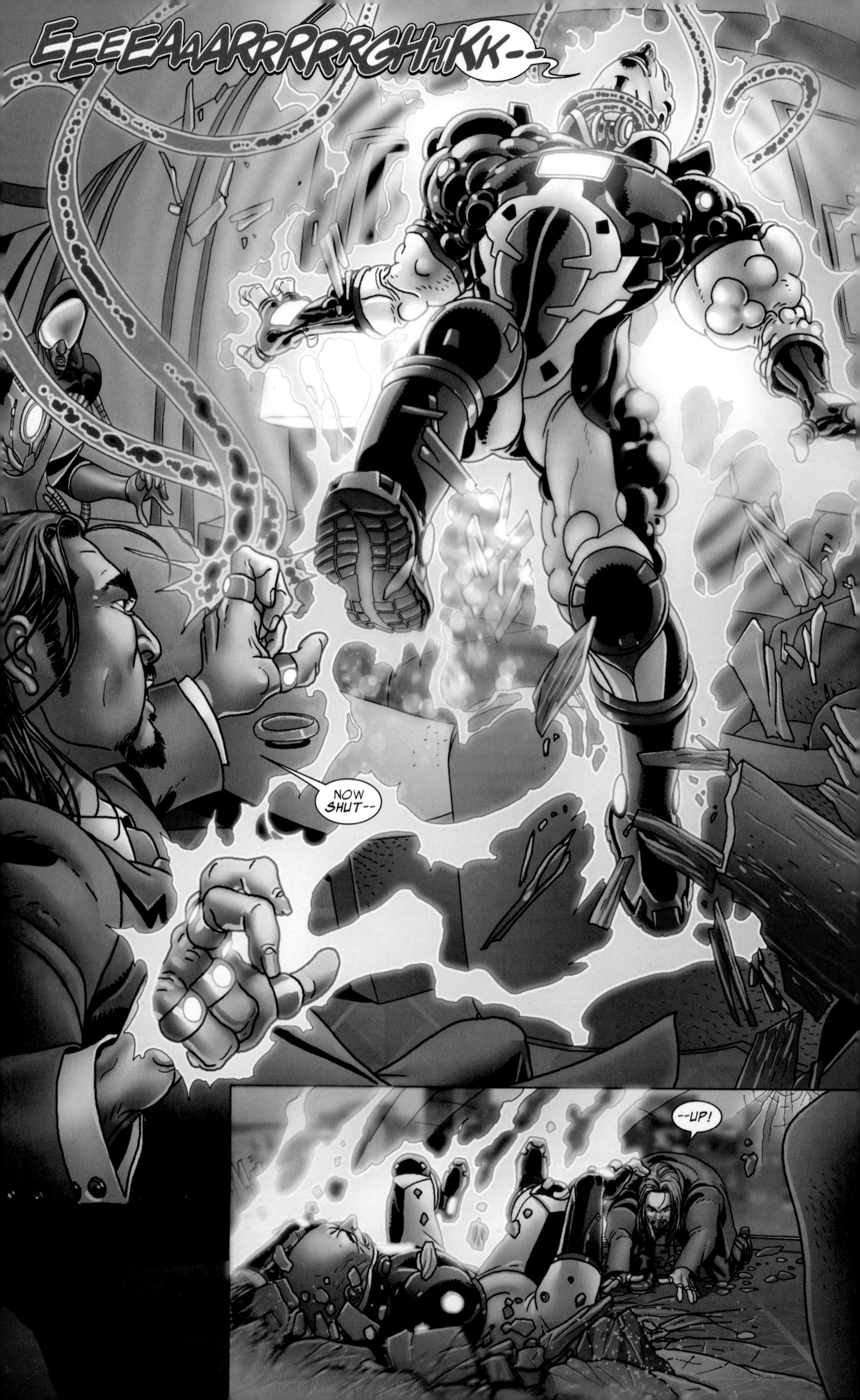
EEEEAAARRRRRRGHHKK--
NOW SHUT--
--UP!

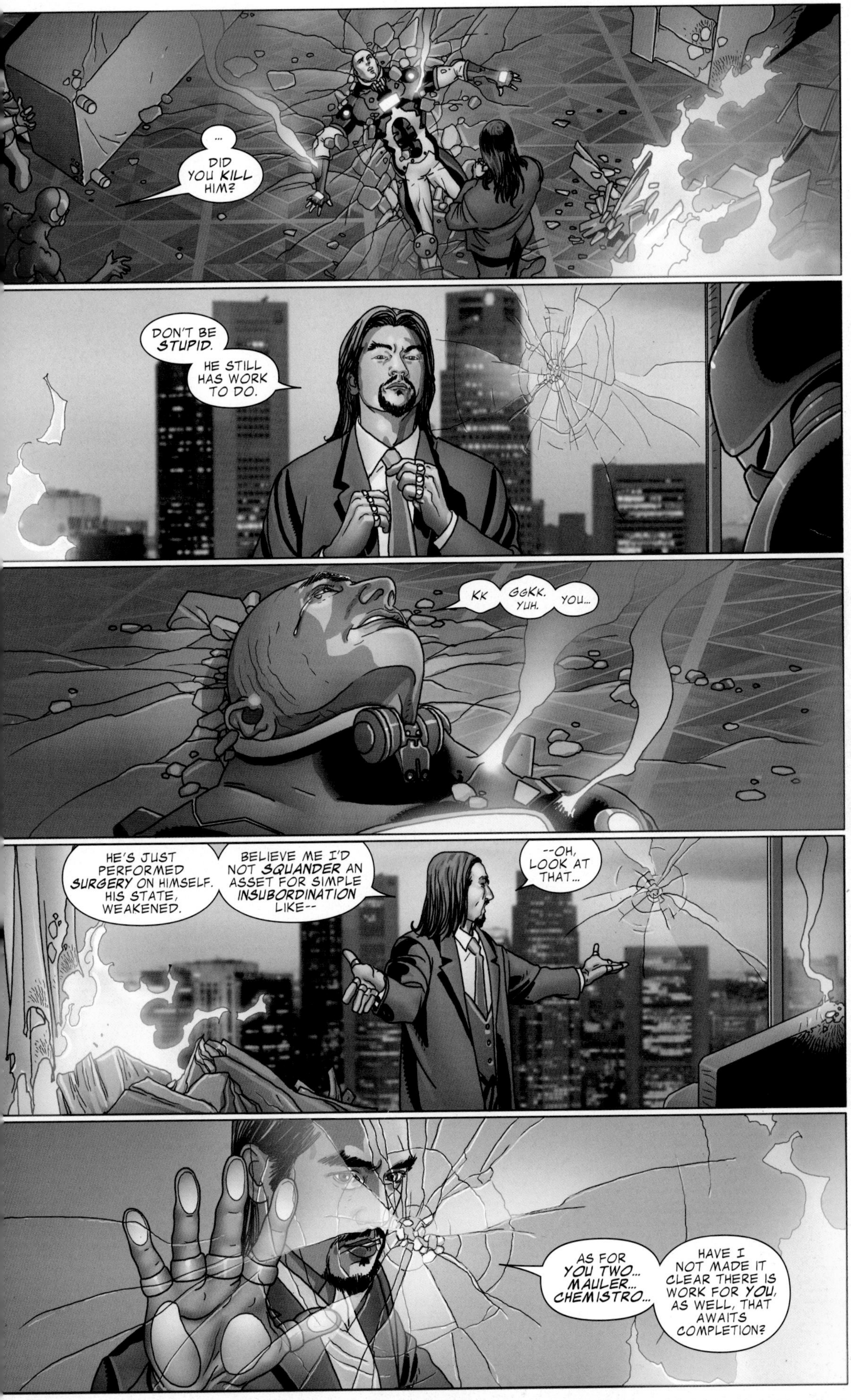

...
DID YOU KILL HIM?
DON'T BE STUPID.
HE STILL HAS WORK TO DO.
KK
GGKK. YUH.
YOU...
HE'S JUST PERFORMED SURGERY ON HIMSELF. HIS STATE, WEAKENED.
BELIEVE ME I'D NOT SQUANDER AN ASSET FOR SIMPLE INSUBORDINATION LIKE--
--OH, LOOK AT THAT...
AS FOR YOU TWO... MAULER... CHEMISTRO...
HAVE I NOT MADE IT CLEAR THERE IS WORK FOR YOU, AS WELL, THAT AWAITS COMPLETION?

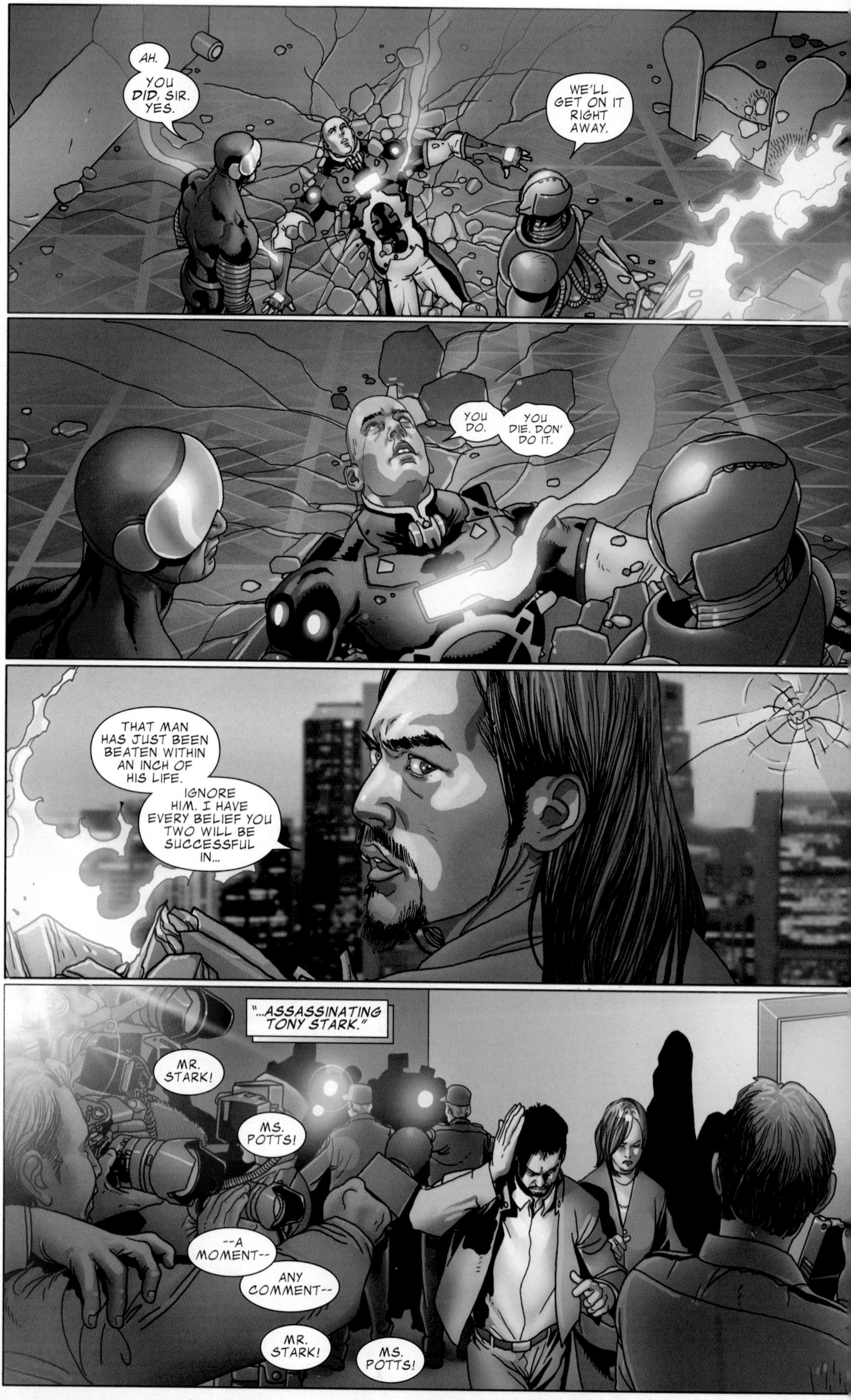
AH.
YOU DID, SIR. YES.
WE'LL GET ON IT RIGHT AWAY.
YOU DO.
YOU DIE. DON' DO IT.
THAT MAN HAS JUST BEEN BEATEN WITHIN AN INCH OF HIS LIFE.
IGNORE HIM. I HAVE EVERY BELIEF YOU TWO WILL BE SUCCESSFUL IN...
"...ASSASSINATING TONY STARK."
MR. STARK!
MS. POTTS!
--A MOMENT--
ANY COMMENT--
MR. STARK!
MS. POTTS!

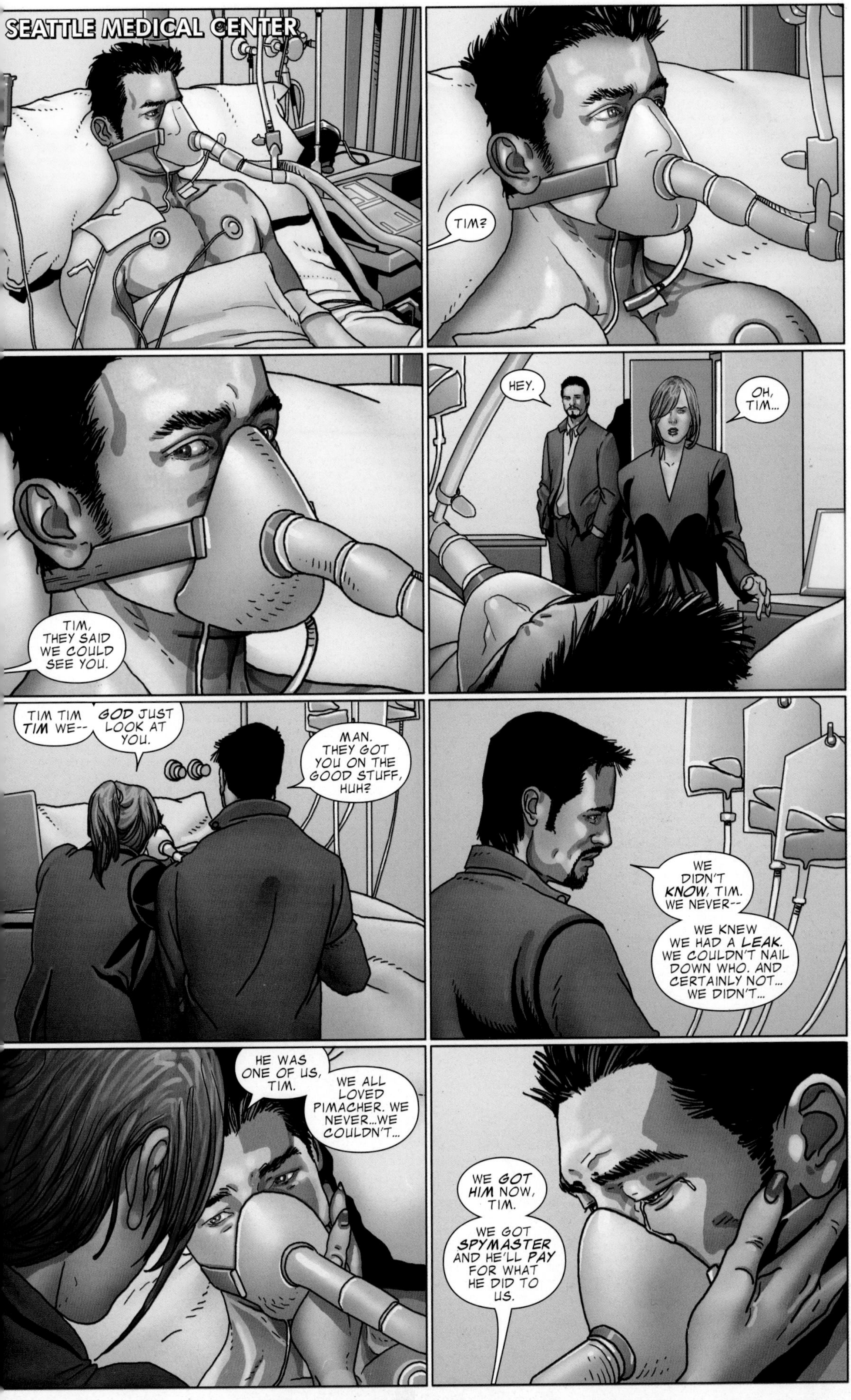
SEATTLE MEDICAL CENTER.
TIM?
TIM, THEY SAID WE COULD SEE YOU.
HEY.
OH, TIM...
TIM TIM TIM WE--
GOD JUST LOOK AT YOU.
MAN. THEY GOT YOU ON THE GOOD STUFF, HUH?
WE DIDN'T KNOW, TIM. WE NEVER--
WE KNEW WE HAD A LEAK. WE COULDN'T NAIL DOWN WHO. AND CERTAINLY NOT... WE DIDN'T...
HE WAS ONE OF US, TIM.
WE ALL LOVED PIMACHER. WE NEVER...WE COULDN'T...
WE GOT HIM NOW, TIM.
WE GOT SPYMASTER AND HE'LL PAY FOR WHAT HE DID TO US.

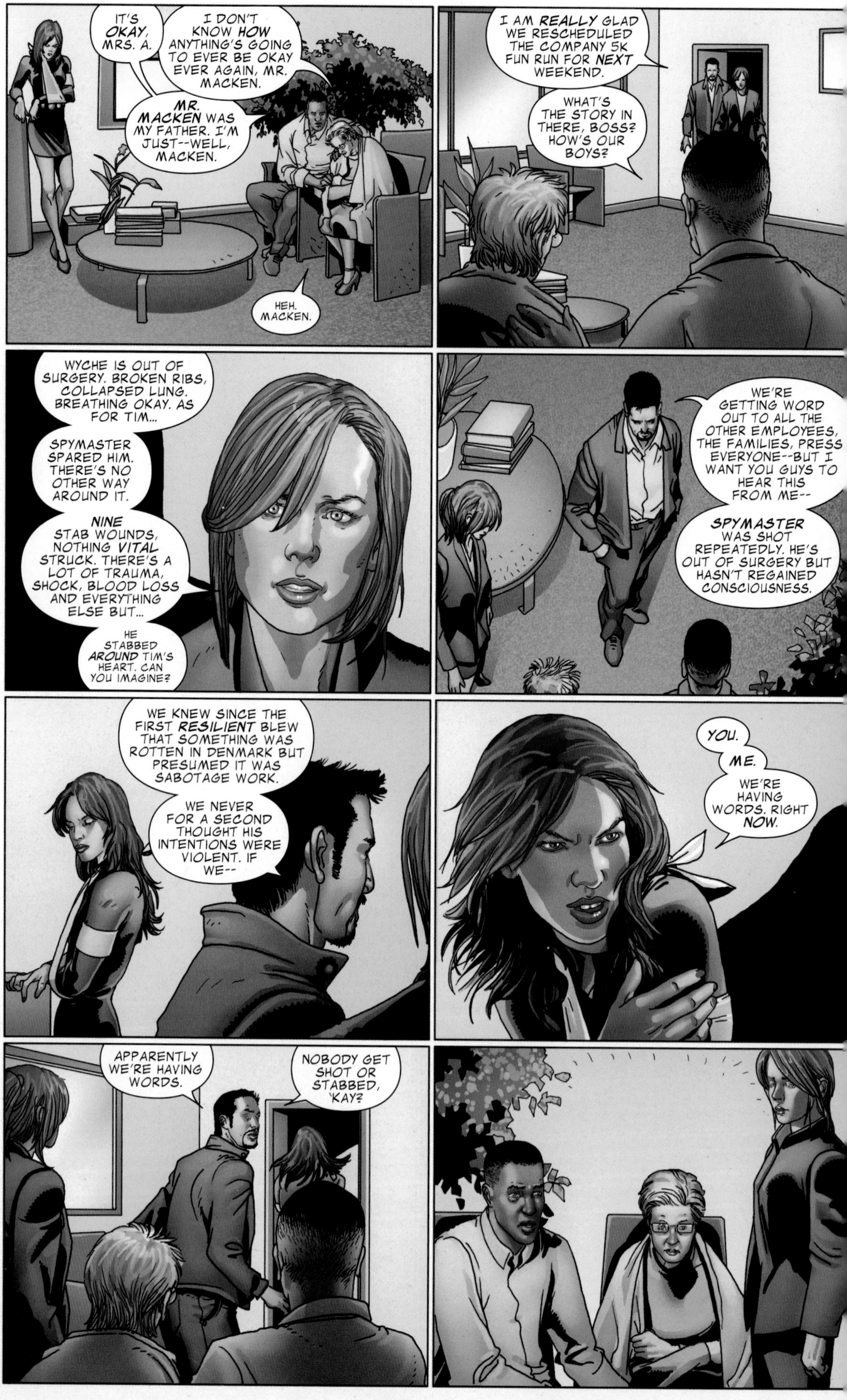
IT'S OKAY, MRS. A.
I DON'T KNOW HOW ANYTHING'S GOING TO EVER BE OKAY EVER AGAIN, MR. MACKEN.
MR. MACKEN WAS MY FATHER. I'M JUST--WELL, MACKEN.
HEH. MACKEN.
I AM REALLY GLAD WE RESCHEDULED THE COMPANY 5K FUN RUN FOR NEXT WEEKEND.
WHAT'S THE STORY IN THERE, BOSS? HOW'S OUR BOYS?
WYCHE IS OUT OF SURGERY. BROKEN RIBS, COLLAPSED LUNG. BREATHING OKAY. AS FOR TIM...
SPYMASTER SPARED HIM. THERE'S NO OTHER WAY AROUND IT.
NINE STAB WOUNDS, NOTHING VITAL STRUCK. THERE'S A LOT OF TRAUMA, SHOCK, BLOOD LOSS AND EVERYTHING ELSE BUT...
HE STABBED AROUND TIM'S HEART. CAN YOU IMAGINE?
WE'RE GETTING WORD OUT TO ALL THE OTHER EMPLOYEES, THE FAMILIES, PRESS EVERYONE--BUT I WANT YOU GUYS TO HEAR THIS FROM ME--
SPYMASTER WAS SHOT REPEATEDLY. HE'S OUT OF SURGERY BUT HASN'T REGAINED CONSCIOUSNESS.
WE KNEW SINCE THE FIRST RESILIENT BLEW THAT SOMETHING WAS ROTTEN IN DENMARK BUT PRESUMED IT WAS SABOTAGE WORK.
WE NEVER FOR A SECOND THOUGHT HIS INTENTIONS WERE VIOLENT. IF WE--
YOU.
ME.
WE'RE HAVING WORDS. RIGHT NOW.
APPARENTLY WE'RE HAVING WORDS.
NOBODY GET SHOT OR STABBED, 'KAY?

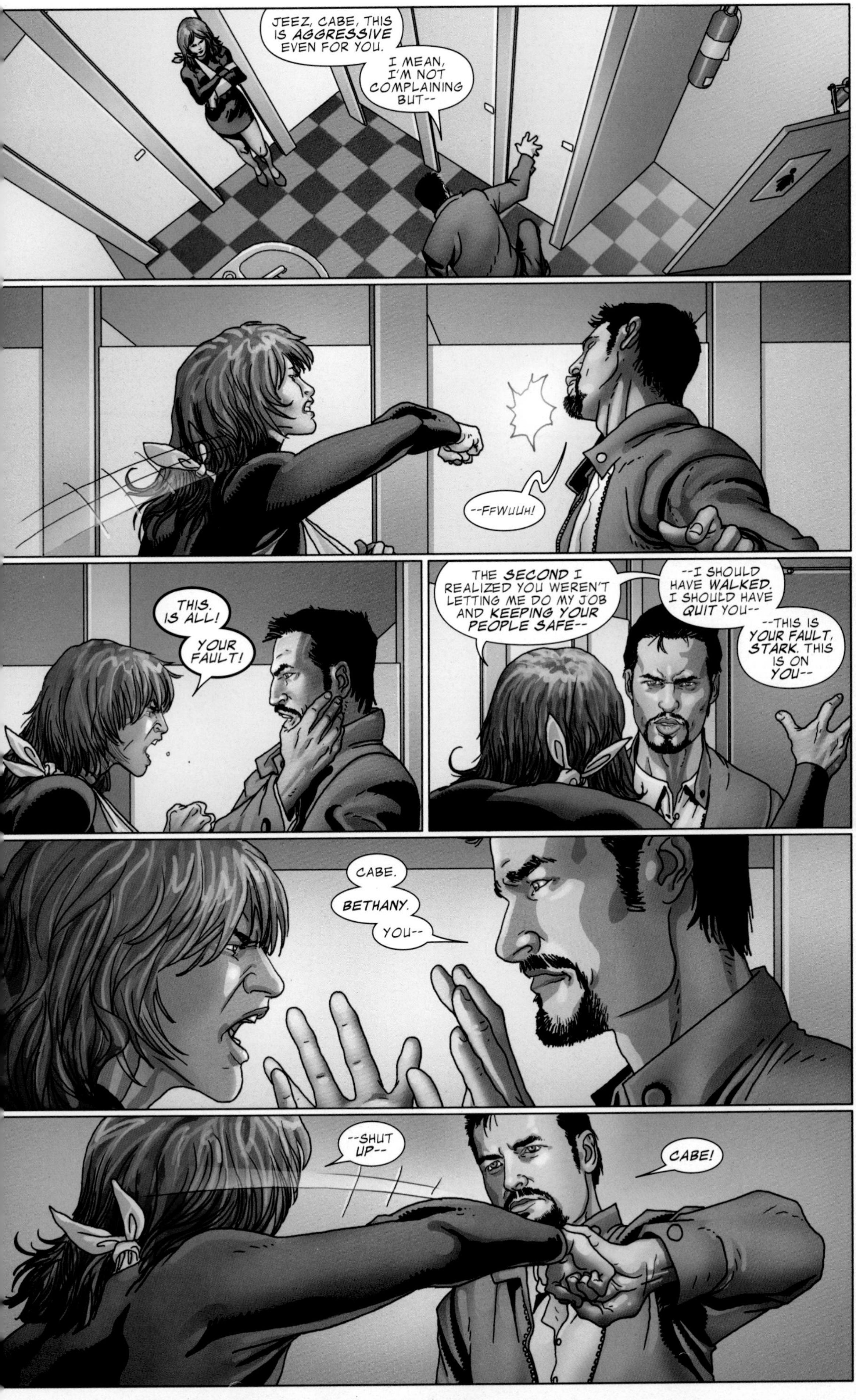
JEEZ, CABE, THIS IS AGGRESSIVE EVEN FOR YOU.
I MEAN, I'M NOT COMPLAINING BUT--
--FFWUUH!
THIS. IS ALL!
YOUR FAULT!
THE SECOND I REALIZED YOU WEREN'T LETTING ME DO MY JOB AND KEEPING YOUR PEOPLE SAFE--
--I SHOULD HAVE WALKED. I SHOULD HAVE QUIT YOU--
--THIS IS YOUR FAULT, STARK. THIS IS ON YOU--
CABE.
BETHANY.
YOU--
--SHUT UP--
CABE!

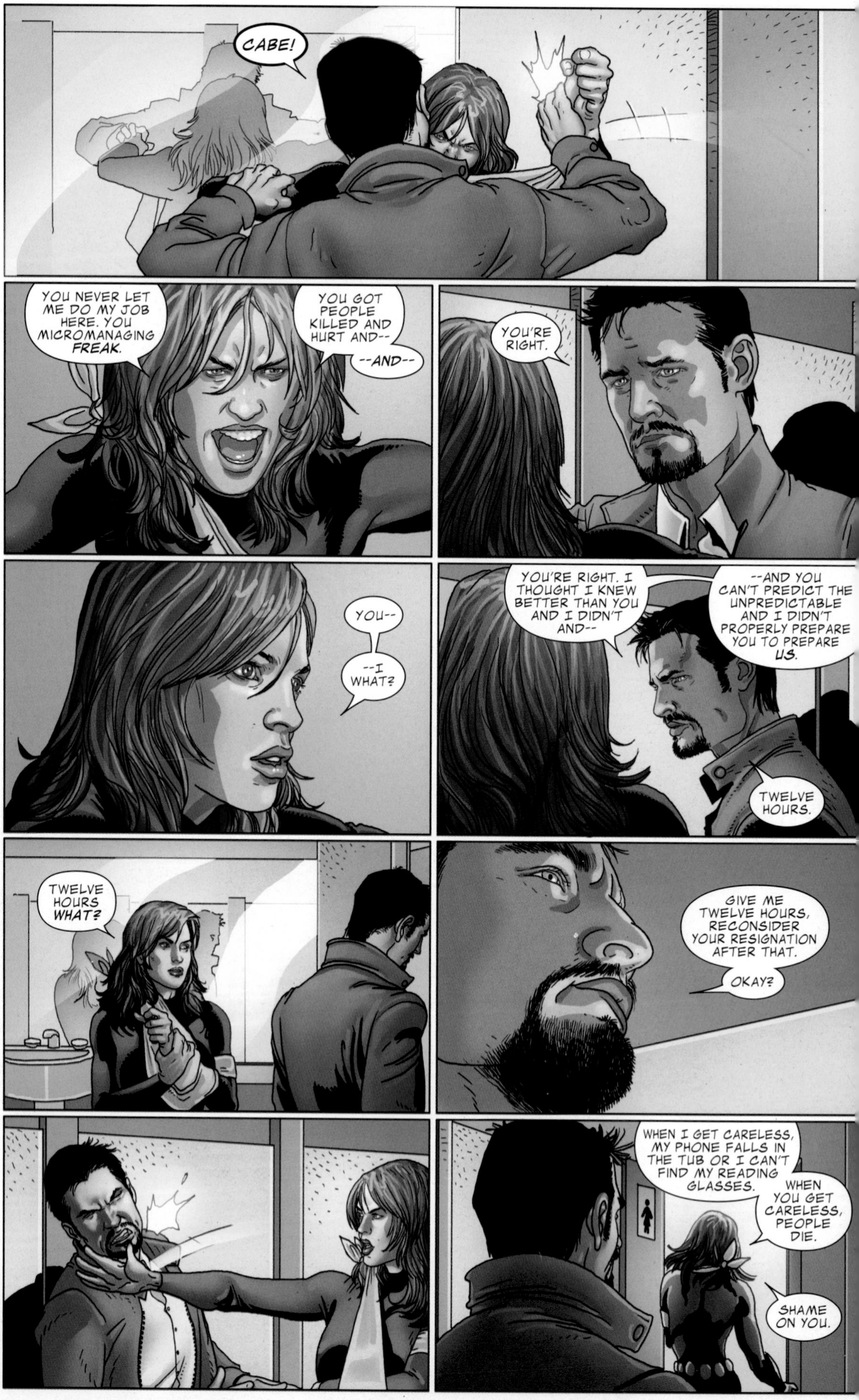

CABE!
YOU NEVER LET ME DO MY JOB HERE. YOU MICROMANAGING FREAK.
YOU GOT PEOPLE KILLED AND HURT AND--
--AND--
YOU'RE RIGHT.
YOU--
--I WHAT?
YOU'RE RIGHT. I THOUGHT I KNEW BETTER THAN YOU AND I DIDN'T AND--
--AND YOU CAN'T PREDICT THE UNPREDICTABLE AND I DIDN'T PROPERLY PREPARE YOU TO PREPARE US.
TWELVE HOURS.
TWELVE HOURS WHAT?
GIVE ME TWELVE HOURS, RECONSIDER YOUR RESIGNATION AFTER THAT.
OKAY?
WHEN I GET CARELESS, MY PHONE FALLS IN THE TUB OR I CAN'T FIND MY READING GLASSES.
WHEN YOU GET CARELESS, PEOPLE DIE.
SHAME ON YOU.

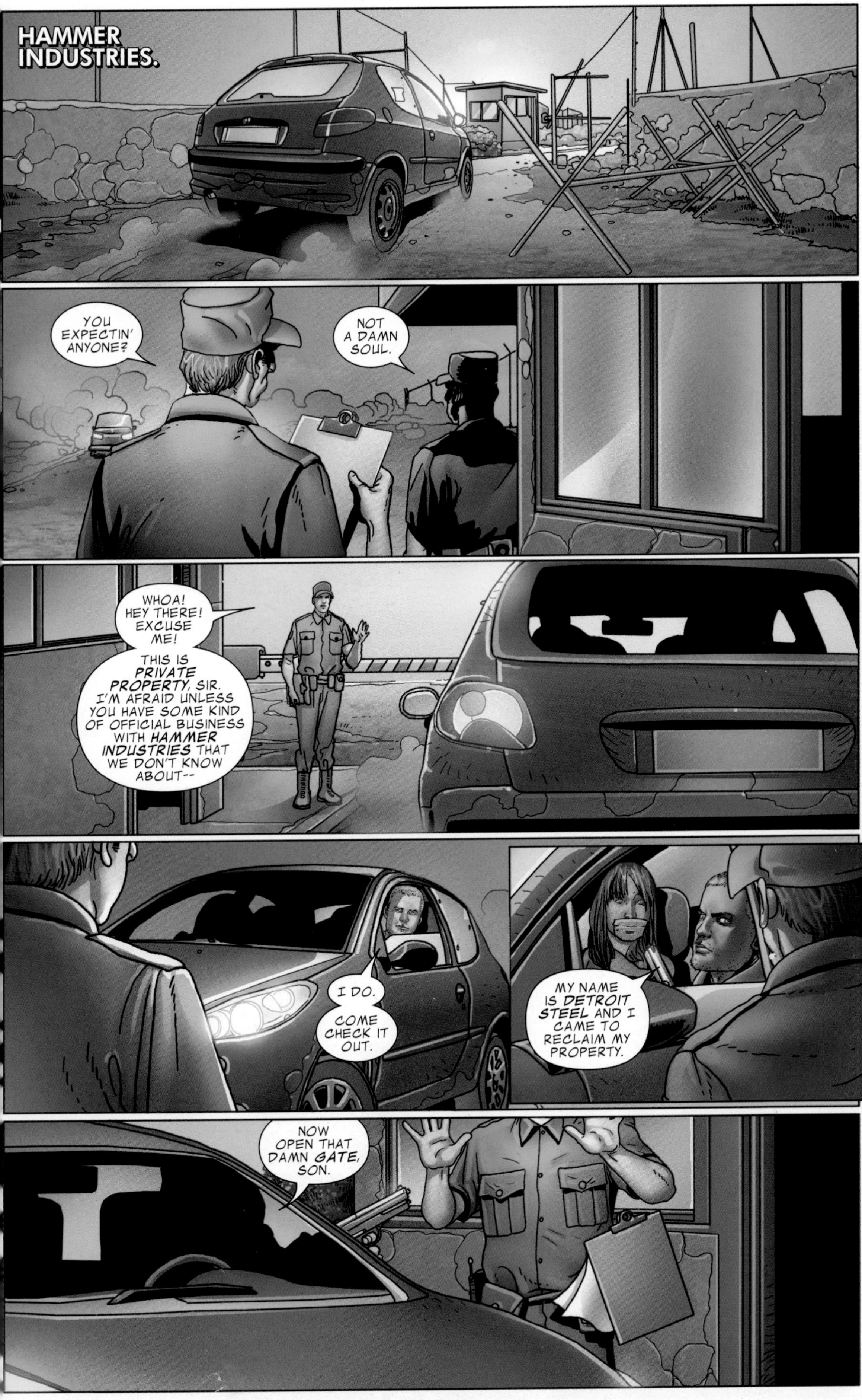
HAMMER INDUSTRIES.
YOU EXPECTIN' ANYONE?
NOT A DAMN SOUL.
WHOA! HEY THERE! EXCUSE ME!
THIS IS PRIVATE PROPERTY, SIR. I'M AFRAID UNLESS YOU HAVE SOME KIND OF OFFICIAL BUSINESS WITH HAMMER INDUSTRIES THAT WE DON'T KNOW ABOUT--
I DO.
COME CHECK IT OUT.
MY NAME IS DETROIT STEEL AND I CAME TO RECLAIM MY PROPERTY.
NOW OPEN THAT DAMN GATE, SON.

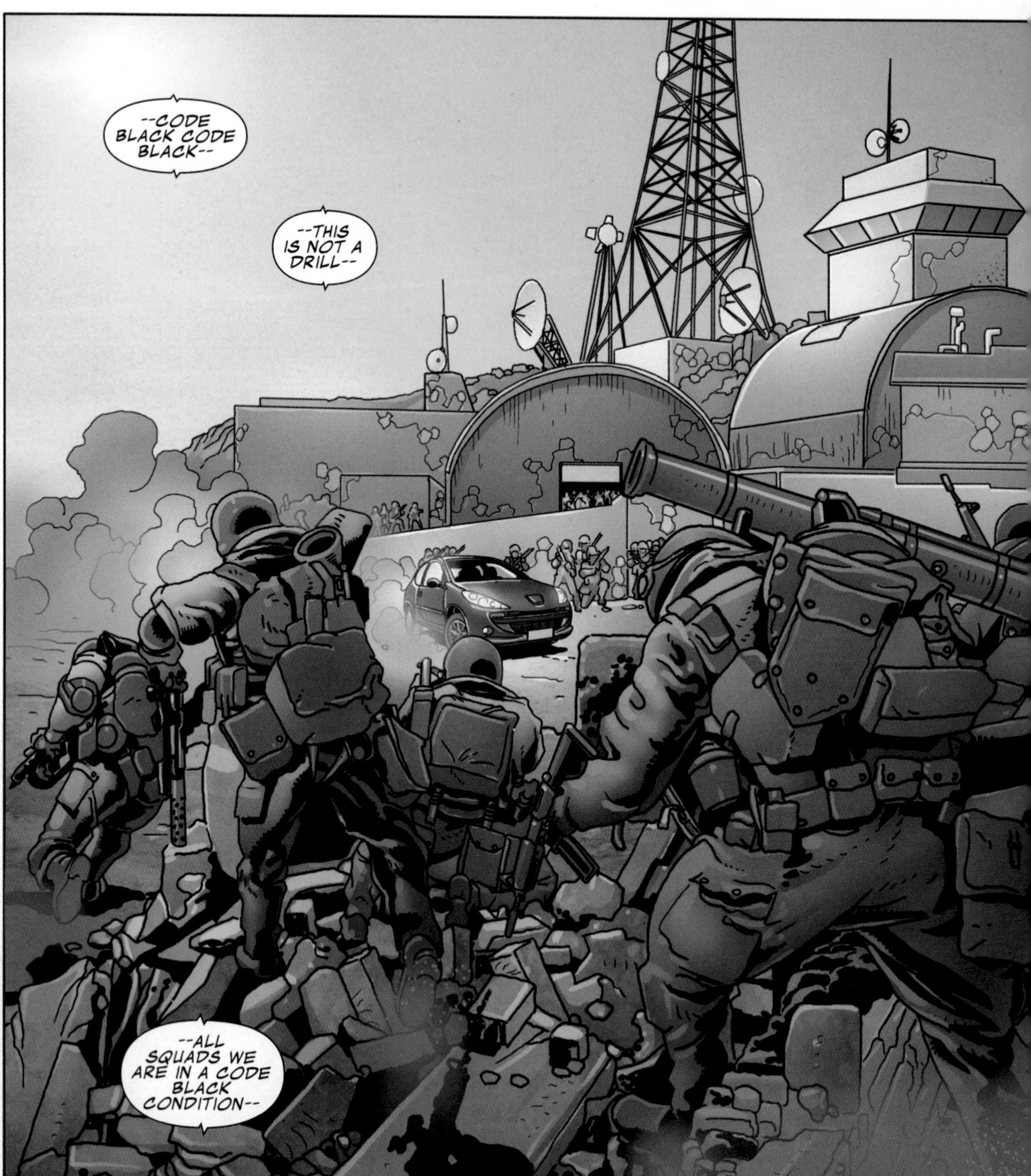
--CODE BLACK CODE BLACK--
--THIS IS NOT A DRILL--
--ALL SQUADS WE ARE IN A CODE BLACK CONDITION--

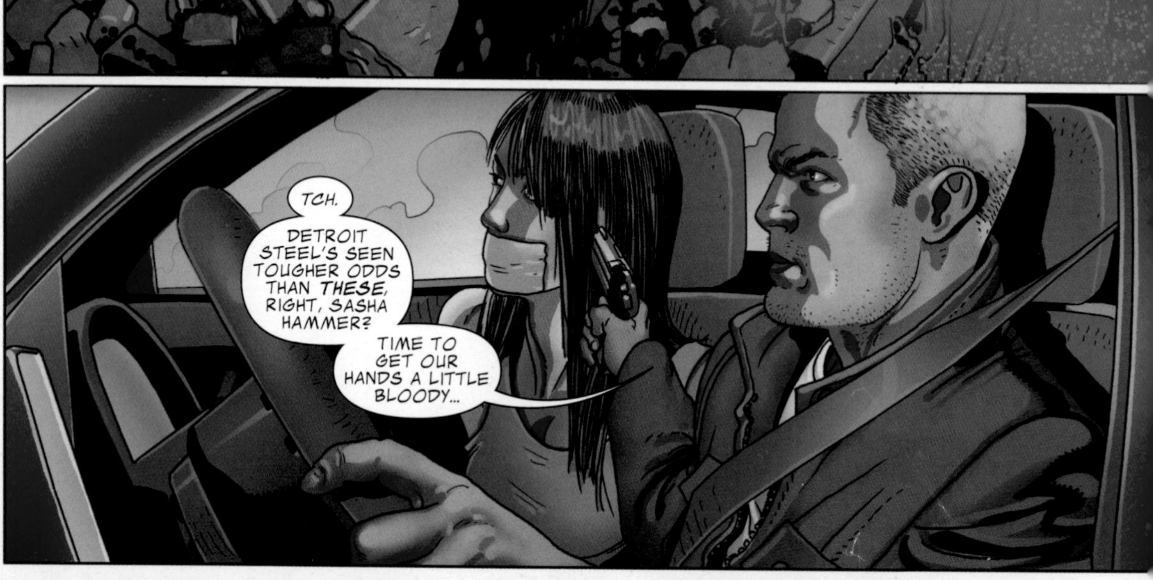
TCH.
DETROIT STEEL'S SEEN TOUGHER ODDS THAN THESE, RIGHT, SASHA HAMMER?
TIME TO GET OUR HANDS A LITTLE BLOODY...

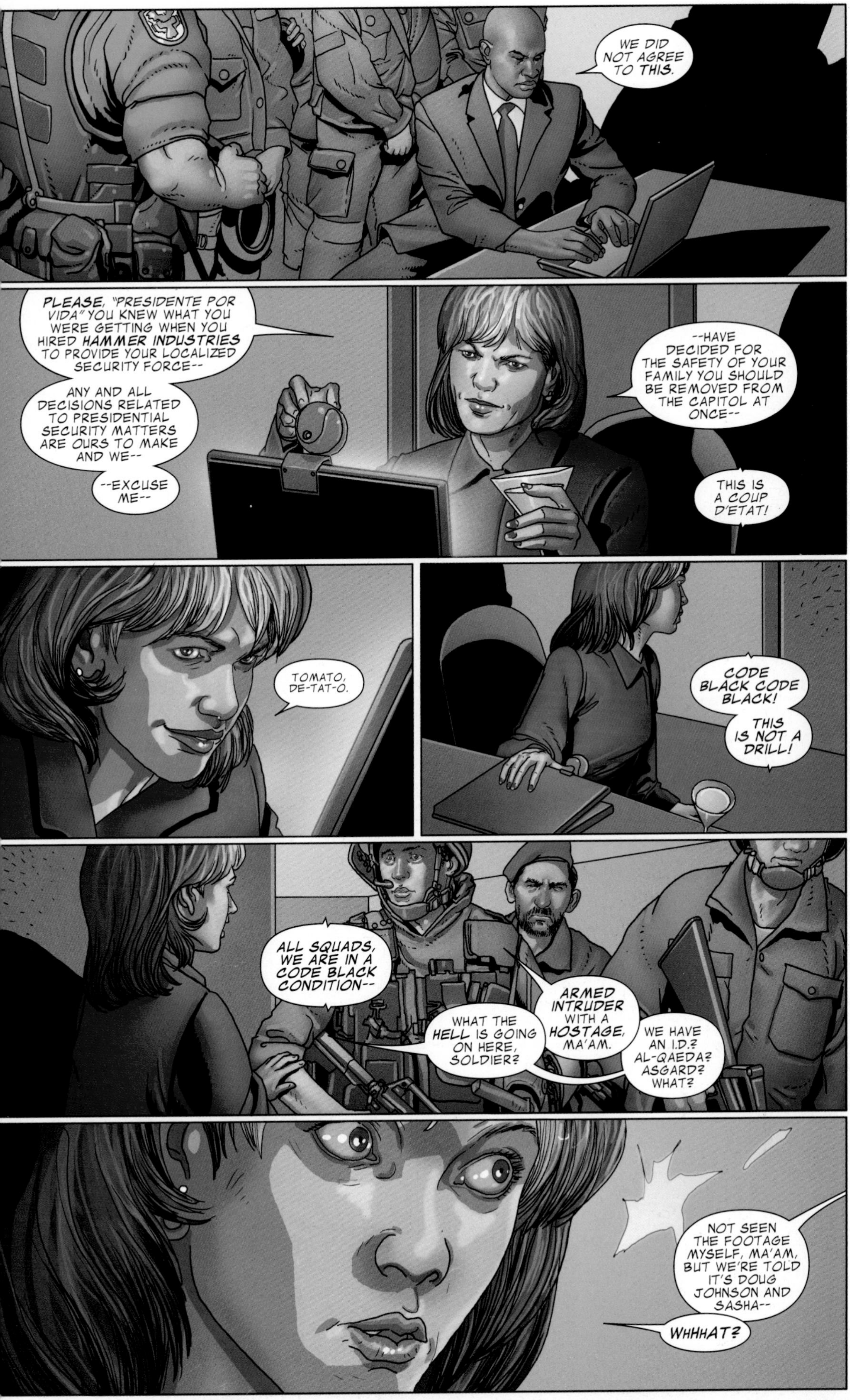
WE DID NOT AGREE TO THIS.
PLEASE, "PRESIDENTE POR VIDA" YOU KNEW WHAT YOU WERE GETTING WHEN YOU HIRED HAMMER INDUSTRIES TO PROVIDE YOUR LOCALIZED SECURITY FORCE--
ANY AND ALL DECISIONS RELATED TO PRESIDENTIAL SECURITY MATTERS ARE OURS TO MAKE AND WE--
--EXCUSE ME--
--HAVE DECIDED FOR THE SAFETY OF YOUR FAMILY YOU SHOULD BE REMOVED FROM THE CAPITOL AT ONCE--
THIS IS A COUP D'ETAT!
TOMATO, DE-TAT-O.
CODE BLACK CODE BLACK!
THIS IS NOT A DRILL!
ALL SQUADS, WE ARE IN A CODE BLACK CONDITION--
WHAT THE HELL IS GOING ON HERE, SOLDIER?
ARMED INTRUDER WITH A HOSTAGE, MA'AM.
WE HAVE AN I.D.? AL-QAEDA? ASGARD? WHAT?
NOT SEEN THE FOOTAGE MYSELF, MA'AM, BUT WE'RE TOLD IT'S DOUG JOHNSON AND SASHA--
WHHHAT?

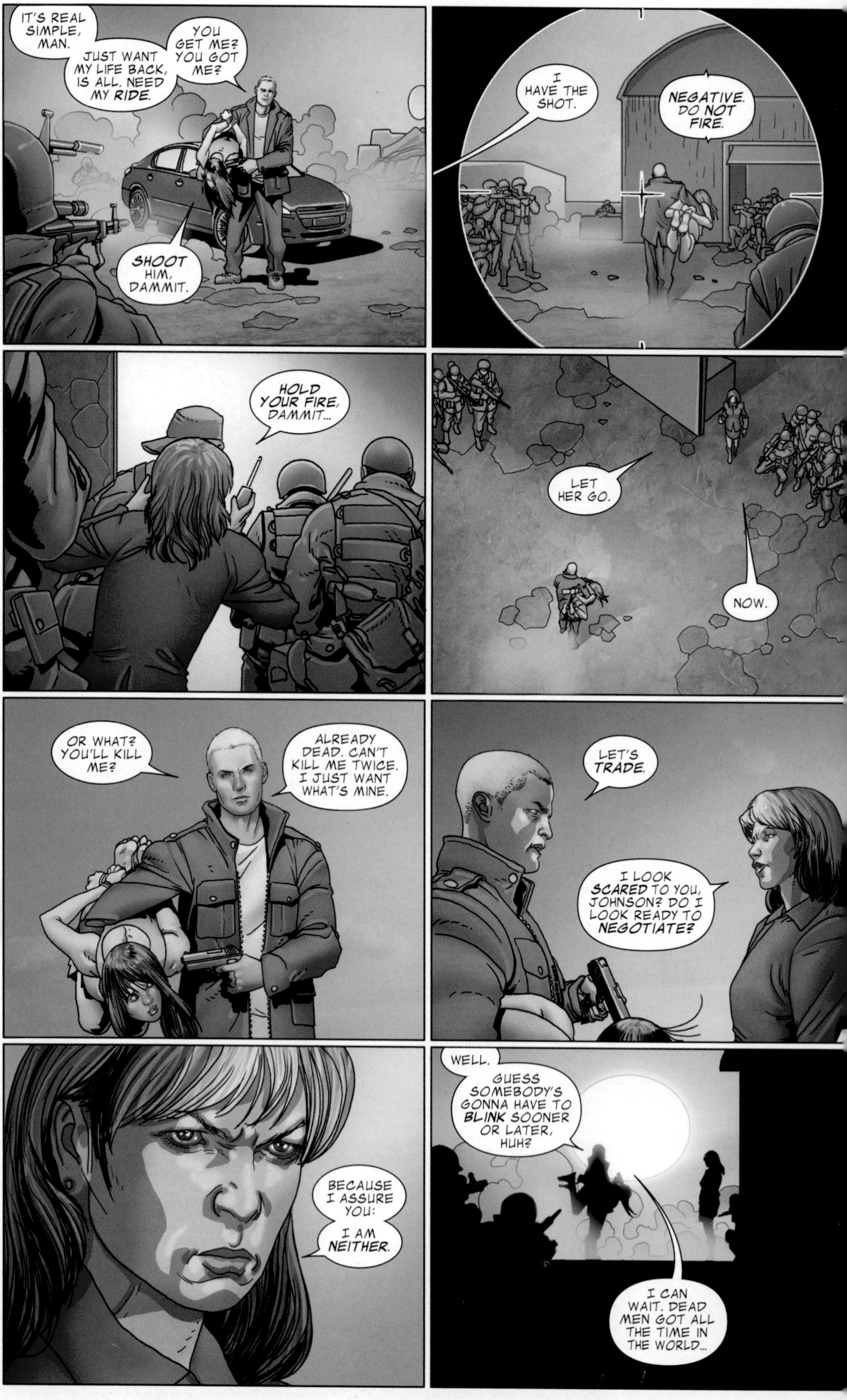
IT'S REAL SIMPLE, MAN.
JUST WANT MY LIFE BACK, IS ALL. NEED MY RIDE.
YOU GET ME? YOU GOT ME?
SHOOT HIM, DAMMIT.
I HAVE THE SHOT.
NEGATIVE. DO NOT FIRE.
HOLD YOUR FIRE, DAMMIT...
LET HER GO.
NOW.
OR WHAT? YOU'LL KILL ME?
ALREADY DEAD. CAN'T KILL ME TWICE. I JUST WANT WHAT'S MINE.
LET'S TRADE.
I LOOK SCARED TO YOU, JOHNSON? DO I LOOK READY TO NEGOTIATE?
BECAUSE I ASSURE YOU:
I AM NEITHER.
WELL.
GUESS SOMEBODY'S GONNA HAVE TO BLINK SOONER OR LATER, HUH?
I CAN WAIT. DEAD MEN GOT ALL THE TIME IN THE WORLD...

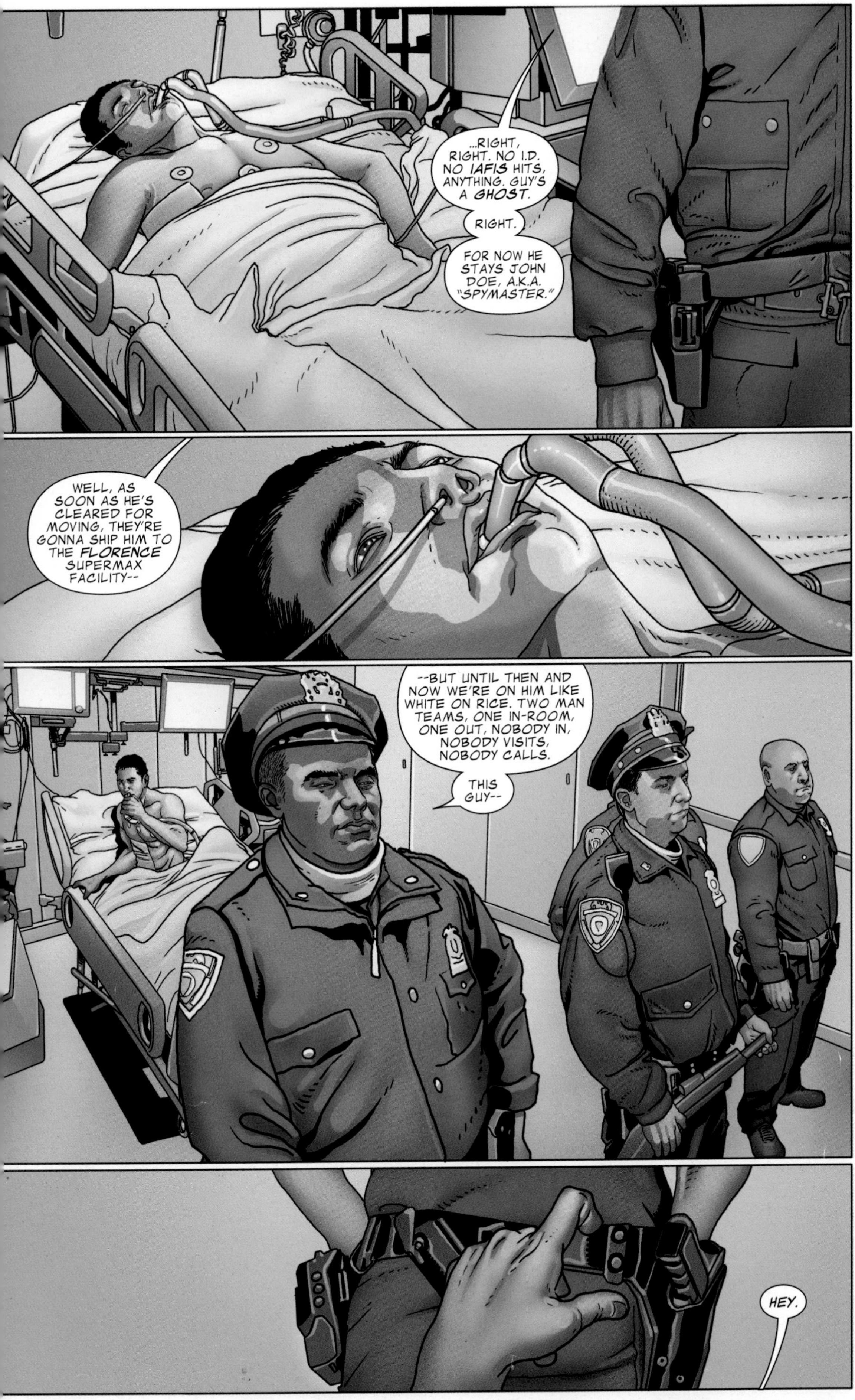
...RIGHT, RIGHT. NO I.D. NO IAFIS HITS, ANYTHING. GUY'S A GHOST.
RIGHT.
FOR NOW HE STAYS JOHN DOE, A.K.A. "SPYMASTER."
WELL, AS SOON AS HE'S CLEARED FOR MOVING, THEY'RE GONNA SHIP HIM TO THE FLORENCE SUPERMAX FACILITY--
--BUT UNTIL THEN AND NOW WE'RE ON HIM LIKE WHITE ON RICE. TWO MAN TEAMS, ONE IN-ROOM, ONE OUT, NOBODY IN, NOBODY VISITS, NOBODY CALLS.
THIS GUY--
HEY.

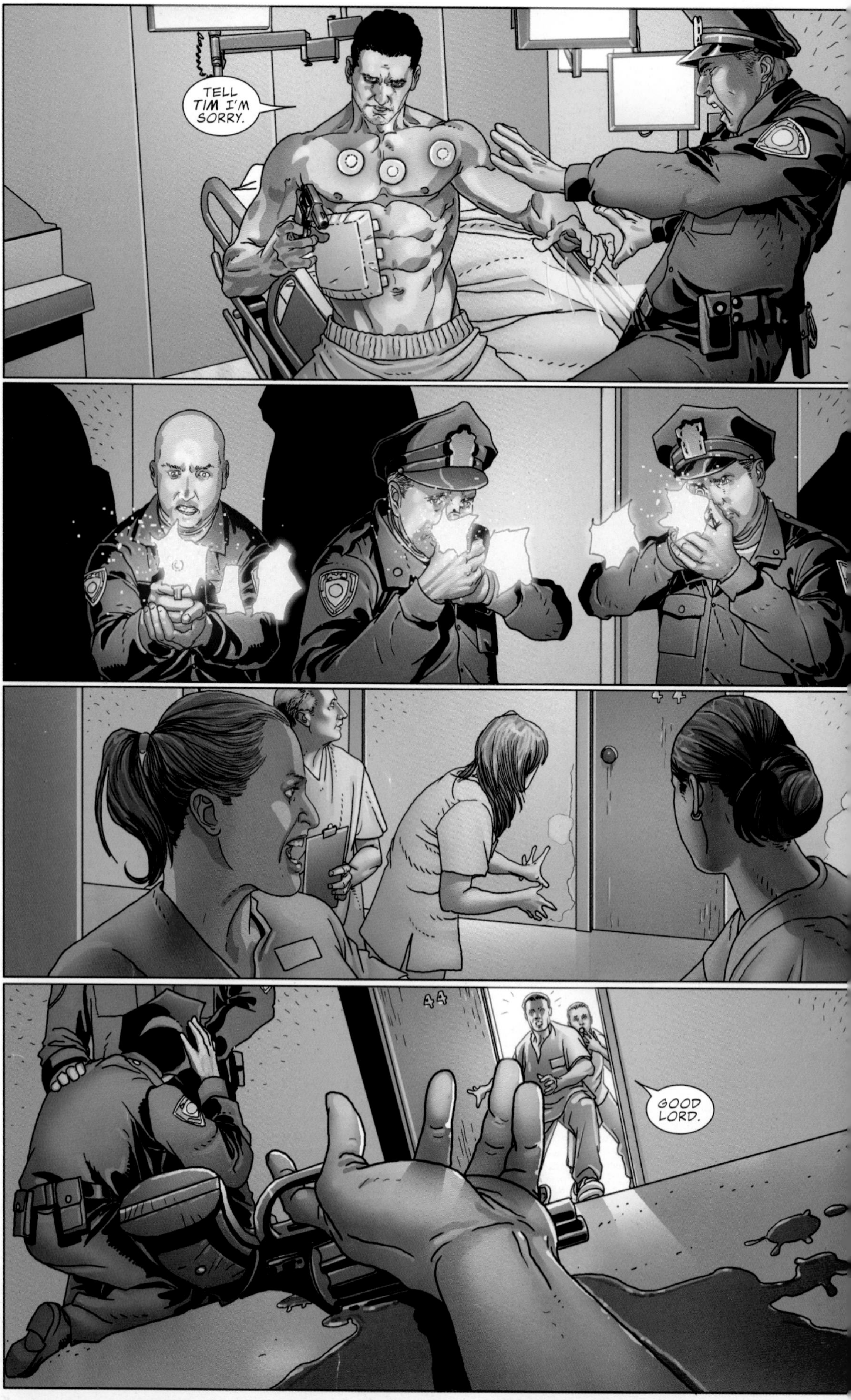
TELL TIM I'M SORRY.
GOOD LORD.

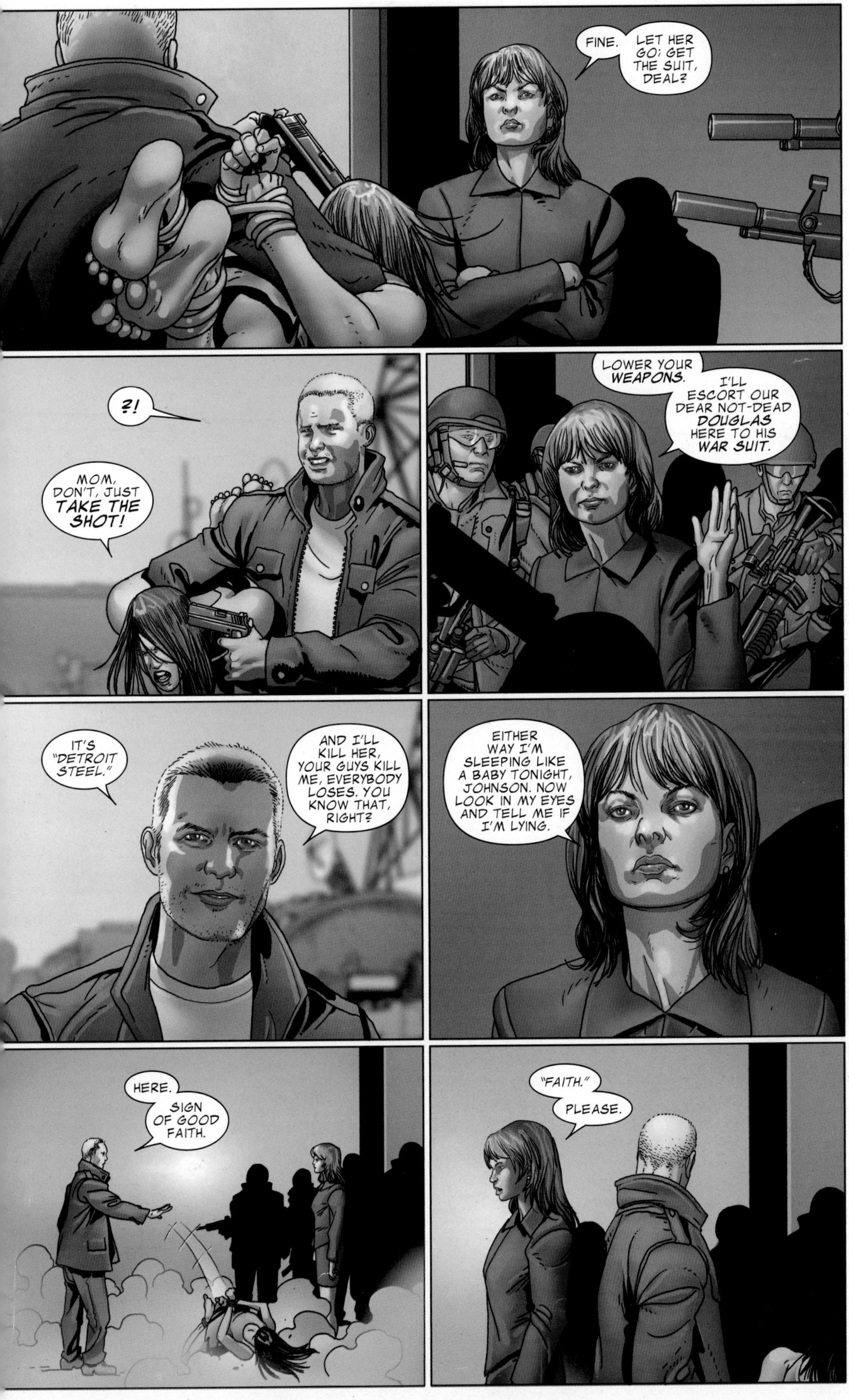
FINE.
LET HER GO; GET THE SUIT, DEAL?
?!
MOM, DON'T, JUST TAKE THE SHOT!
LOWER YOUR WEAPONS.
I'LL ESCORT OUR DEAR NOT-DEAD DOUGLAS HERE TO HIS WAR SUIT.
IT'S "DETROIT STEEL."
AND I'LL KILL HER, YOUR GUYS KILL ME, EVERYBODY LOSES. YOU KNOW THAT, RIGHT?
EITHER WAY I'M SLEEPING LIKE A BABY TONIGHT, JOHNSON. NOW LOOK IN MY EYES AND TELL ME IF I'M LYING.
HERE.
SIGN OF GOOD FAITH.
"FAITH."
PLEASE.

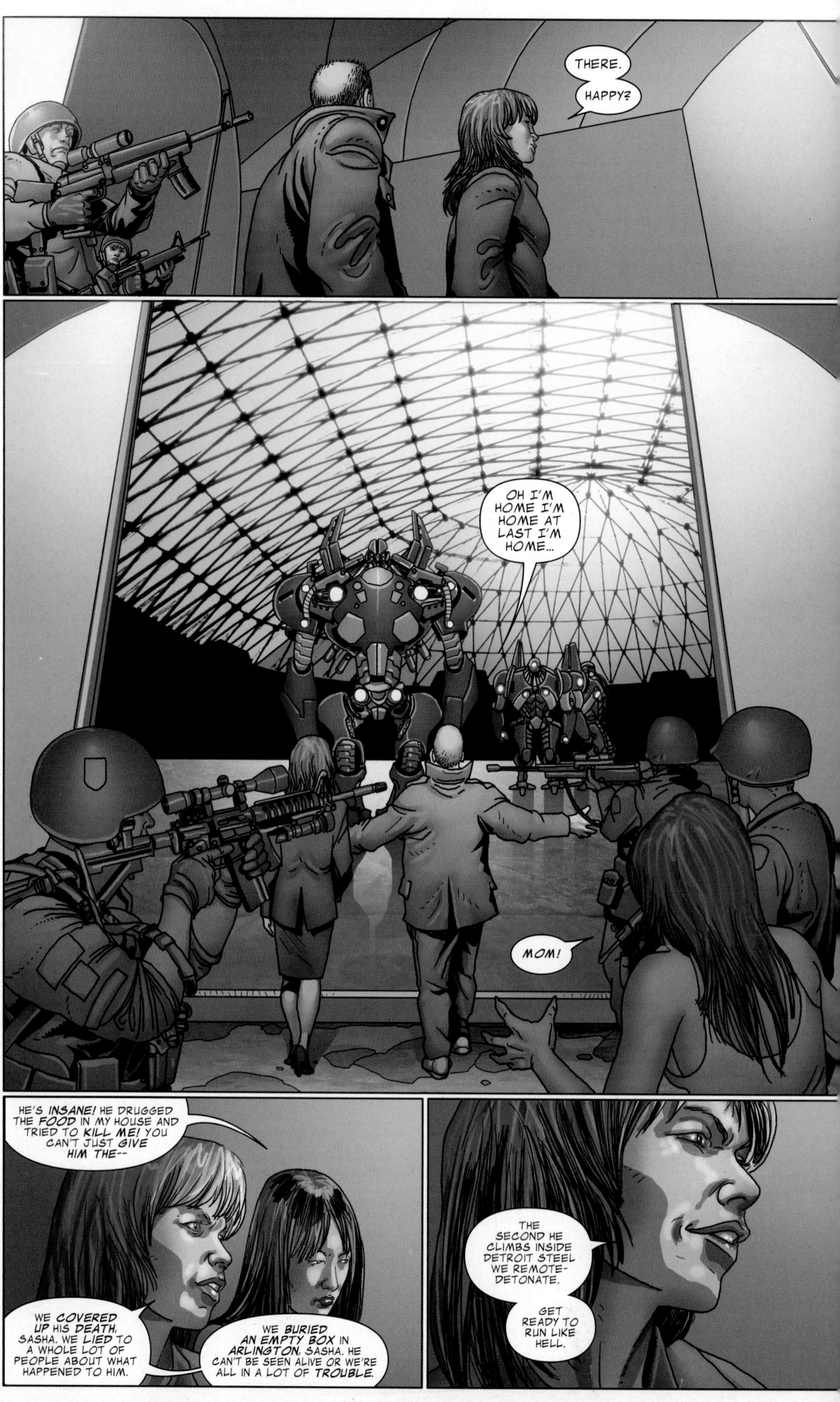
THERE.
HAPPY?
OH I'M HOME I'M HOME AT LAST I'M HOME...
MOM!
HE'S INSANE! HE DRUGGED THE FOOD IN MY HOUSE AND TRIED TO KILL ME! YOU CAN'T JUST GIVE HIM THE--
WE COVERED UP HIS DEATH, SASHA. WE LIED TO A WHOLE LOT OF PEOPLE ABOUT WHAT HAPPENED TO HIM.
WE BURIED AN EMPTY BOX IN ARLINGTON, SASHA. HE CAN'T BE SEEN ALIVE OR WE'RE ALL IN A LOT OF TROUBLE.
THE SECOND HE CLIMBS INSIDE DETROIT STEEL WE REMOTE-DETONATE.
GET READY TO RUN LIKE HELL.

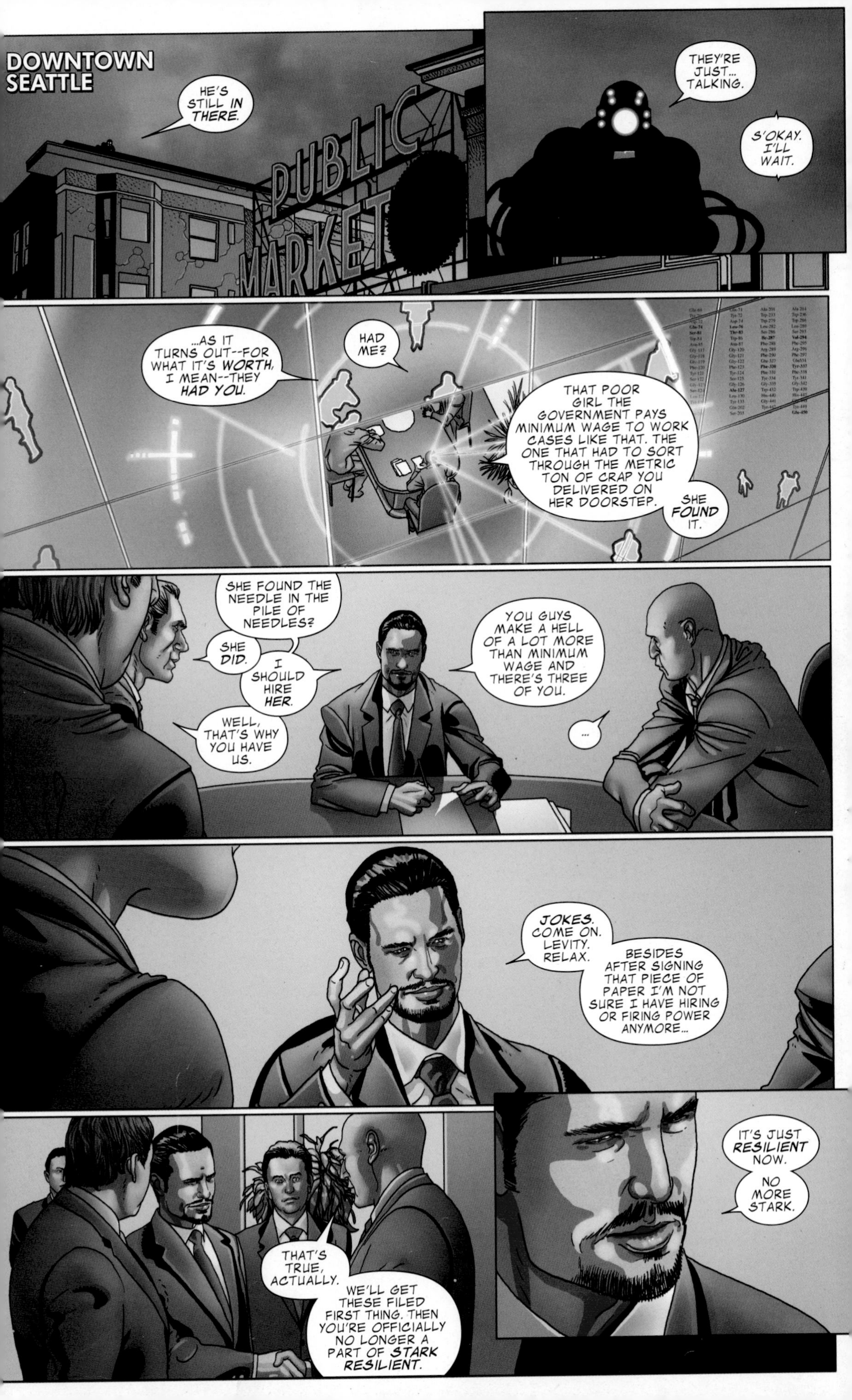
DOWNTOWN SEATTLE
HE'S STILL IN THERE.
PUBLIC MARKET
THEY'RE JUST... TALKING.
S'OKAY. I'LL WAIT.
...AS IT TURNS OUT--FOR WHAT IT'S WORTH, I MEAN--THEY HAD YOU.
HAD ME?
THAT POOR GIRL THE GOVERNMENT PAYS MINIMUM WAGE TO WORK CASES LIKE THAT. THE ONE THAT HAD TO SORT THROUGH THE METRIC TON OF CRAP YOU DELIVERED ON HER DOORSTEP.
SHE FOUND IT.
SHE FOUND THE NEEDLE IN THE PILE OF NEEDLES?
SHE DID.
I SHOULD HIRE HER.
WELL, THAT'S WHY YOU HAVE US.
YOU GUYS MAKE A HELL OF A LOT MORE THAN MINIMUM WAGE AND THERE'S THREE OF YOU.
...
JOKES. COME ON. LEVITY. RELAX.
BESIDES AFTER SIGNING THAT PIECE OF PAPER I'M NOT SURE I HAVE HIRING OR FIRING POWER ANYMORE...
THAT'S TRUE, ACTUALLY.
WE'LL GET THESE FILED FIRST THING. THEN YOU'RE OFFICIALLY NO LONGER A PART OF STARK RESILIENT.
IT'S JUST RESILIENT NOW.
NO MORE STARK.

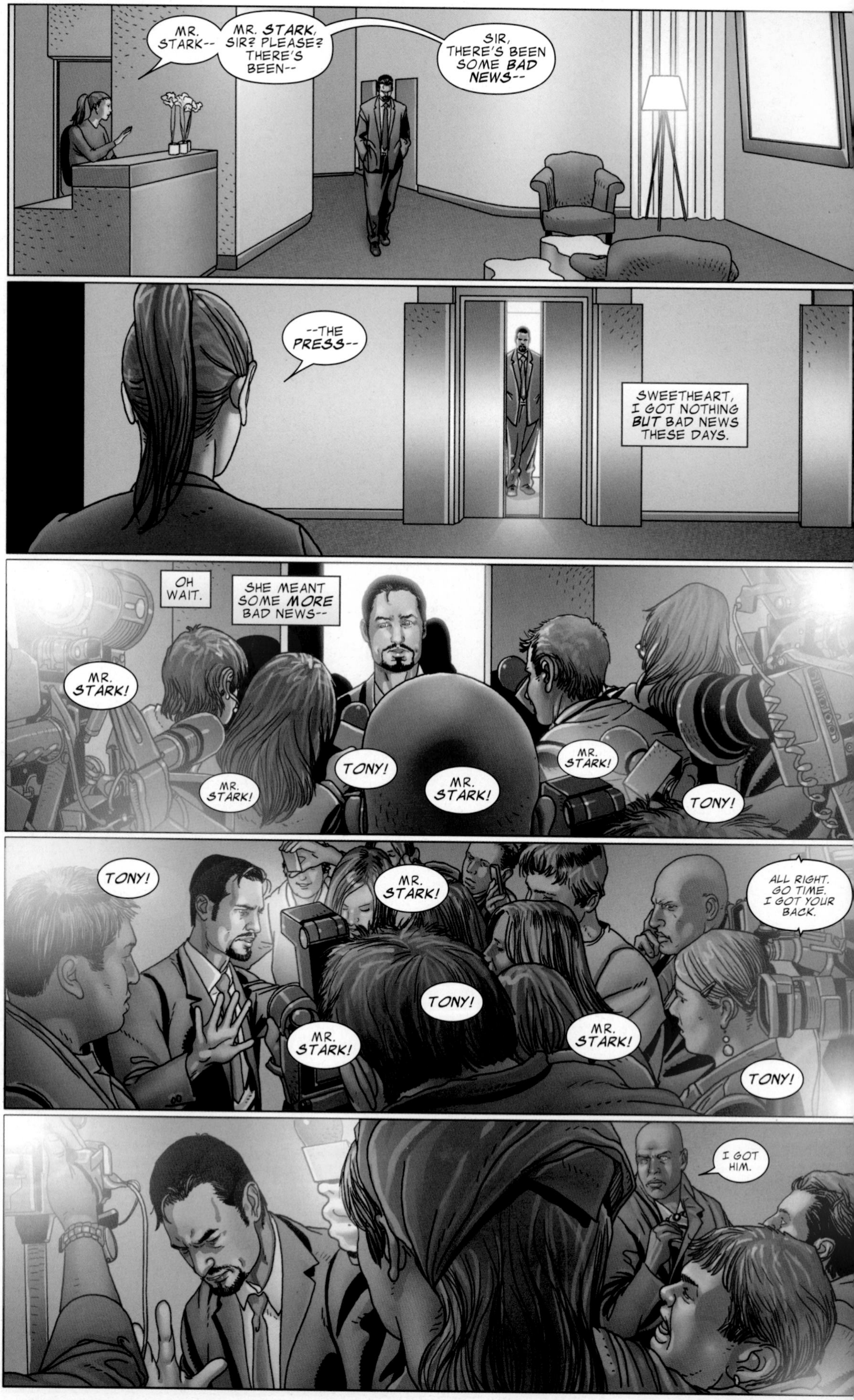
MR. STARK--
MR. STARK, SIR? PLEASE? THERE'S BEEN--
SIR, THERE'S BEEN SOME BAD NEWS--
--THE PRESS--
SWEETHEART, I GOT NOTHING BUT BAD NEWS THESE DAYS.
OH WAIT.
SHE MEANT SOME MORE BAD NEWS--
MR. STARK!
TONY!
MR. STARK!
MR. STARK!
MR. STARK!
TONY!
TONY!
MR. STARK!
ALL RIGHT. GO TIME. I GOT YOUR BACK.
TONY!
MR. STARK!
MR. STARK!
TONY!
I GOT HIM.

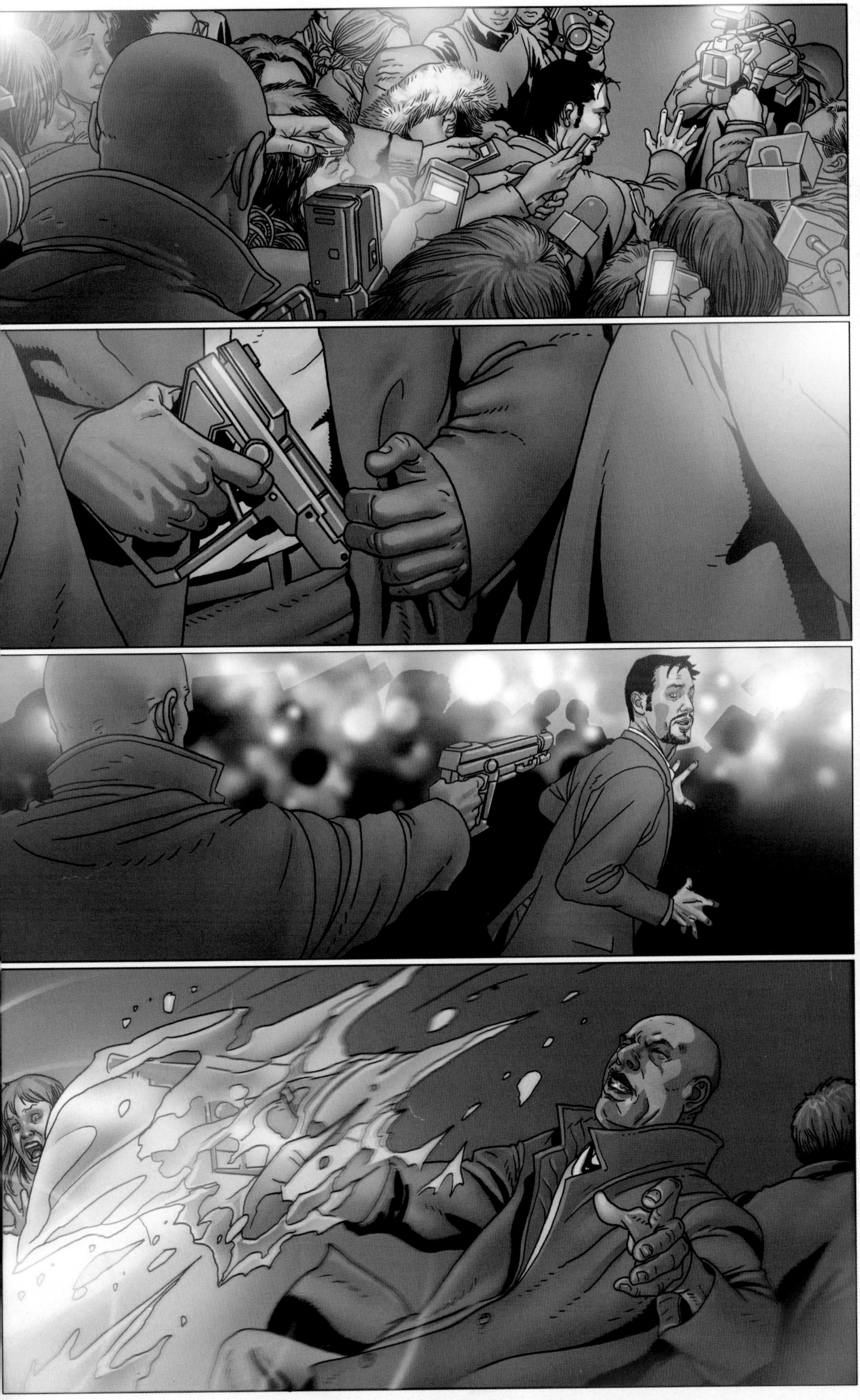

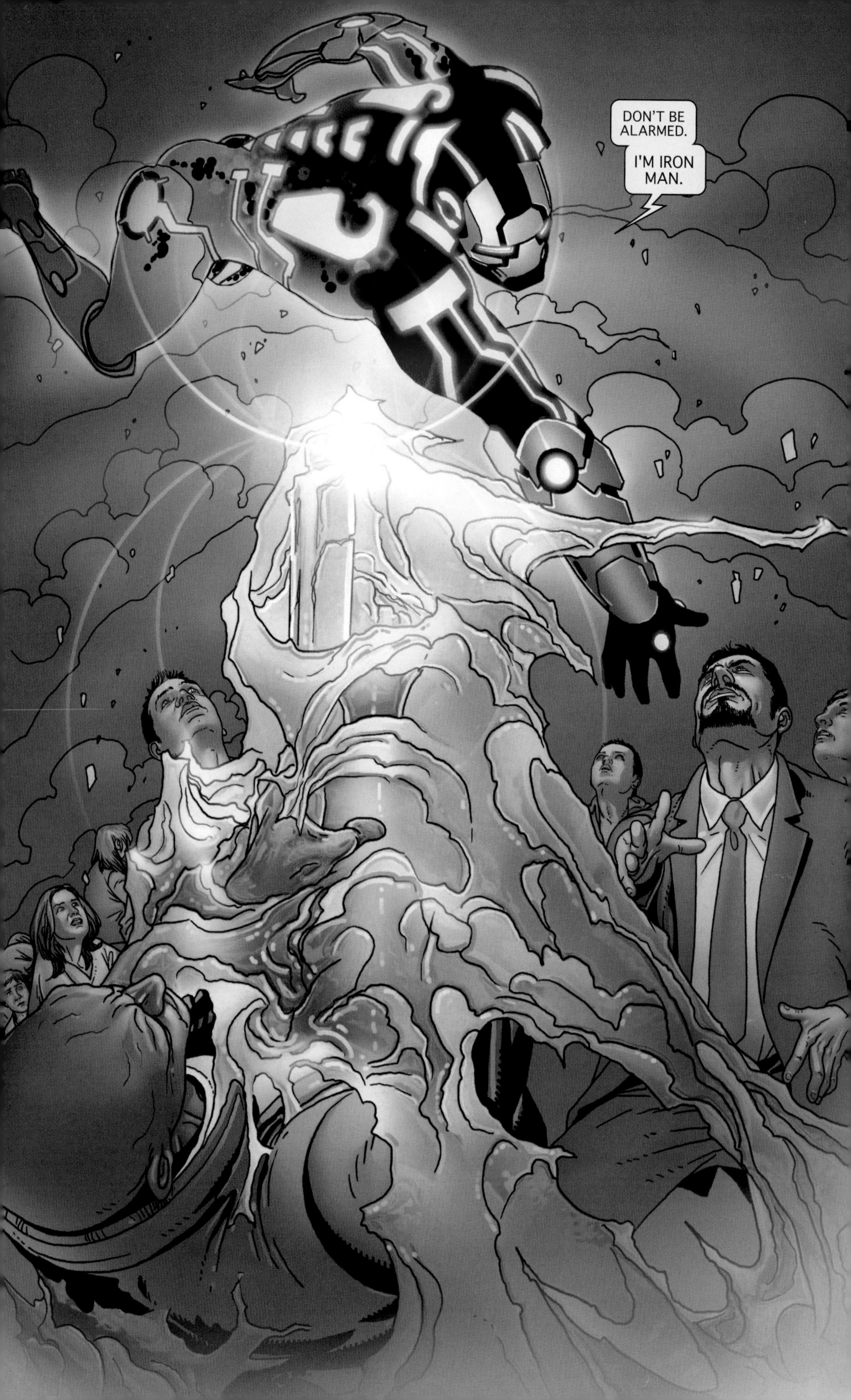
DON'T BE ALARMED.
I'M IRON MAN.

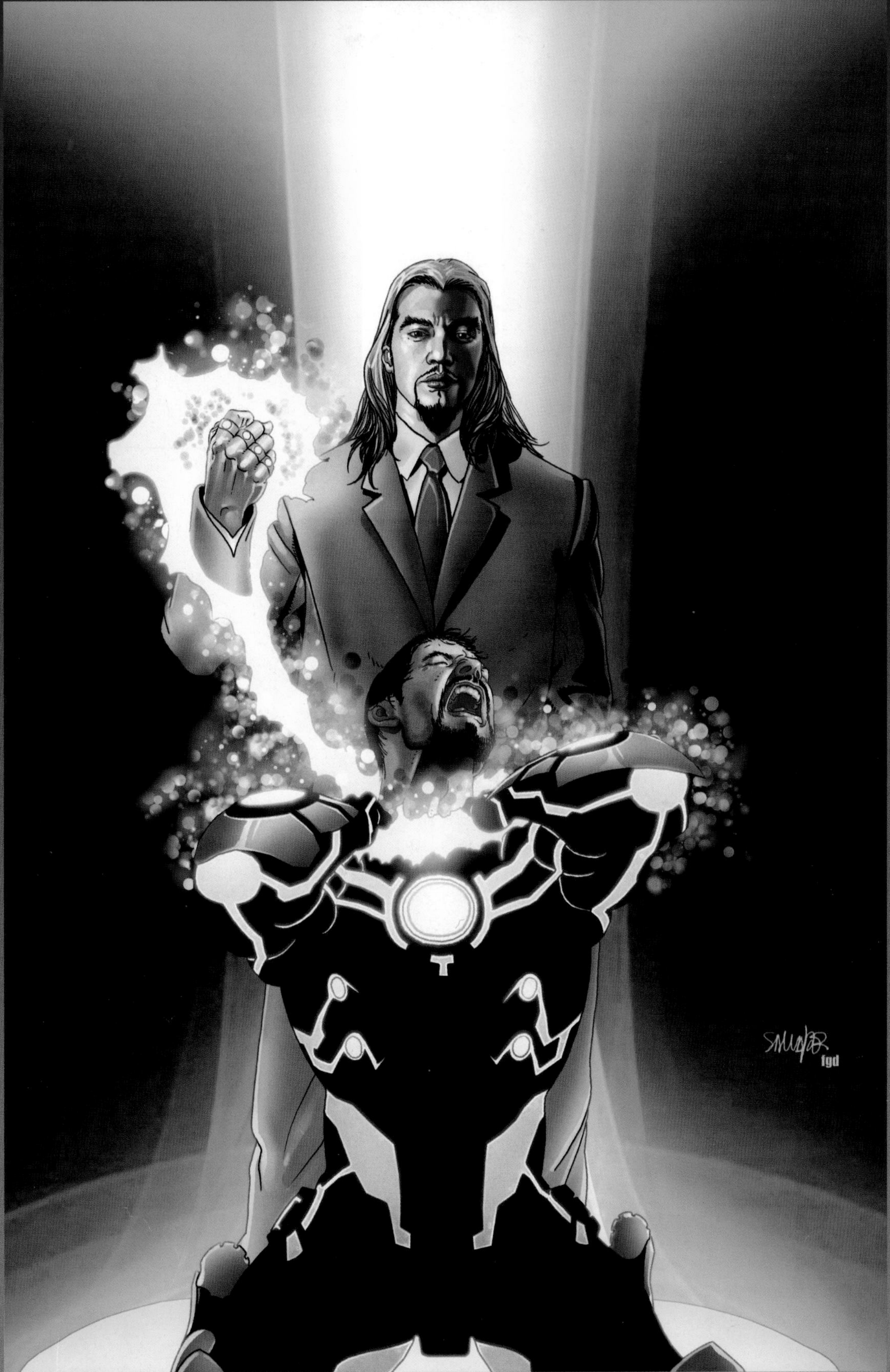
SALVADOR
fgd

PART FIVE:
THE DEAD AND THE DYING 520

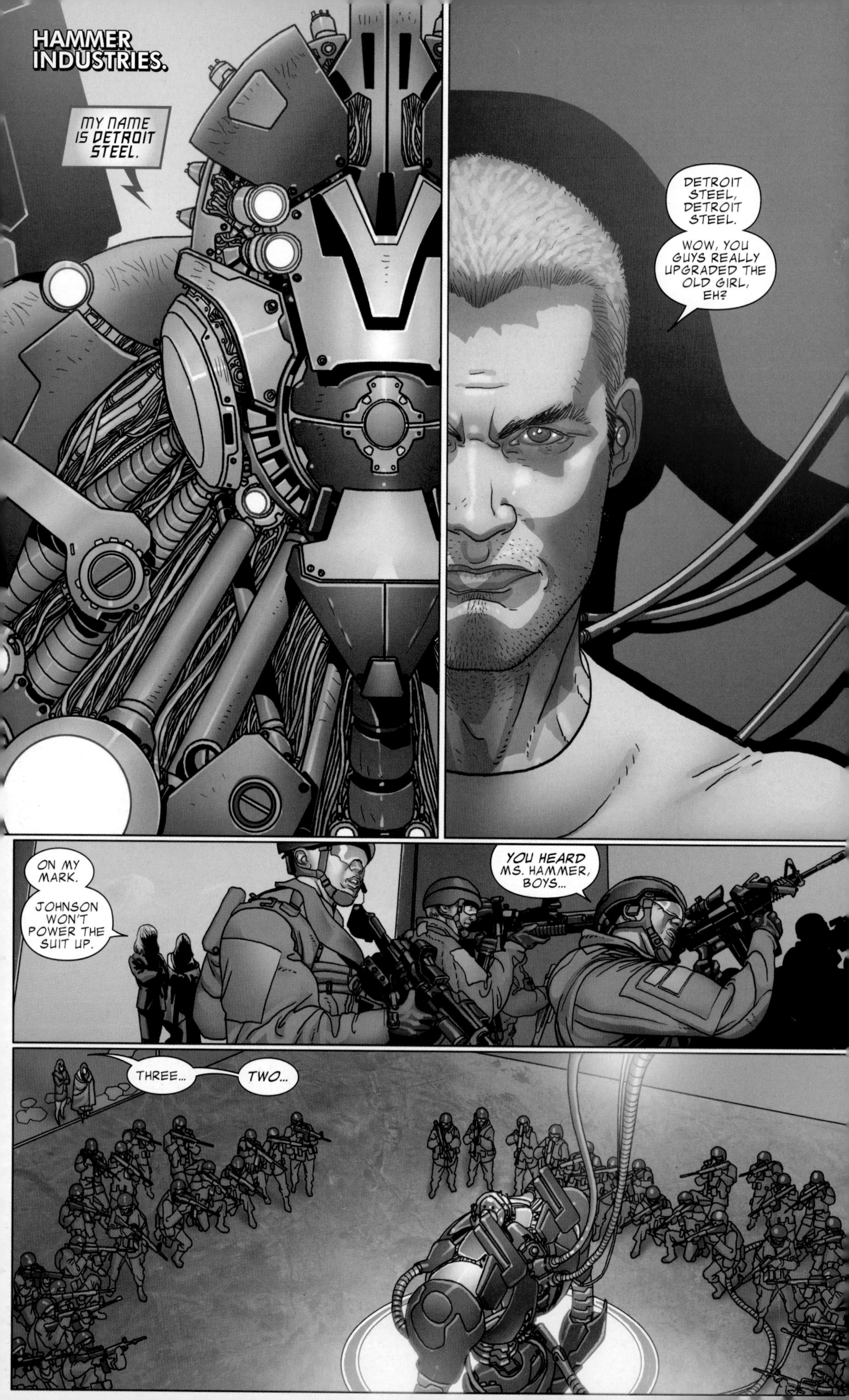
HAMMER INDUSTRIES.
MY NAME IS DETROIT STEEL.
DETROIT STEEL, DETROIT STEEL.
WOW, YOU GUYS REALLY UPGRADED THE OLD GIRL, EH?
ON MY MARK.
JOHNSON WON'T POWER THE SUIT UP.
YOU HEARD MS. HAMMER, BOYS...
THREE...
TWO...

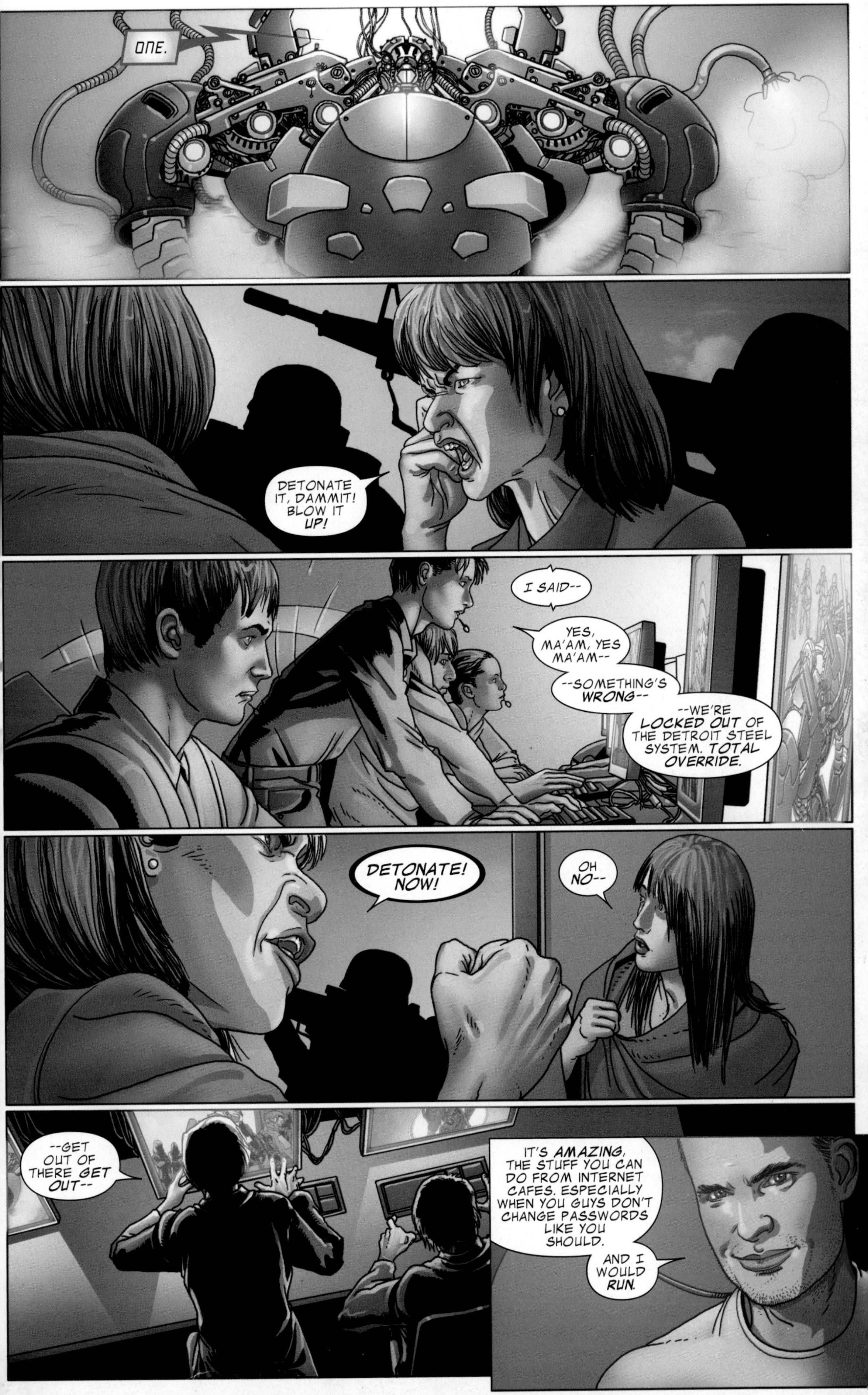
ONE.
DETONATE IT, DAMMIT! BLOW IT UP!
I SAID--
YES, MA'AM, YES MA'AM--
--SOMETHING'S WRONG--
--WE'RE LOCKED OUT OF THE DETROIT STEEL SYSTEM. TOTAL OVERRIDE.
DETONATE! NOW!
OH NO--
--GET OUT OF THERE GET OUT--
IT'S AMAZING, THE STUFF YOU CAN DO FROM INTERNET CAFES. ESPECIALLY WHEN YOU GUYS DON'T CHANGE PASSWORDS LIKE YOU SHOULD.
AND I WOULD RUN.

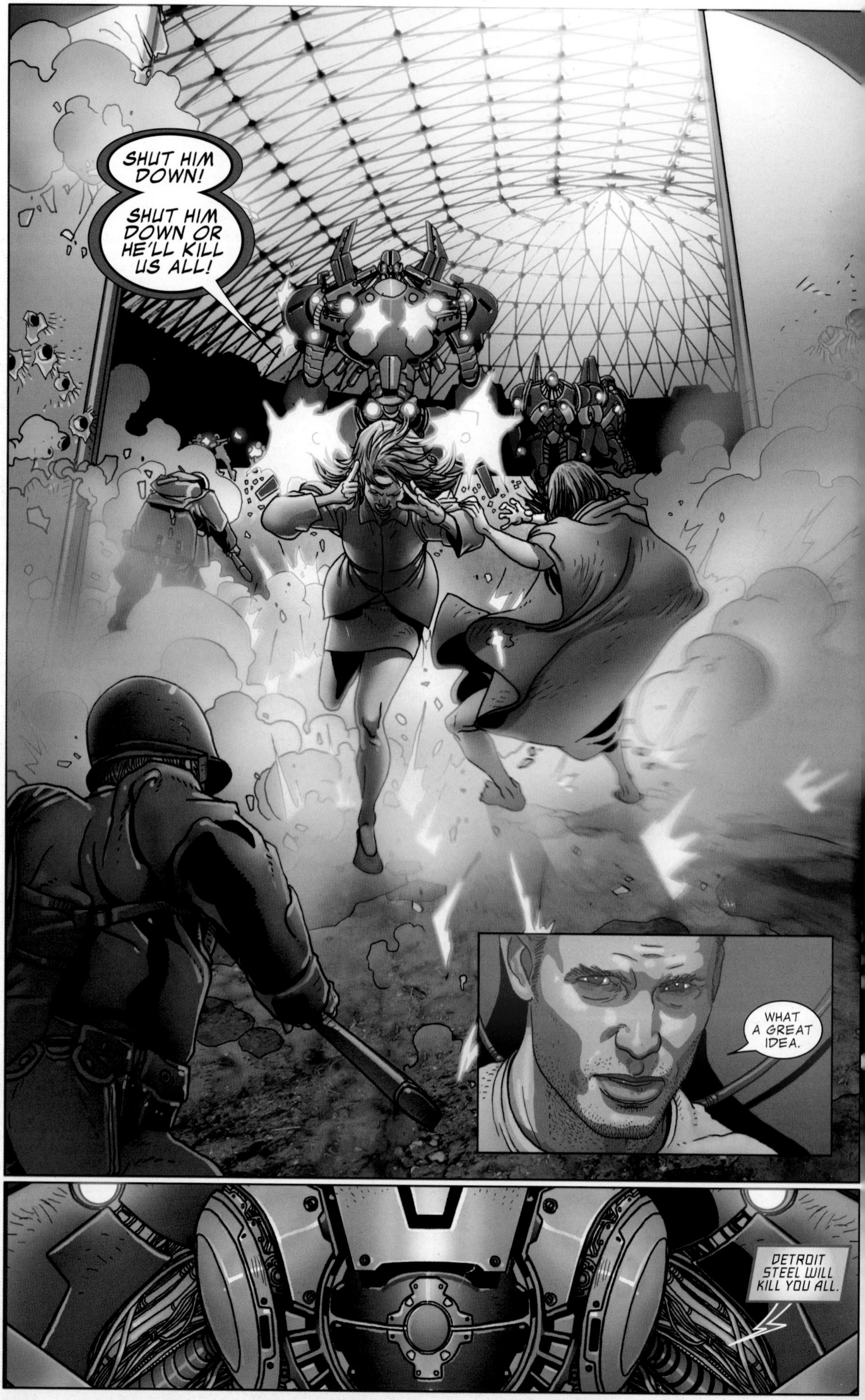
SHUT HIM DOWN!
SHUT HIM DOWN OR HE'LL KILL US ALL!
WHAT A GREAT IDEA.
DETROIT STEEL WILL KILL YOU ALL.

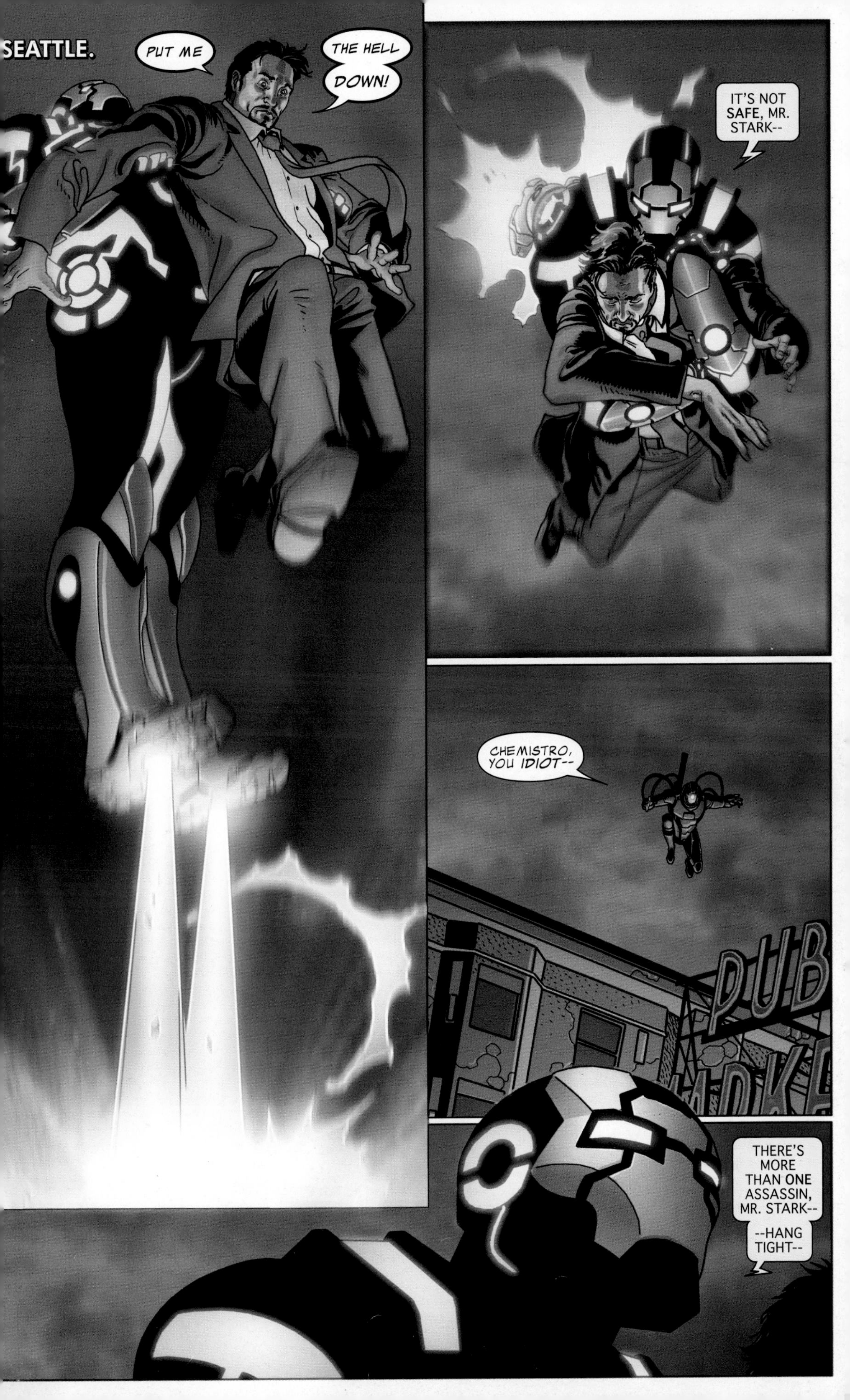
SEATTLE.
PUT ME
THE HELL DOWN!
IT'S NOT SAFE, MR. STARK--
CHEMISTRO, YOU IDIOT--
PUB
THERE'S MORE THAN ONE ASSASSIN, MR. STARK--
--HANG TIGHT--

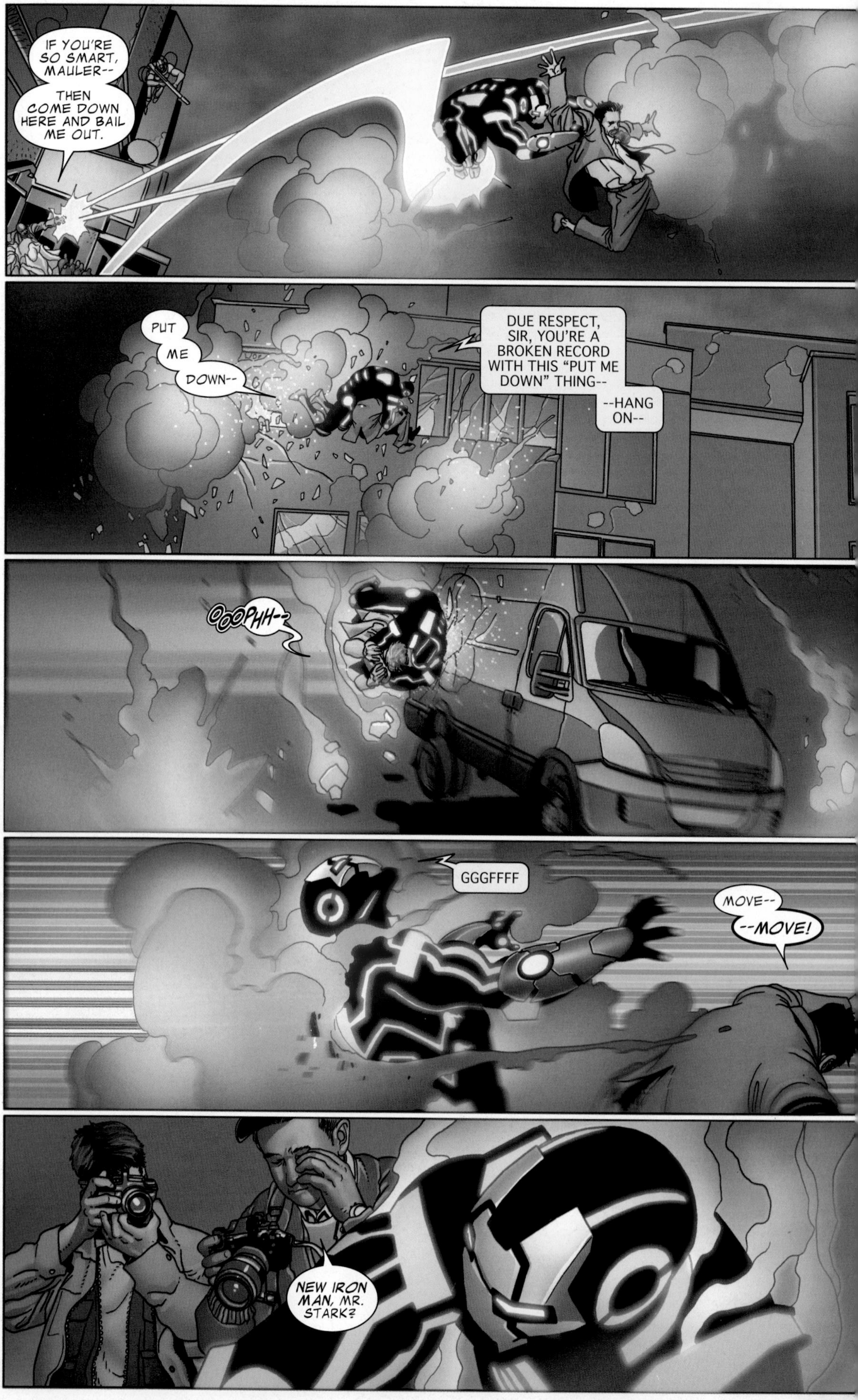
IF YOU'RE SO SMART, MAULER--
THEN COME DOWN HERE AND BAIL ME OUT.
PUT
ME
DOWN--
DUE RESPECT, SIR, YOU'RE A BROKEN RECORD WITH THIS "PUT ME DOWN" THING--
--HANG ON--
OOOPHH--
GGGFFFF
MOVE--
--MOVE!
NEW IRON MAN, MR. STARK?

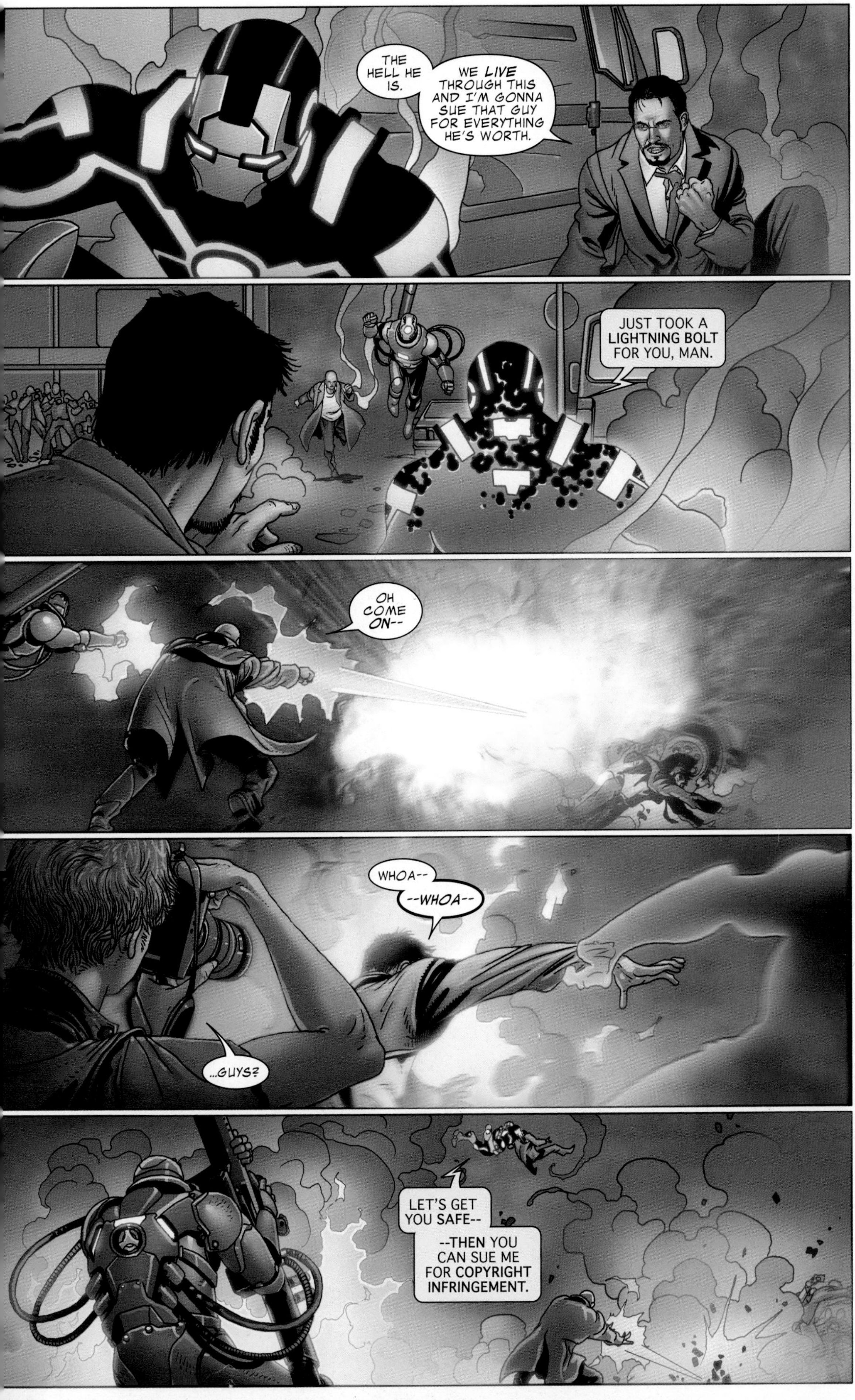
THE HELL HE IS.
WE LIVE THROUGH THIS AND I'M GONNA SUE THAT GUY FOR EVERYTHING HE'S WORTH.
JUST TOOK A LIGHTNING BOLT FOR YOU, MAN.
OH COME ON--
WHOA--
--WHOA--
...GUYS?
LET'S GET YOU SAFE--
--THEN YOU CAN SUE ME FOR COPYRIGHT INFRINGEMENT.

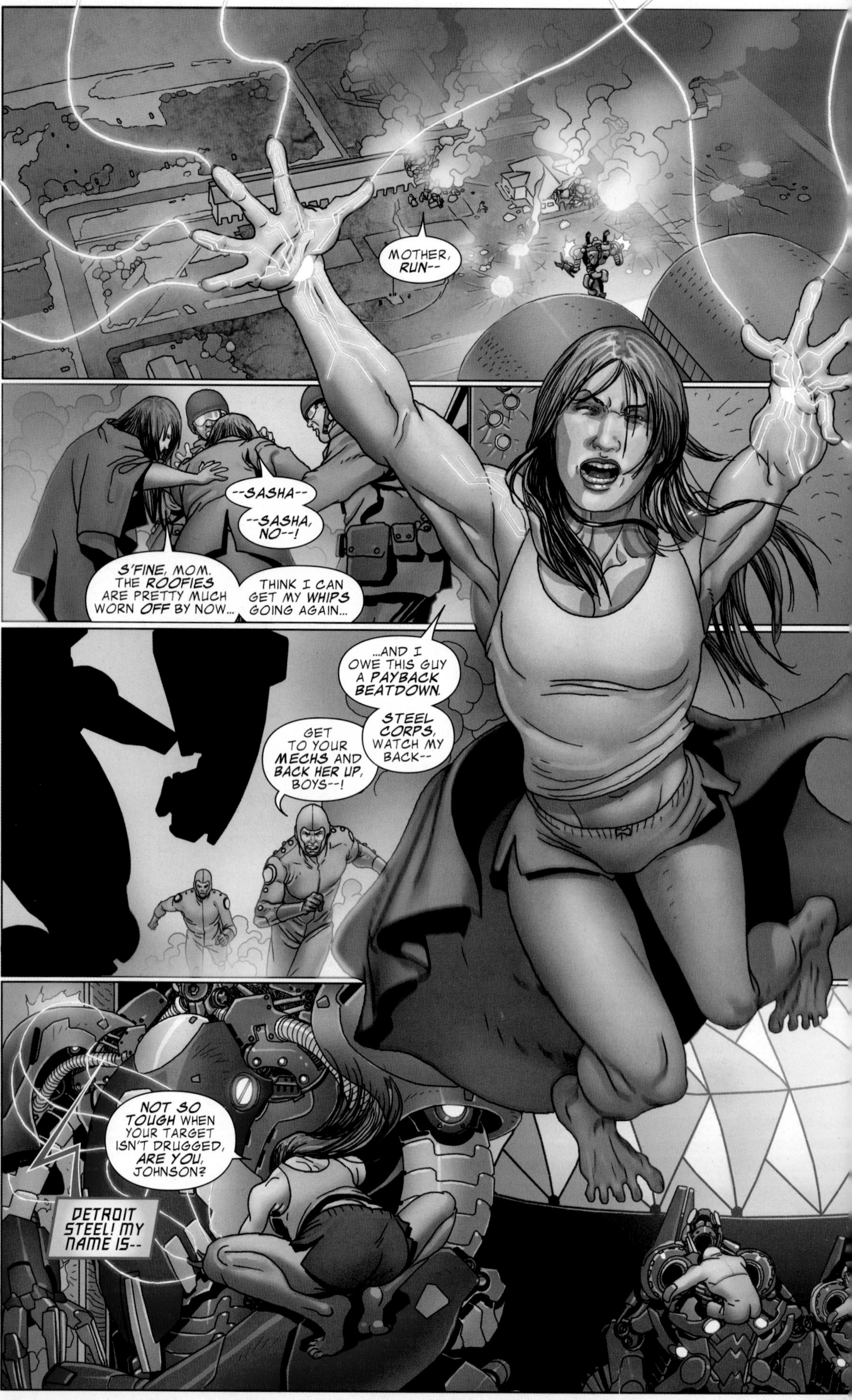
MOTHER, RUN--
--SASHA--
--SASHA, NO--!
S'FINE, MOM. THE ROOFIES ARE PRETTY MUCH WORN OFF BY NOW...
THINK I CAN GET MY WHIPS GOING AGAIN...
...AND I OWE THIS GUY A PAYBACK BEATDOWN.
STEEL CORPS, WATCH MY BACK--
GET TO YOUR MECHS AND BACK HER UP, BOYS--!
NOT SO TOUGH WHEN YOUR TARGET ISN'T DRUGGED, ARE YOU, JOHNSON?
DETROIT STEEL! MY NAME IS--

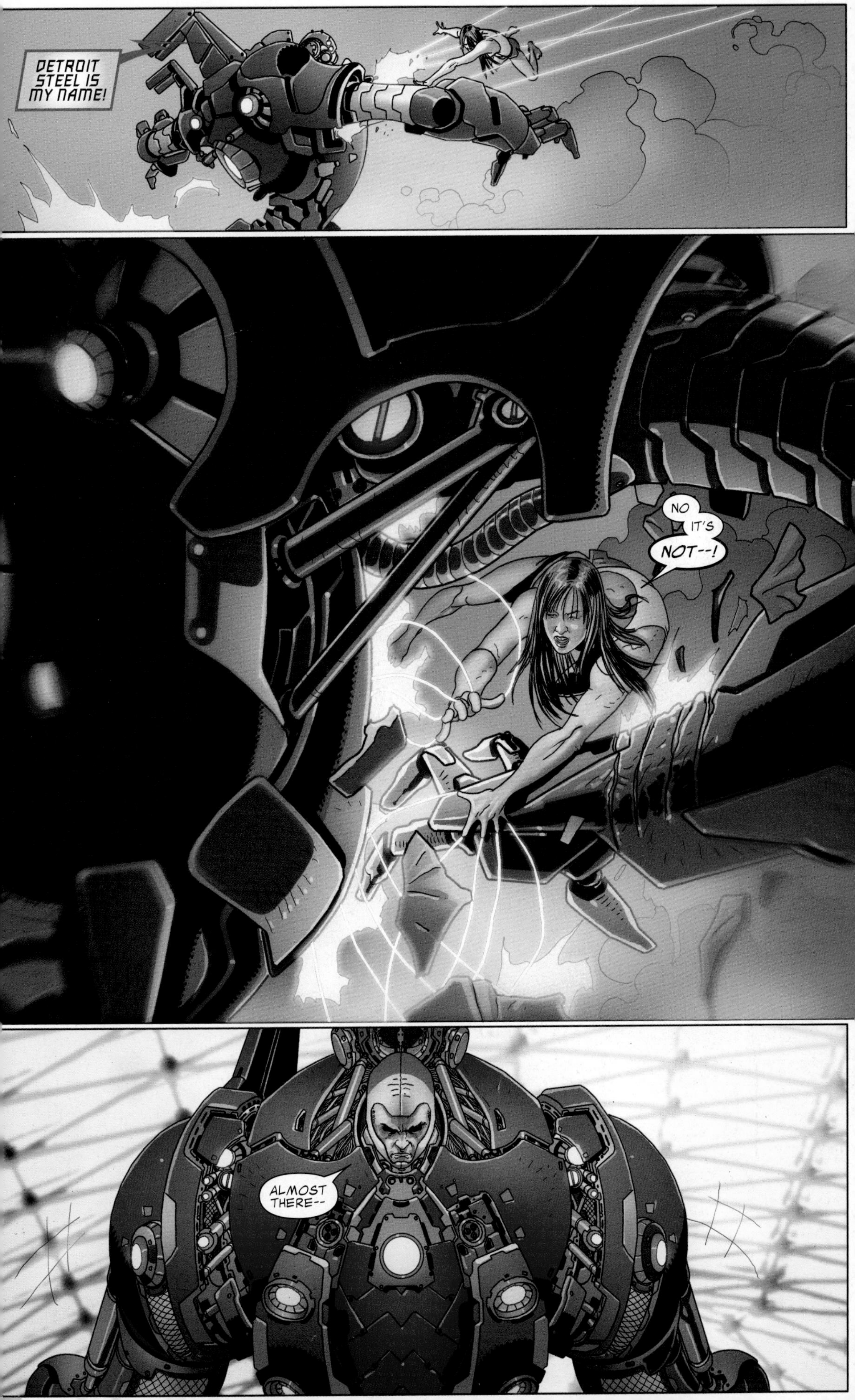
DETROIT STEEL IS MY NAME!
NO IT'S NOT--!
ALMOST THERE--

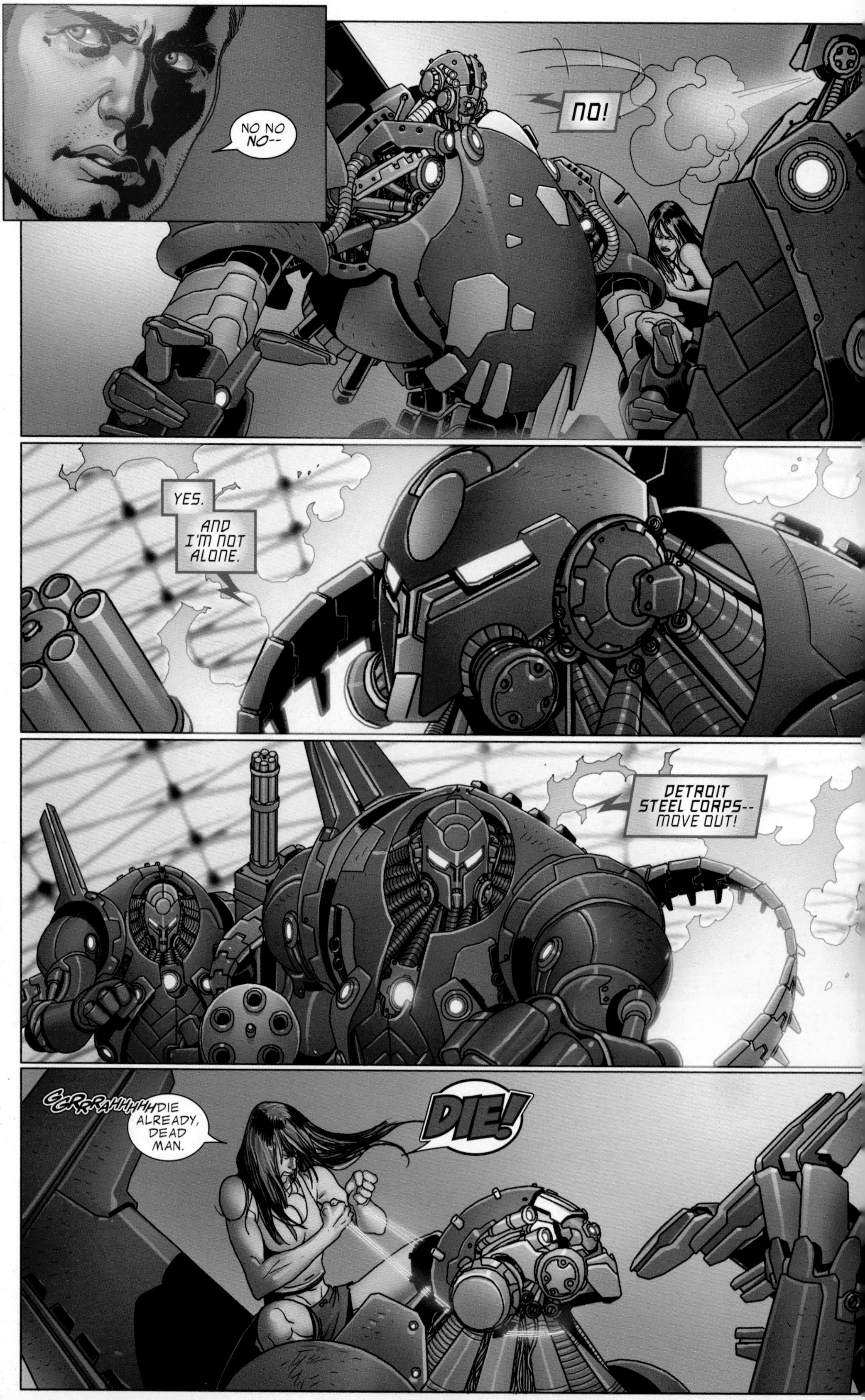
NO NO NO--
NO!
YES.
AND I'M NOT ALONE.
DETROIT STEEL CORPS-- MOVE OUT!
GRRRAHHHHH
DIE ALREADY, DEAD MAN.
DIE!

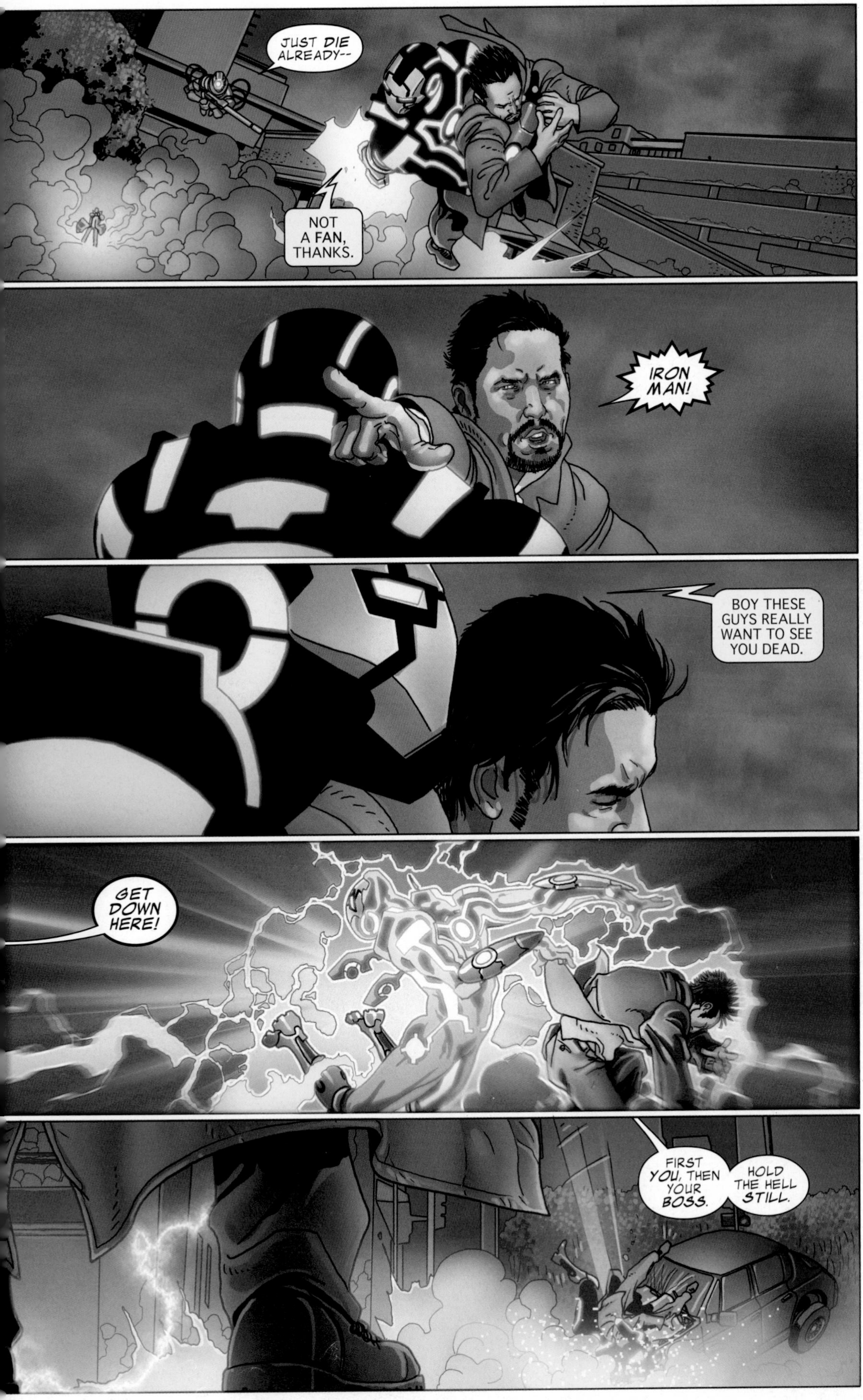
JUST DIE ALREADY--
NOT A FAN, THANKS.
IRON MAN!
BOY THESE GUYS REALLY WANT TO SEE YOU DEAD.
GET DOWN HERE!
FIRST YOU, THEN YOUR BOSS.
HOLD THE HELL STILL.

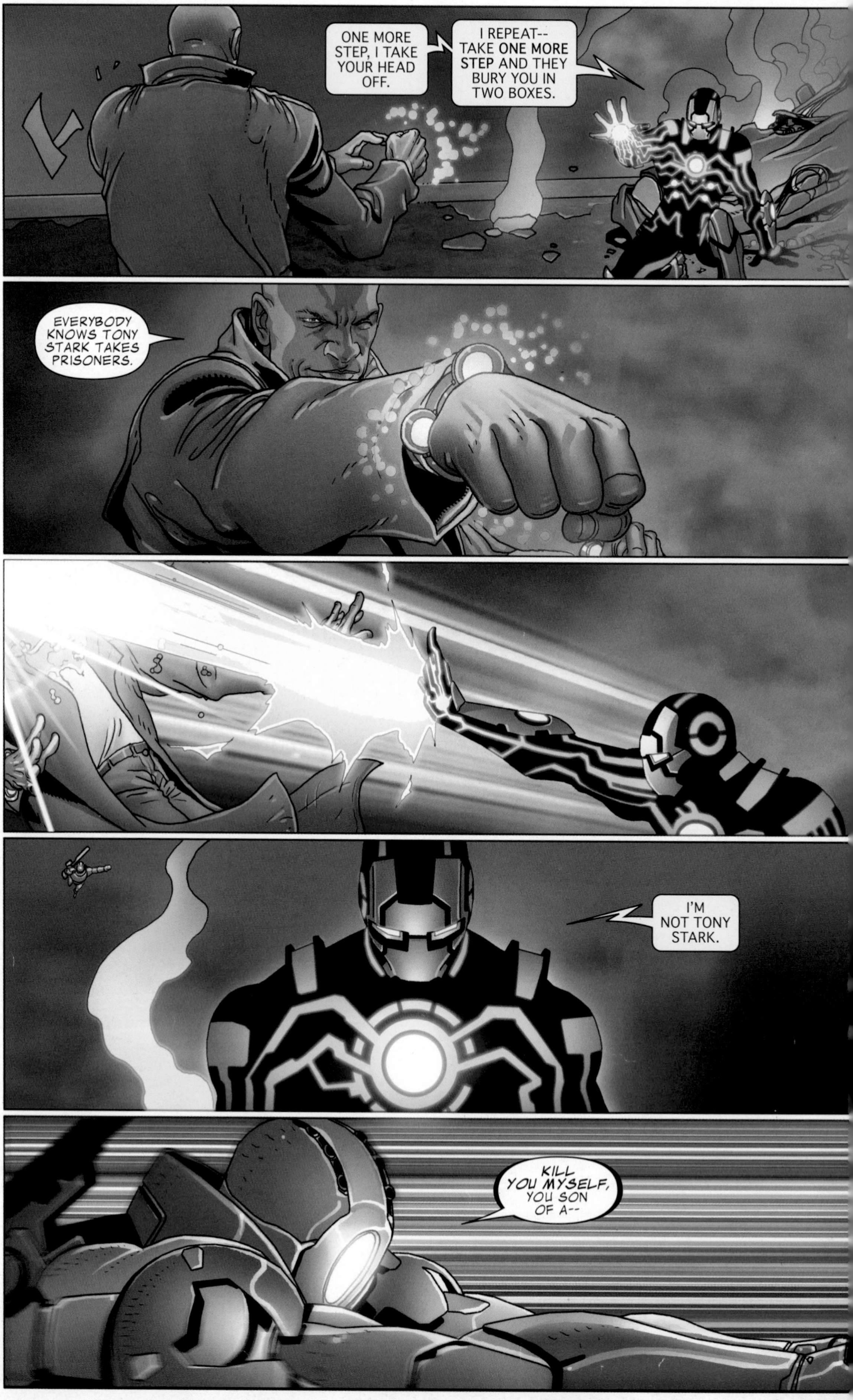
ONE MORE STEP, I TAKE YOUR HEAD OFF.
I REPEAT-- TAKE ONE MORE STEP AND THEY BURY YOU IN TWO BOXES.
EVERYBODY KNOWS TONY STARK TAKES PRISONERS.
I'M NOT TONY STARK.
KILL YOU MYSELF, YOU SON OF A--

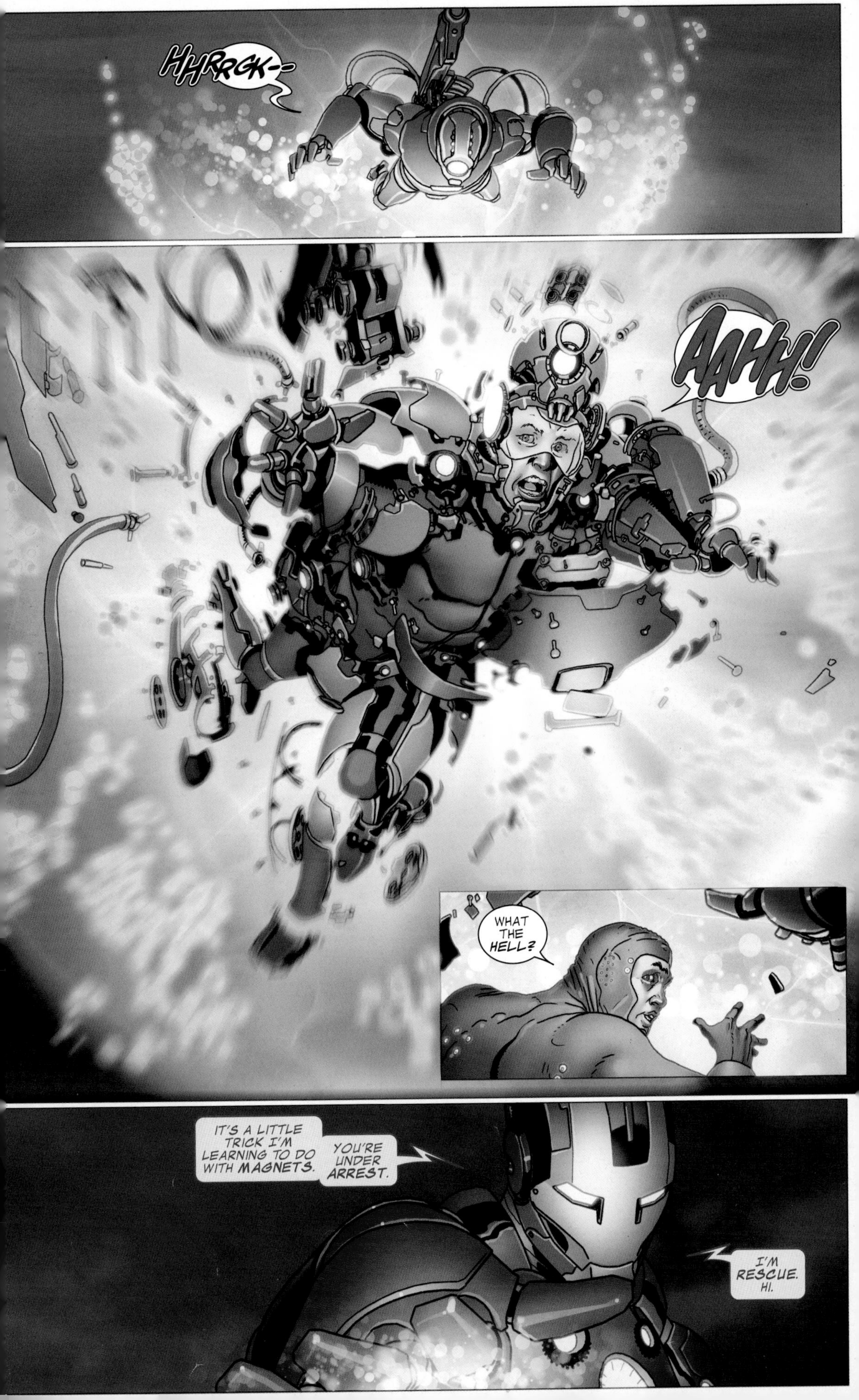
HHRRGK--
AAHH!
WHAT THE HELL?
IT'S A LITTLE TRICK I'M LEARNING TO DO WITH MAGNETS.
YOU'RE UNDER ARREST.
I'M RESCUE. HI.

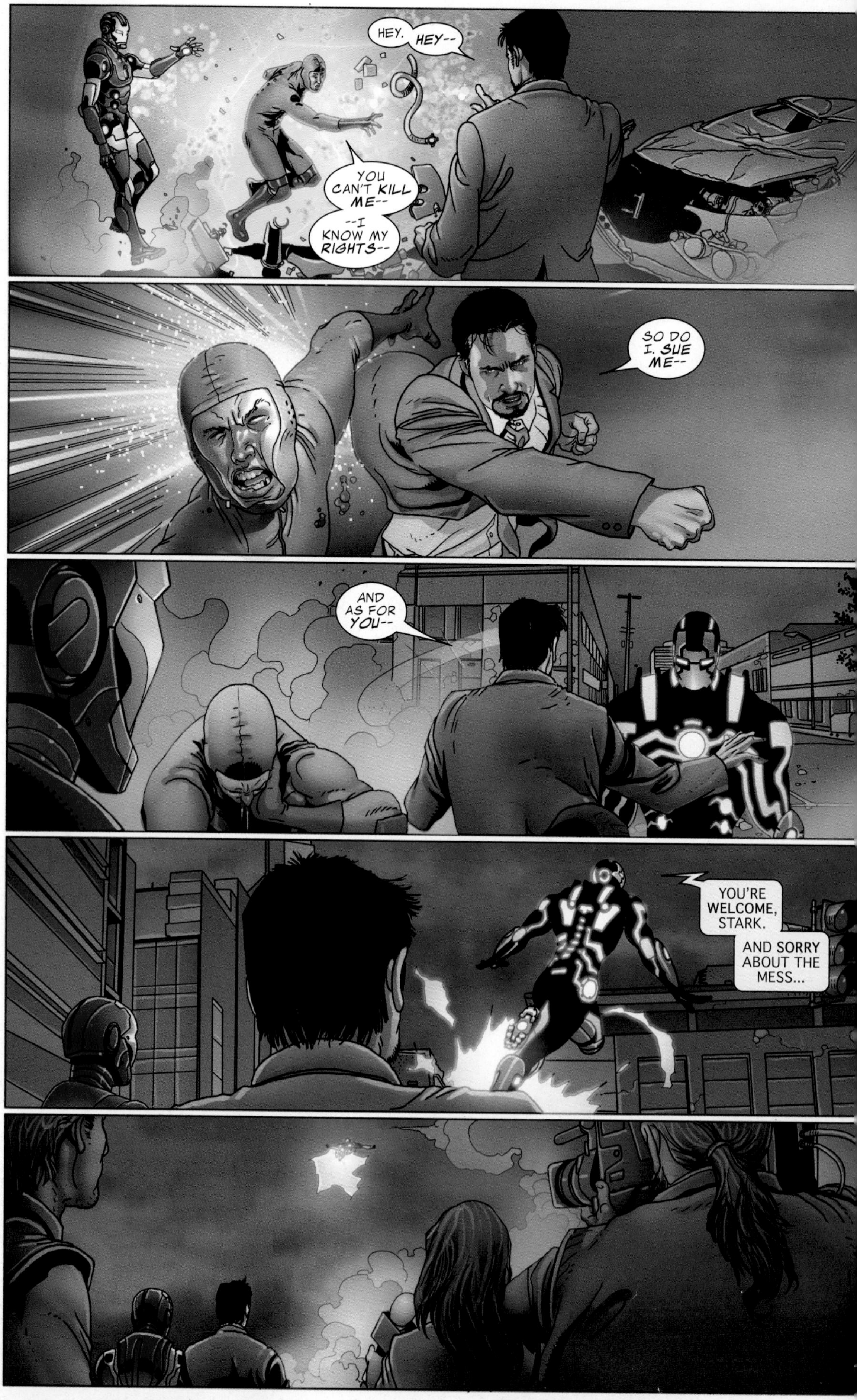
HEY.
HEY--
YOU CAN'T KILL ME--
--I KNOW MY RIGHTS--
SO DO I. SUE ME--
AND AS FOR YOU--
YOU'RE WELCOME, STARK.
AND SORRY ABOUT THE MESS...

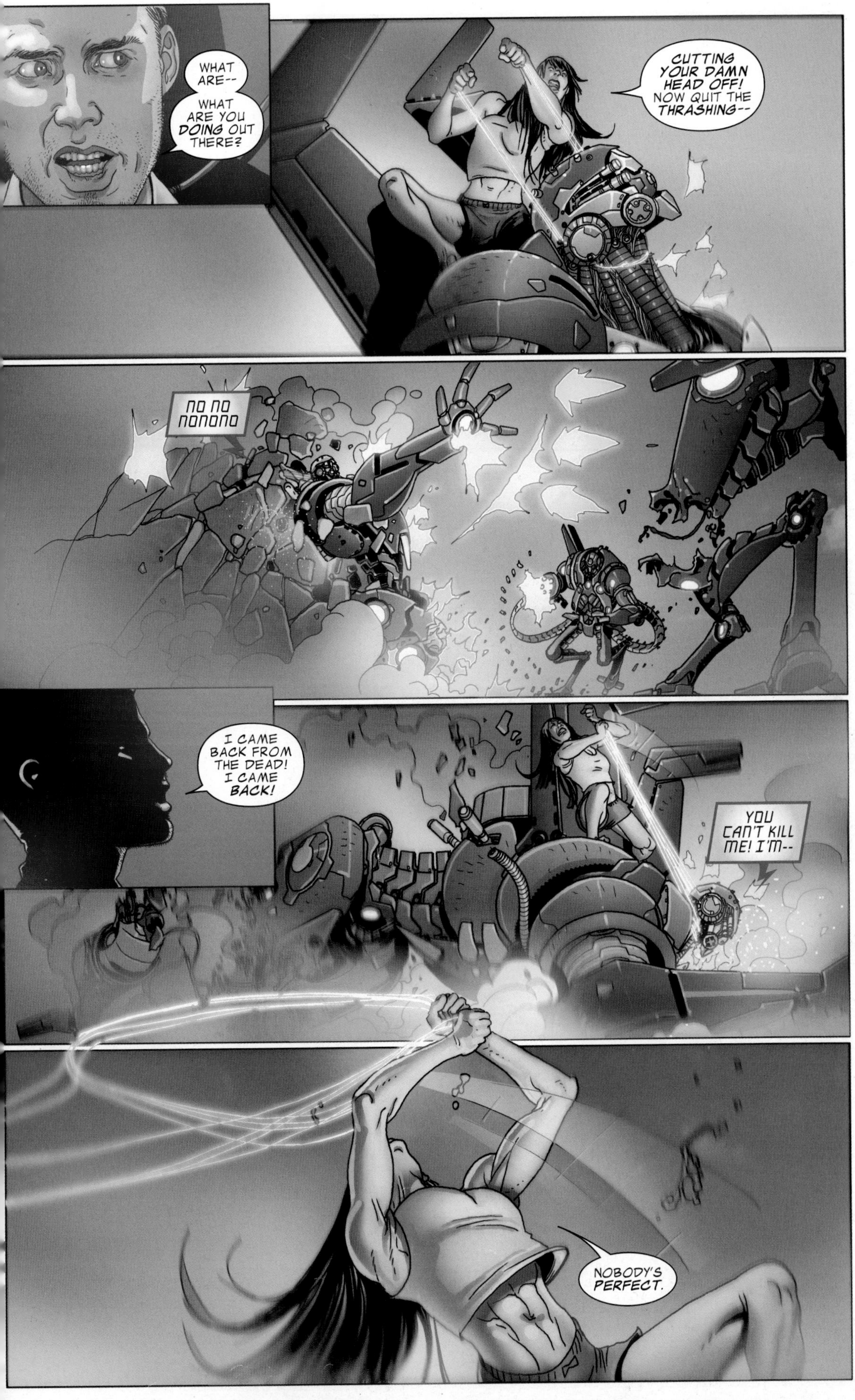
WHAT ARE-- WHAT ARE YOU DOING OUT THERE?
CUTTING YOUR DAMN HEAD OFF! NOW QUIT THE THRASHING--
NO NO NONONO
I CAME BACK FROM THE DEAD! I CAME BACK!
YOU CAN'T KILL ME! I'M--
NOBODY'S PERFECT.

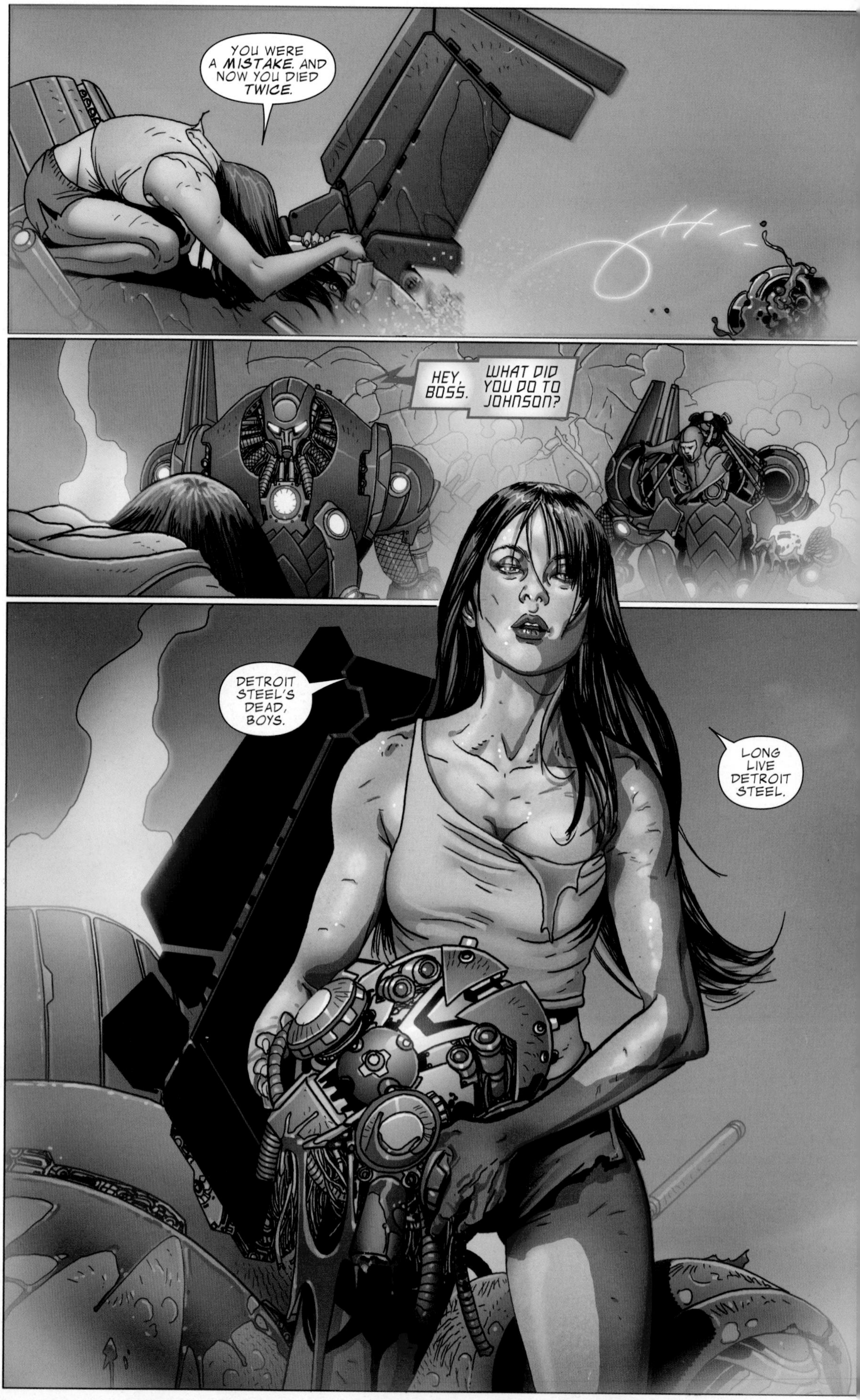
YOU WERE A MISTAKE. AND NOW YOU DIED TWICE.
HEY, BOSS.
WHAT DID YOU DO TO JOHNSON?
DETROIT STEEL'S DEAD, BOYS.
LONG LIVE DETROIT STEEL.

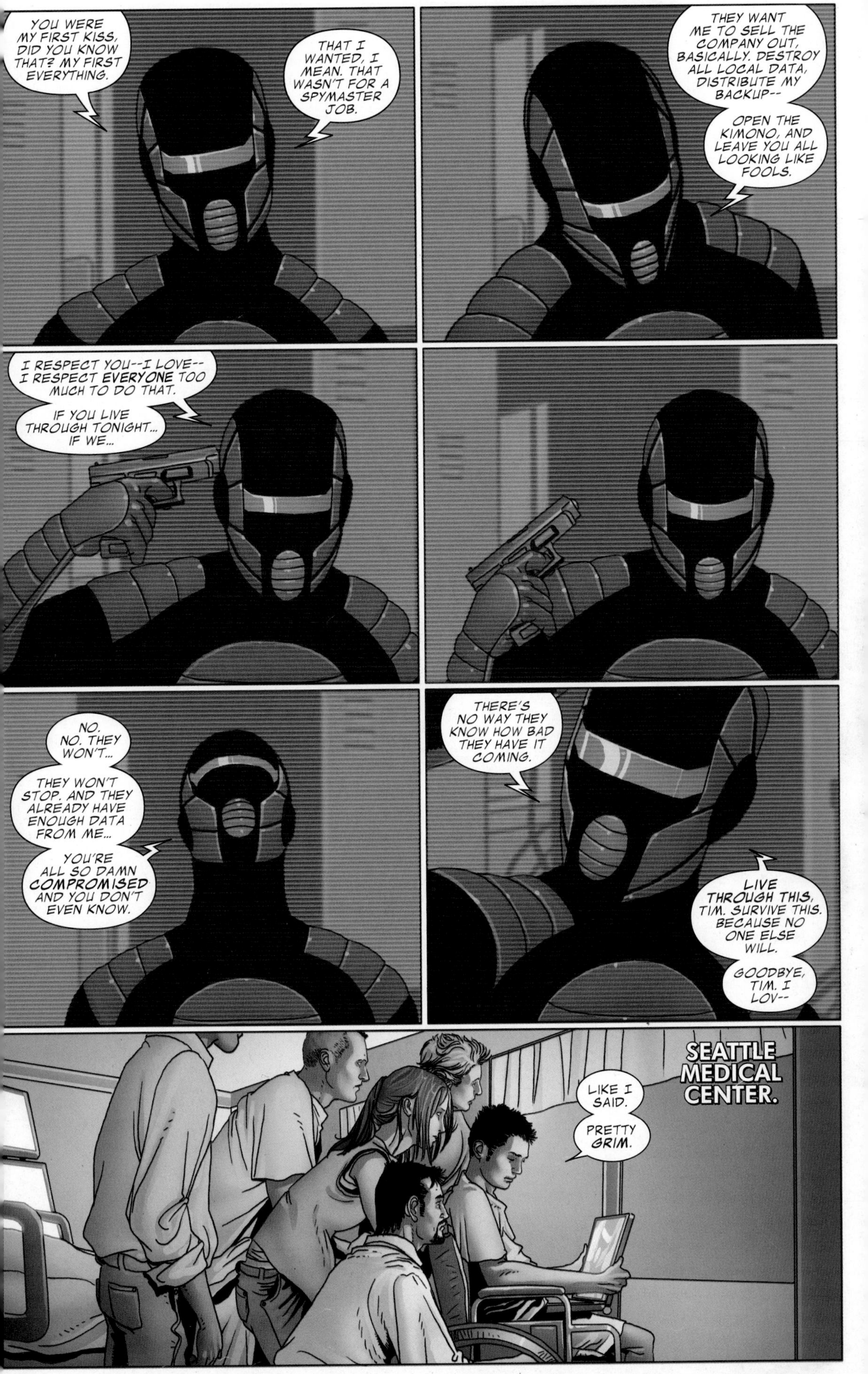
YOU WERE MY FIRST KISS, DID YOU KNOW THAT? MY FIRST EVERYTHING.
THAT I WANTED, I MEAN. THAT WASN'T FOR A SPYMASTER JOB.
THEY WANT ME TO SELL THE COMPANY OUT, BASICALLY. DESTROY ALL LOCAL DATA, DISTRIBUTE MY BACKUP--
OPEN THE KIMONO, AND LEAVE YOU ALL LOOKING LIKE FOOLS.
I RESPECT YOU--I LOVE-- I RESPECT EVERYONE TOO MUCH TO DO THAT.
IF YOU LIVE THROUGH TONIGHT... IF WE...
NO. NO. THEY WON'T...
THEY WON'T STOP. AND THEY ALREADY HAVE ENOUGH DATA FROM ME...
YOU'RE ALL SO DAMN COMPROMISED AND YOU DON'T EVEN KNOW.
THERE'S NO WAY THEY KNOW HOW BAD THEY HAVE IT COMING.
LIVE THROUGH THIS, TIM. SURVIVE THIS. BECAUSE NO ONE ELSE WILL.
GOODBYE, TIM. I LOV--
SEATTLE MEDICAL CENTER.
LIKE I SAID.
PRETTY GRIM.

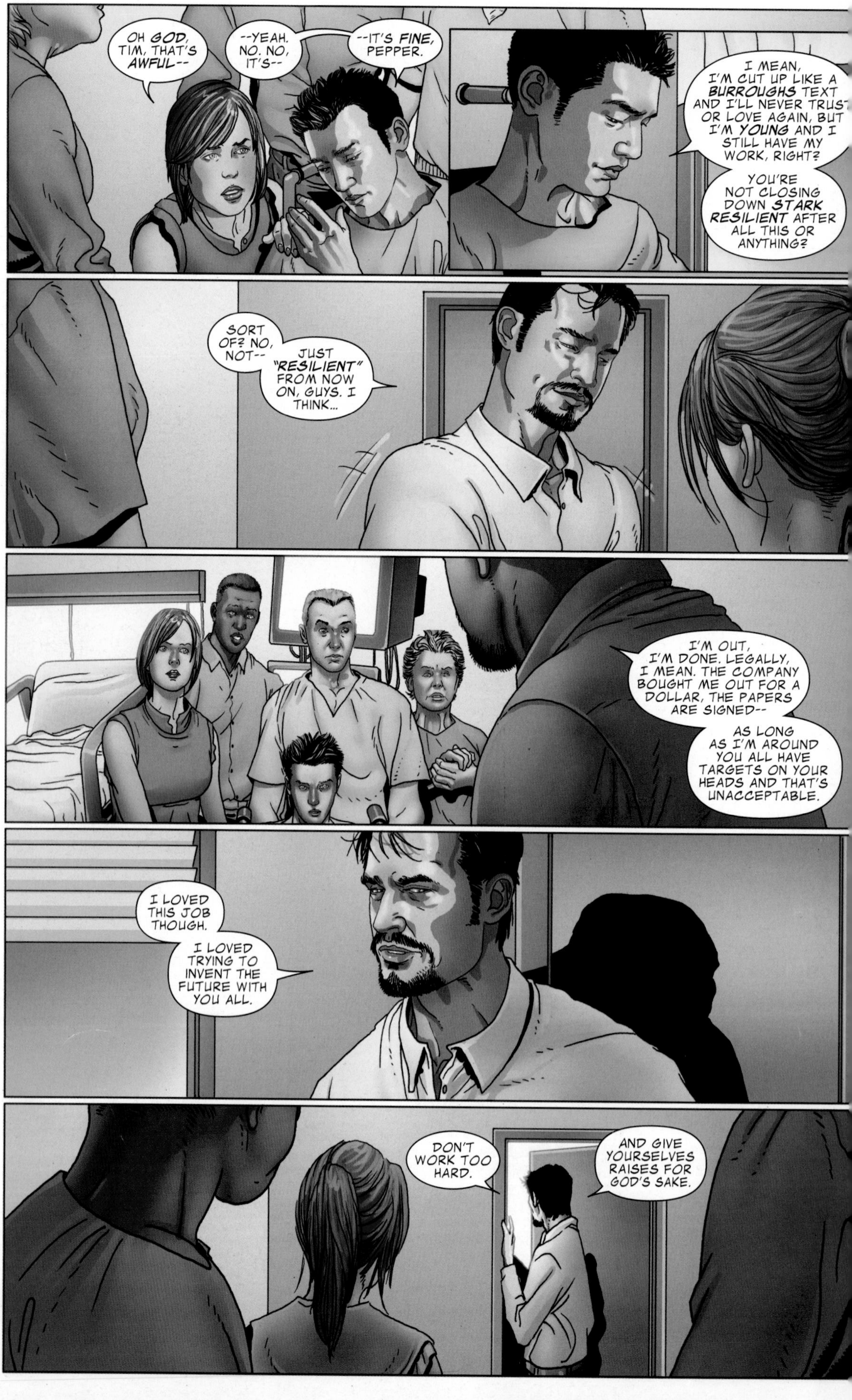
OH GOD, TIM, THAT'S AWFUL--
--YEAH. NO. NO, IT'S--
--IT'S FINE, PEPPER.
I MEAN, I'M CUT UP LIKE A BURROUGHS TEXT AND I'LL NEVER TRUST OR LOVE AGAIN, BUT I'M YOUNG AND I STILL HAVE MY WORK, RIGHT?
YOU'RE NOT CLOSING DOWN STARK RESILIENT AFTER ALL THIS OR ANYTHING?
SORT OF? NO, NOT--
JUST "RESILIENT" FROM NOW ON, GUYS. I THINK...
I'M OUT, I'M DONE. LEGALLY, I MEAN. THE COMPANY BOUGHT ME OUT FOR A DOLLAR, THE PAPERS ARE SIGNED--
AS LONG AS I'M AROUND YOU ALL HAVE TARGETS ON YOUR HEADS AND THAT'S UNACCEPTABLE.
I LOVED THIS JOB THOUGH.
I LOVED TRYING TO INVENT THE FUTURE WITH YOU ALL.
DON'T WORK TOO HARD.
AND GIVE YOURSELVES RAISES FOR GOD'S SAKE.

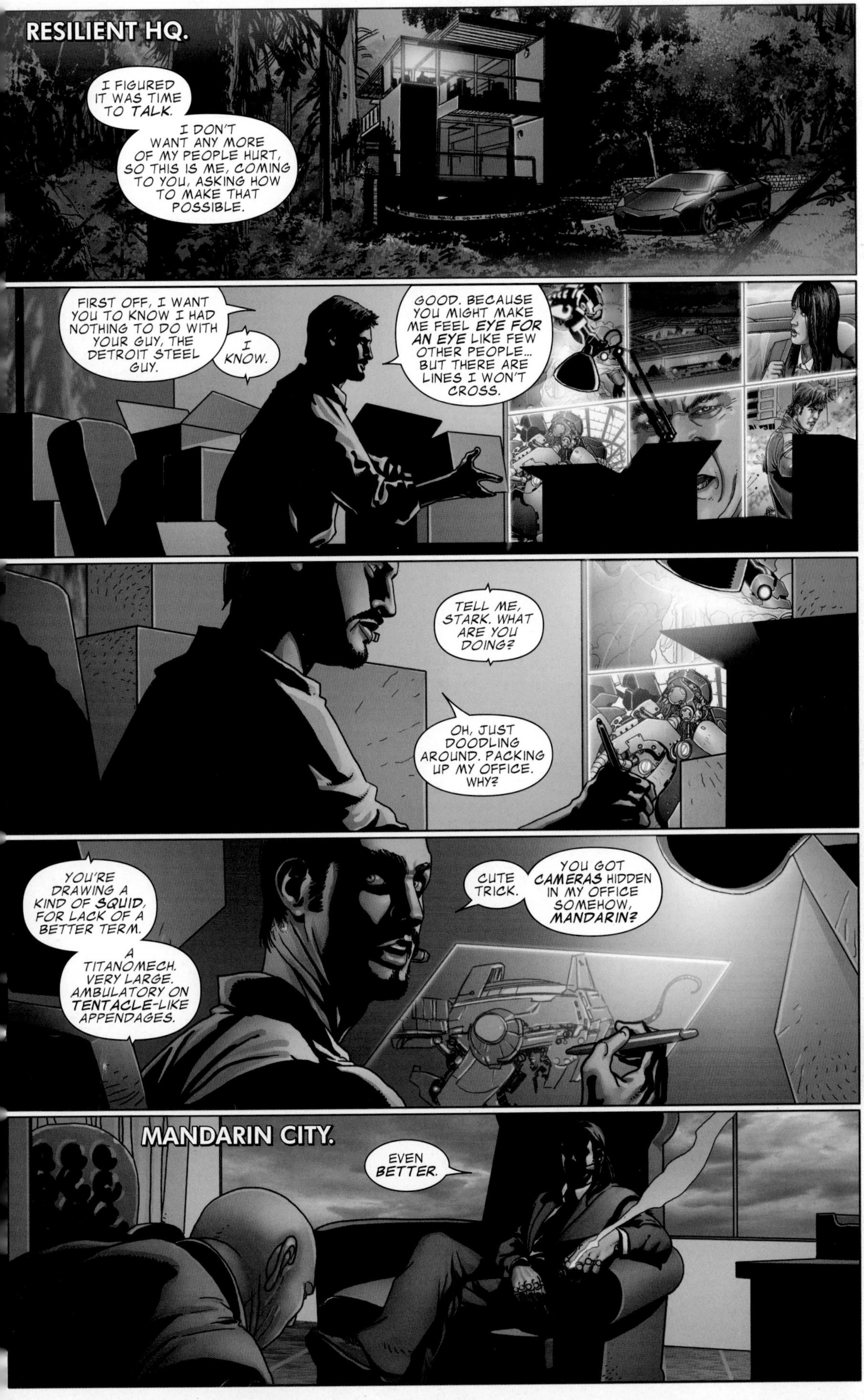
RESILIENT HQ.
I FIGURED IT WAS TIME TO TALK.
I DON'T WANT ANY MORE OF MY PEOPLE HURT, SO THIS IS ME, COMING TO YOU, ASKING HOW TO MAKE THAT POSSIBLE.
FIRST OFF, I WANT YOU TO KNOW I HAD NOTHING TO DO WITH YOUR GUY, THE DETROIT STEEL GUY.
I KNOW.
GOOD. BECAUSE YOU MIGHT MAKE ME FEEL EYE FOR AN EYE LIKE FEW OTHER PEOPLE... BUT THERE ARE LINES I WON'T CROSS.
TELL ME, STARK. WHAT ARE YOU DOING?
OH, JUST DOODLING AROUND. PACKING UP MY OFFICE. WHY?
YOU'RE DRAWING A KIND OF SQUID, FOR LACK OF A BETTER TERM.
A TITANOMECH. VERY LARGE. AMBULATORY ON TENTACLE-LIKE APPENDAGES.
CUTE TRICK.
YOU GOT CAMERAS HIDDEN IN MY OFFICE SOMEHOW, MANDARIN?
MANDARIN CITY.
EVEN BETTER.

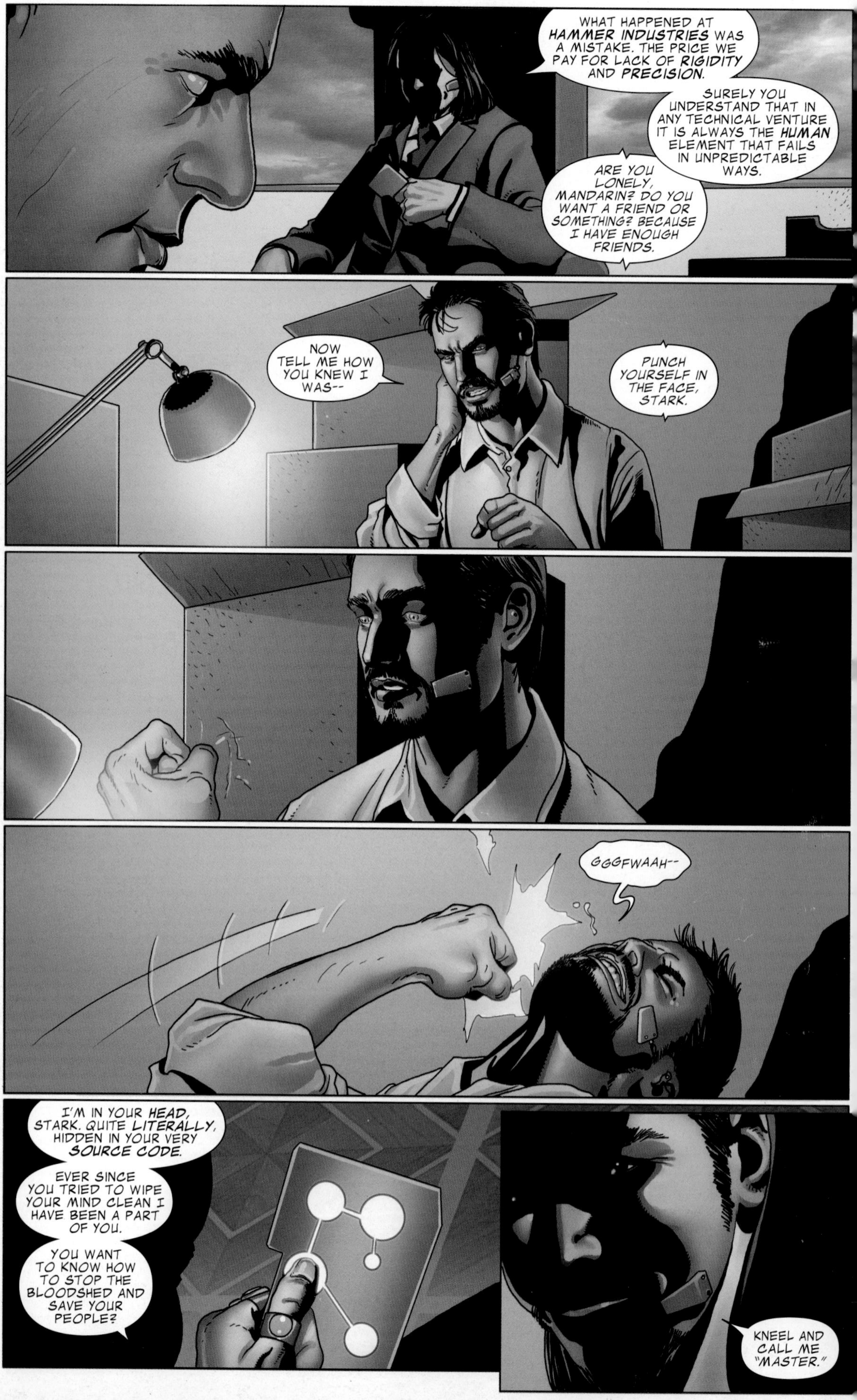
WHAT HAPPENED AT HAMMER INDUSTRIES WAS A MISTAKE. THE PRICE WE PAY FOR LACK OF RIGIDITY AND PRECISION.
SURELY YOU UNDERSTAND THAT IN ANY TECHNICAL VENTURE IT IS ALWAYS THE HUMAN ELEMENT THAT FAILS IN UNPREDICTABLE WAYS.
ARE YOU LONELY, MANDARIN? DO YOU WANT A FRIEND OR SOMETHING? BECAUSE I HAVE ENOUGH FRIENDS.
NOW TELL ME HOW YOU KNEW I WAS--
PUNCH YOURSELF IN THE FACE, STARK.
GGGFWAAH--
I'M IN YOUR HEAD, STARK. QUITE LITERALLY. HIDDEN IN YOUR VERY SOURCE CODE.
EVER SINCE YOU TRIED TO WIPE YOUR MIND CLEAN I HAVE BEEN A PART OF YOU.
YOU WANT TO KNOW HOW TO STOP THE BLOODSHED AND SAVE YOUR PEOPLE?
KNEEL AND CALL ME "MASTER."

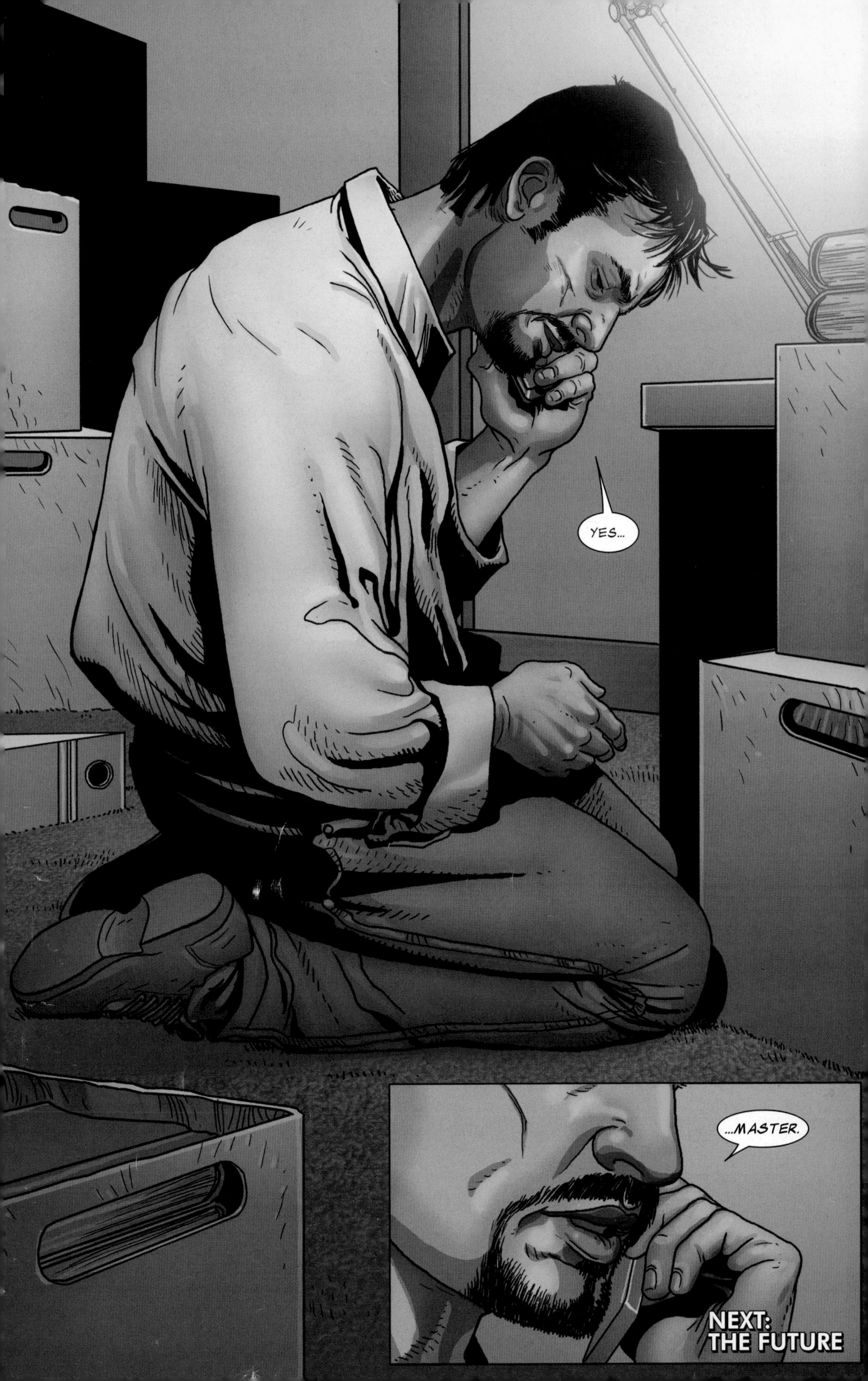
YES...
...MASTER.
NEXT:
THE FUTURE

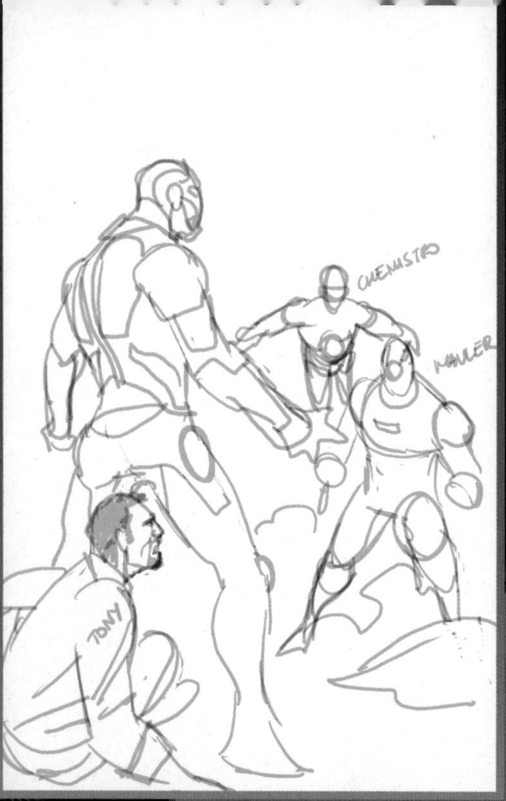
CHEMISTRO
MAULER
TONY

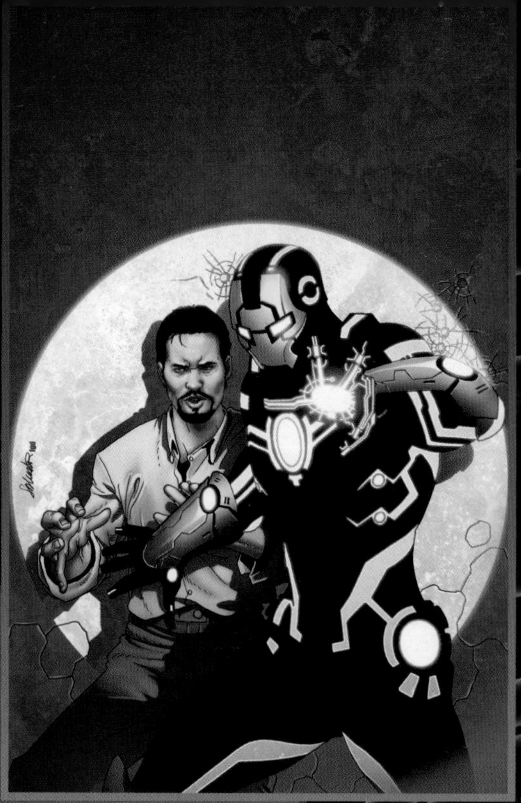

#519

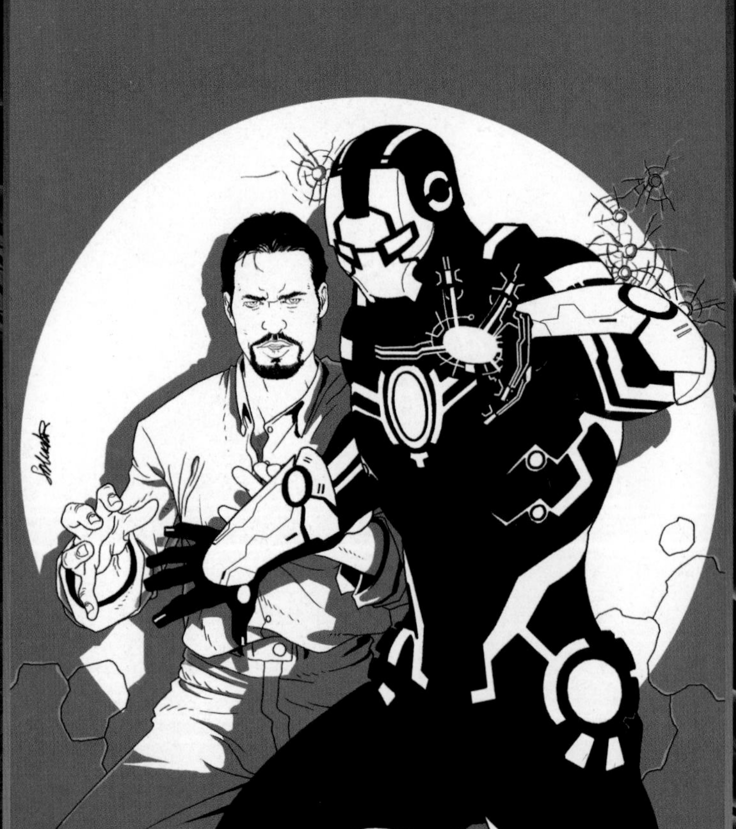

COVER PROCESS
BY SALVADOR LARROCA

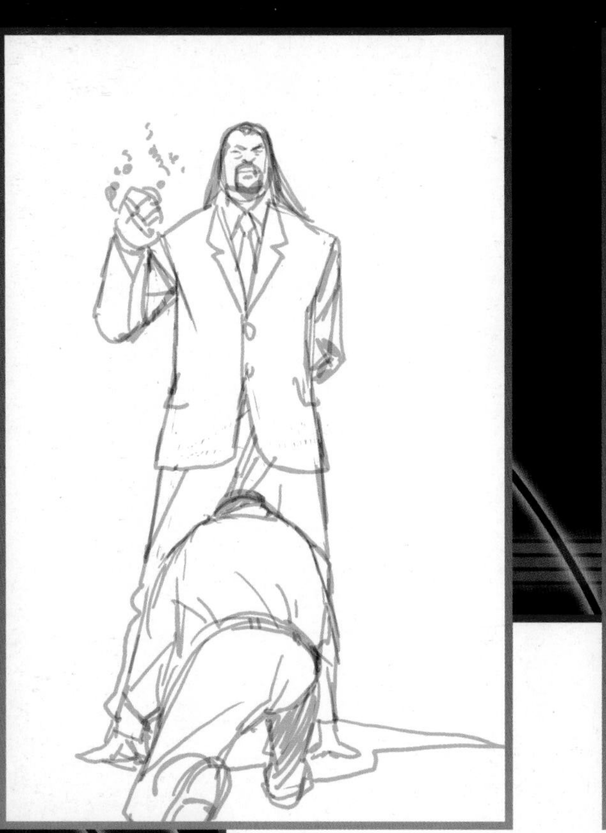

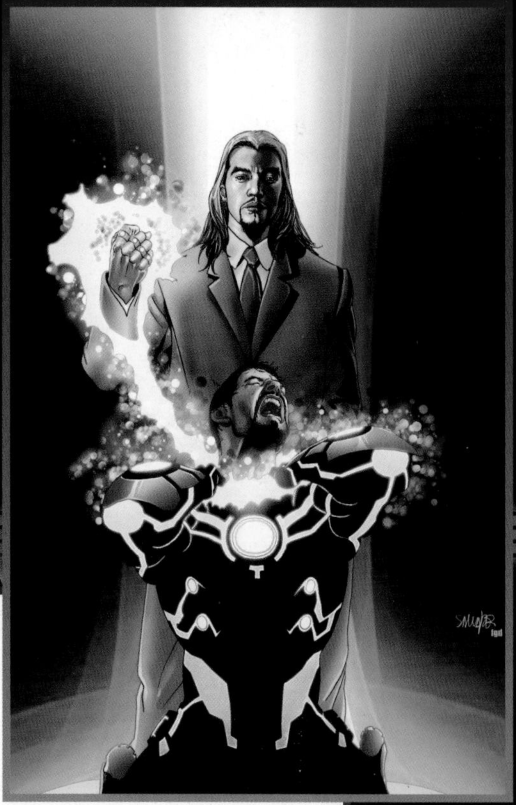

#520

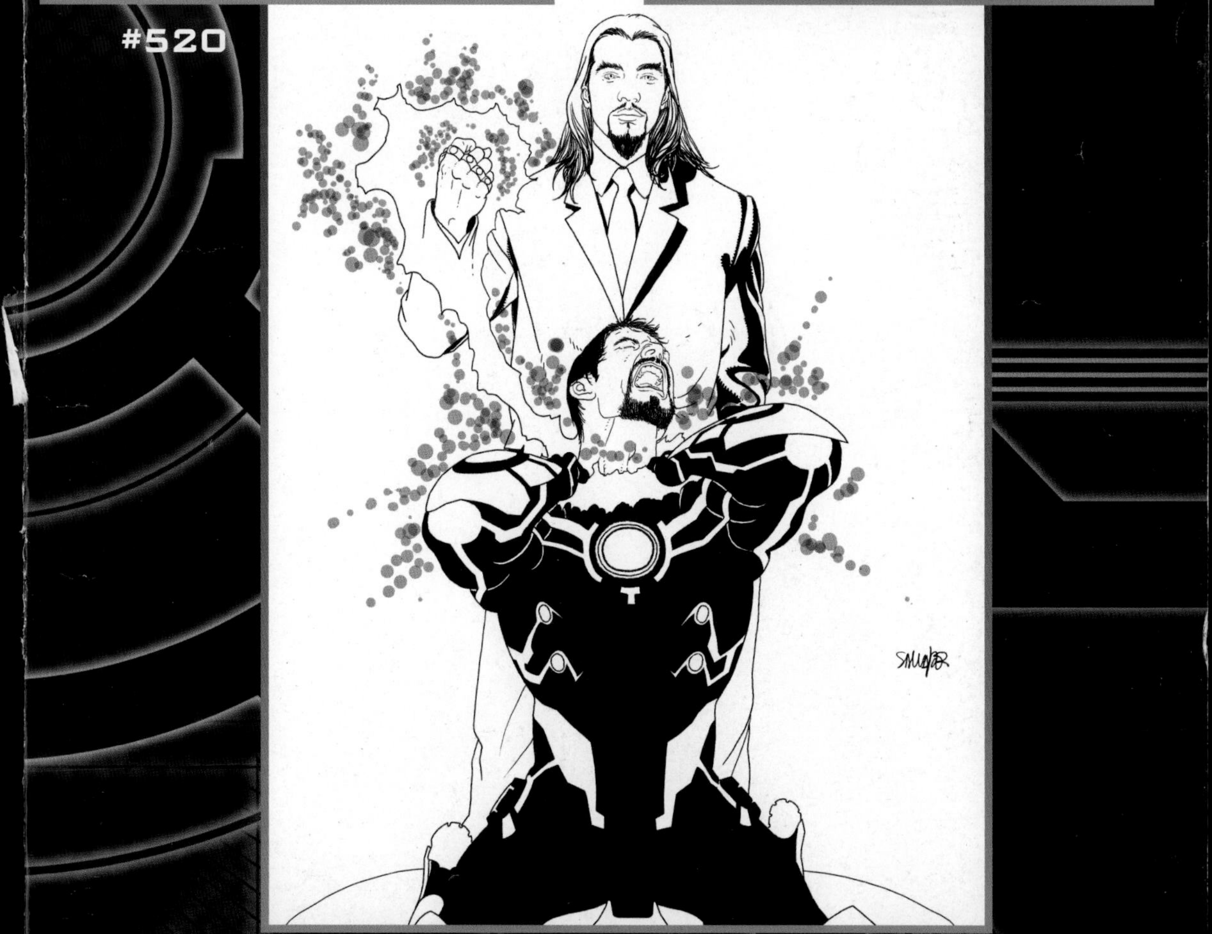